Social Science Methods for Psychodynamic Inquiry

Also by William R. Meyers

CITIZEN PARTICIPATION IN MENTAL HEALTH: RESEARCH AND SOCIAL POLICY (*co-authored*)

THE EVALUATION ENTERPRISE

Social Science Methods for Psychodynamic Inquiry

The Unconscious on the World Scene

William R. Meyers
University of Cincinnati, USA

palgrave
macmillan

First published 2015 by
PALGRAVE MACMILLAN

Palgrave Macmillan in the UK is an imprint of Macmillan Publishers Limited, registered in England, company number 785998, of Houndmills, Basingstoke, Hampshire RG21 6XS.

Palgrave Macmillan in the US is a division of St Martin's Press LLC, 175 Fifth Avenue, New York, NY 10010.

Palgrave Macmillan is the global academic imprint of the above companies and has companies and representatives throughout the world.

Palgrave® and Macmillan® are registered trademarks in the United States, the United Kingdom, Europe and other countries.

ISBN 978–1–137–52489–8

This book is printed on paper suitable for recycling and made from fully managed and sustained forest sources. Logging, pulping and manufacturing processes are expected to conform to the environmental regulations of the country of origin.

A catalogue record for this book is available from the British Library.

A catalog record for this book is available from the Library of Congress.

Typeset by MPS Limited, Chennai, India.

For my wife, Pat, the light of my life.

Contents

List of Tables

Acknowledgments

I would like to thank the following people, who kindly and helpfully read and commented on one or more chapters for me at various stages: Richard Berk, Audrey Buller, Ralph Buncher, Christine Gerety, Sarah Gideonse, Sarah Knox, Bradford Mank, Peter Rose, Jennifer Sheehy-Skeffington, and Howard Stafford.

I am also deeply indebted to the following people who, with extraordinary generosity, read and commented on most or all of the manuscript, sometimes more than once, and gave me very good counsel over an extended period: Arthur Kendall, Steven Meyers, Bennett Simon, Susan Sorenson, Peter Suedfeld, Jacques Szaluta, and Joel Warm.

The extended collaboration with David Beisel, Ivo Feierabend, Martina Klicperova-Baker, and Jana Svehlova, described in Chapter 9, was a pleasure and an honor.

Chapter 8 is, in significant part, my re-analysis of data gathered with and by Christine Gerety, and I am grateful for her help and friendship.

I am grateful to Joel Bakan for allowing me to quote so extensively from his fine book, *The Corporation*, in Chapter 11.

I feel very fortunate to have found superb editors at Palgrave Macmillan. Nicola Jones' insights into substantive matters, and her quality of judgment were extraordinary, and helped improve the clarity and organization of the manuscript in important ways. Elizabeth Forrest did outstanding work on a variety of improvements of the text itself. I am greatly in their debt.

Jayne MacArthur, freelance copyeditor, did an extraordinary job, with tact, precision, and sensitivity to language, and I would recommend her highly to anyone.

I am deeply grateful to my family: Steven Meyers for his extensive and very helpful work on the manuscript, Sally Meyers Faust for her constant encouragement, and my wife Pat O'Connor for her profound understanding and enduring support.

1
Introduction: Social Science Methods for Psychodynamic Inquiry on the World Scene

Though this be madness, yet there is method in 't.
William Shakespeare, *Hamlet*

The Central Issue

The central issue I address in this book is how to conduct research on psychodynamic matters on the world scene in a scientifically valid and credible way. This is of utmost importance considering the chaotic, irrational, and menacing elements in world affairs currently.

What the Book Does

I present a variety of social science research methods and concepts that can place psychodynamic inquiry into world events on a more scientific basis. I want to further our understanding of the roots of dangerous irrationality, which I believe stems from feelings, beliefs and fantasies that are outside of conscious awareness. I consider "clinically sophisticated" and "psychodynamically oriented" to be synonyms. Five of my own research studies, presented in the book, serve as indications of what can be done by researchers in this area.

Value to the Reader

I hope this book will be useful to clinical and counseling psychologists, both students and practitioners. The methods presented extend the range of what they can do with clinical training, giving them the new tools they need to conduct psychodynamic inquiries on the larger world scene. These tools can also help students and practitioners qualify for a broader range of jobs. I say this as a teacher of methodology, and as a former business and organizational consultant.

I hope this book will also be useful to social scientists and social science students in their methodology coursework and in their professional practice. It shows how to apply the research tools they ordinarily already have (usually survey methods or experimentation), plus a number of additional ones I explain, to more psychodynamic matters on the world scene. That understanding would expand their range of professional opportunities.

I also hope that the lay reader will benefit by getting a better understanding of which research "findings" and assertions about these world events to believe, and which to reject as unsupported by good methodology.

Some Definitions

By "unconscious" I mean "well out of awareness and not easily brought into awareness." This is a fairly standard usage. "Irrational", however, means many things to many people. I propose that for our purposes we use only one specific meaning*: irrational actions in our usage are behaviors on the world scene that are so highly destructive or self-destructive, or extremely bizarre, that they suggest the presence of motives and fantasies outside of conscious awareness.*

Therefore, simple miscalculations, errors in logic or in estimating probabilities, or simple non-optimal decisions in general, would not ordinarily be irrational in my sense of the word. They could instead be the result of inherent cognitive and intellectual limitations, stress, social pressure, lack of general knowledge, or lack of specific required data.

How can we identify actions that do seem to be irrational according to our definition? Chapter 3 suggests some of the types of behavior that researchers could look at.

The Problem We Face: There is Rampant Irrationality

On 21 February 2006, a Sunni dissident group in Iraq bombed the beautiful Golden Dome Mosque, sacred to the Shiites of Iraq (Worth, 2006). This atrocity proved self-defeating: it elicited the retaliatory bombing of 27 Sunni mosques by Shiite groups. Episodes of blindly destructive, self-defeating behavior on the world scene, even in recent years—Bosnia, Kosovo, the Middle East, Darfur, Sudan, Myanmar—suggest to me that among the intense emotional forces involved are some that lay outside of conscious awareness: there is a deep inner irrationality on the political scene.

Even on a smaller scale, there is profound irrationality. On Good Friday, 22 April 2011, in San Fernando, a town north of Manila, 24 Filipinos had themselves crucified to atone for their sins. This ritual occurs there every year on Good Friday, and is now attended by thousands of tourists (MSNBC, 2007; Reuters, 2011).

There is widespread and profound irrationality on the international political scene, and self-destructive outbursts that defy reason in many parts of the world. In Ireland there have been the waves of child rape and torture by clerics; the vicious exploitation of unmarried women in the Magdalene laundries; and the lethal neglect and starvation of children at the Tuam (Catholic) and Bethany (Protestant) orphanages. In Rotherham, England, there was recently uncovered the rape, beatings, and abuse of over 1400 children by Pakistani pedophile gangs over a 16-year period. I will analyze these in more detail below.

In the Middle East, the Islamic State of Iraq and Syria (ISIS) are crucifying and beheading captives. In Nigeria, Boko Haram has kidnapped and enslaved a large group of schoolgirls. In Paris, editors and cartoonists at *Charlie Hebdo* have been assassinated, and in Hamburg the offices of the *Morning Post* have been fire-bombed for reprinting the cartoons. In Saudi Arabia, Raif Badawi was sentenced to 1000 lashes for his liberal writings. We are in deep waters here but it is evident that some of the ideation behind these vicious and ruthless acts is outside of conscious awareness, and the formulations of depth psychology are needed as *part* of the explanation for this violence. For example we need to investigate the likelihood that in these cases the individual's sense of self has merged with the radical ideology, so that a perceived insult to Mohammed, or to Islam, is *experienced* as a direct threat to the integrity of the self, felt as an insulting and deeply threatening *personal* attack—not only by the *Charlie Hebdo* cartoons, but also by the videos and photos, widely circulated, of the humiliation and torture at Abu Ghraib—attacks that must be avenged with violence. And revenge motives usually contain intensely sadistic elements, which are clearly evident in the systematic murders of helpless people at the *Charlie Hebdo* offices, and in the public floggings for alleged infractions against Islam (*The World Post*, 2015). There are likely to be other elements too, for example a sense of exaltation at having been *personally* chosen to avenge the insult to the prophet Mohammed seems evident in the *Charlie Hebdo* murders. But all this needs systematic clinically informed psychodynamically oriented investigation.

Kim Jong-un

On 28 December 2011, Kim Jong-un, son of Kim Jong-il, ritualistically dubbed "The Great Successor," became the ruler of North Korea. No one knows what an untested juvenile will do with absolute power and nuclear arms. Kim Jong-un continues to be a strange and worrisome force. The *New York Times* reported "a blunt and explicit threat on Thursday from North Korea that its weapons programs would 'target' the United States, and that it would proceed with a third and 'higher-level' nuclear test...An official statement said, 'We do not hide that a variety of satellites and long-range rockets which will be launched by the D.P.R.K. one after another and a nuclear test of higher level will target against the U.S., the sworn enemy of the Korean people'" (Sanger and Sang-Hun, 2013). According to press reports citing announcements in the official press of North Korea (Choe, 2013; Fisher, 2013a), Kim Jong-un recently executed his uncle as an enemy of the people.

The Tsarnaev Brothers

Dzhokhar Tsarnaev, the surviving brother, went on trial on 3 November 2014 for the Boston Marathon bombing. The press reports that teachers and fellow students at Cambridge Rindge and Latin High School where he attended declare that he was in all respects a reasonable and sensible teenager who showed no signs of deviance or mental pathology. My own informants in Cambridge who know Tsarnaev's teachers report that the teachers did experience him in this way.

But we now know that underneath "the mask of sanity" there was a person who made the bombs, carefully ensuring that the inner workings were surrounded by metal fragments, ball bearings, and nails, designed to become shrapnel, and who visualized with satisfaction the pain and destruction these bombs would inflict on his fellow human beings. It seems evident to me that pleasure in inflicting terror and devastation bespeaks unconscious forces that go far beyond rational ideological commitment, a motive for power, or insufficient cognitive complexity, although these may also be factors.

Climate Change Denial

Another example of profound irrationality concerns the nature of the denial of climate change. To counter the overwhelming scientific evidence for climate change caused by human activity, deniers of this change have proposed an extraordinary diversity of wild and mutually contradictory conspiracy theories. According to the popular press, the accused conspirators include climate scientists aiming to get funding, the United Nations seeking to take over the USA, communists and socialists trying to destroy capitalism, Margaret Thatcher and conservative leaders aiming to promote nuclear power, Jacques Chirac and the secret Bilderberg group trying to take over the world, and eugenics groups seeking to depopulate the world. Surely there are paranoid themes in play here, and underlying unconscious fantasies.

Zhirinovsky

The speeches and statements of Russian politician Vladimir Zhirinovsky, which I discuss in detail in Chapter 8, may furnish another example of ideation not fully under conscious control. Zhirinovsky's threats have been called "absurd," "histrionic," and "the work of a buffoon," but, like Hitler in *Mein Kampf*, they could imply the workings of powerful unconscious fantasies that may burst into action given the right circumstances.

Self-destructive Behavior by Political and Cultural Figures

The bizarre and self-destructive behavior of political and cultural figures provides many sad examples of political figures being driven by unconscious forces. The repeated sending of lewd photos over the Internet by Congressman Anthony Weiner; the alleged sexual aggression of Dominique Strauss-Kahn (the Managing Director of the International Monetary Fund), which ruined his chances of becoming President of France; the patronization of escort services by Eliot Spitzer, which cost him the Governorship of New York, were not rational acts. The memories, motivations, and fantasies prompting these actions must lie outside of conscious awareness. Is there evidence, for example, that unconsciously they wanted to be caught? Or instead is there evidence of unconscious fantasies of invincibility? *These are empirical questions. We don't know until we look, and in this book I suggest how to look.*

Tuam, Bethany, Magdalene

Without psychodynamic understanding questions involving motives and ideation outside of conscious awareness cannot be addressed and researched. An example is provided by current revelations about the starvation and lethal neglect of babies at the Tuam (Catholic) and Bethany (Protestant) orphanages in Ireland. This was followed by tossing the dead babies into unmarked graves.

There are also current revelations of the cruel treatment of women, almost captives and slaves, in the secretive Magdalene laundries in Ireland, where an estimated 30,000 unwed mothers, seduced women, homeless women, and prostitutes were consigned to work in miserable conditions, usually for life, and for no wages. In 1993 a mass grave of 155 women was discovered in the convent grounds of one of the laundries, triggering a public protest.

We know from clinical experience that the part of the personality that makes moral judgments is largely unconscious and is the most sadistic part of the personality. As a result, there may be evidence for the characterization of the infants as "children of Satan," and of the unwed mothers in the laundries as "whores." From a methodological point of view, the researcher would look for discussions and documents using terms like these, or any terms indicating that, at the unconscious level, these babies born out of wedlock, and these unwed mothers, were despised by their captors, who, as nuns, had foregone sexuality and motherhood. Or could unconscious envy of the unwed mothers have affected their treatment? Content analyses seeking relevant words and phases in documents and interviews could shed light on this question. These documents could be internal memos, diaries, formal rules and regulations, subsequent exculpatory statements, and the like. To avoid researcher bias, multiple observers would be needed to rate these documents and carry out the interviews. Computerized content analysis could be used to look for certain terms in the documents and interview records, and to measure their frequency. Comparison studies could be made with documents from facilities where the residents were treated kindly. Burial certificates could be examined. The death rates of the babies could be compared with the death rates of babies in the general population. Any assertions that emerged from the research could be exposed to Popperian disconfirmation based on predictions to as yet unexamined data, as described in Chapter 4. These would be grim studies that will deeply move the researcher, so co-researchers, or colleagues, would be needed to lessen the impact a solo researcher might feel and help compensate for emotionally driven distortions in the study findings.

So in many instances we think we know what kinds of data to look for. *But we don't know until we look.* Perhaps the Tuam and Bethany and Magdalene inquiries do not disclose unconscious processes like the ones I have hypothesized. Writings, memos, letters, and conversations could be studied. And perhaps Anthony Weiner, or Eliot Spitzer, or Dominique Strauss-Kahn did not unconsciously want to get caught. Instead, they may have had unconscious fantasies of invincibility, like the little child who wears a Superman costume. Again, writings, memos, emails, conversations, and particular actions could be studied for clues as to unconscious mental processes, including motives and fantasies. *These are empirical questions* to be settled by inquiry using the methods suggested in this book.

These and other bizarre and somber events portrayed in the news media made me increasingly aware of the need to delve into mental processes that are outside of conscious awareness. It seemed unlikely that they could *all* be *fully* explained by theories of *rational* behavior such as the utility maximization that entrances economists, or by cognitive psychological concepts like framing, integrative complexity, social dominance theory, decision theory, or role analysis, important as they are. These concepts, and the research based on them, are important for two reasons: they explain significant parts of many phenomena, and, as cognitive researcher Ran Hassim points out below, they are suffused with ideation outside of conscious awareness. The work on social dominance, on framing, and on integrative complexity particularly impress me. Consequently, in Chapter 5, I propose an explicit set of procedures for setting psychodynamic research findings in the context of other social science concepts. *At the same time, in viewing the various destructive, self-destructive, and bizarre events described above, I concluded that methods are needed for effective inquiry into the* unconscious *mental processes underlying these deeply distressing events.* I also recognized that these inquiries would not be for the faint of heart.

Why These Research Methods are Needed to Study the Roots of Irrational Actions

The unconscious motives and fantasies underlying irrational actions are *paradoxical*: in the unconscious time does not exist, everything is in the present, opposites don't cancel each other out, there is magical thinking. As a result, the structured methods of the clinically informed psychodynamically sophisticated social sciences are necessary for drawing valid inferences about these matters. These methods can illuminate the phenomena, estimate and reduce researcher bias, and subject the researcher's assertions to disconfirmatory testing. *These are not the only useful methods but the particular kinds of methods I suggest are appropriate here because inquiries into unconscious factors in political/social events arouse extreme skepticism in many people, so a clearly articulated standard of proof is needed in these inquiries. The challenge posed by the paradoxical and enigmatic character of unconscious processes adds to the need for this kind of proof, as explained in Chapter 4.* Each of the following chapters sets forth and illustrates methods that will be useful to the researcher.

Knowing and not Knowing

The topics we will examine can be emotionally upsetting, as the reader will see from some of the examples in this book, and, perhaps understandably, many people prefer not to look too deeply into them. As we all know, the modern political and economic scene has been populated with dictators, genocidal wars, and wild, mutually destructive rages between religious and ethnic groups, and a huge range of other bizarre behaviors. I think we all realize *at some level* that not *all* of it can be explained as rational thinking by leaders and followers. In fact, I think we tend to *know and not know* at the same time. This situation suggests to me a "captive mind" syndrome that actively denies the reality of irrational unconscious processes while secretly knowing that they are real.

This syndrome was described by the Polish philosopher and poet (and Nobel Laureate) Czeslaw Milosz in his book *The Captive Mind* (1953 [1990]). He examined the blind belief of European intellectuals such as Sartre in the ethical purity of Marxist "dialectical materialism," despite the widespread bloody persecutions and murders by the Stalinist regime. Milosz's idea was that these intellectuals believed in the purity of the communist state while secretly knowing that it wasn't true.

Tony Judt (2010) applied the concept of "the captive mind" to the contemporary blind belief in "the free market mechanism," despite widespread evidence that it has created a plutocracy in America and is antithetical to the self-interest of most of the believers. The "captive mind" concept involves knowing and not knowing at the same time. These intellectuals give over their belief system to a dominant ethos but in a secret inner compartment of their mind they don't believe in it.

A related point was made by the psychologist David Bakan (1967a), who identified a "mystery–mastery complex," which involves wanting to know and wanting to not know at the same time. Bakan argued that much psychological inquiry is handicapped by self-imposed mental and methodological restrictions aimed at preventing the researcher from finding out things he would rather not know. Bakan argued that introspection is the key to escaping from the mystery–mastery complex. In Chapter 2 we will find evidence that introspection is essential to "mentalization," and empathy.

An underlying issue is that no one likes the idea that there is a part of our mind that is unknown to us and is outside of our control; even worse, others may occasionally get a glimpse of it without our knowing. As Freud said, this is a blow to our self-esteem.

Unconscious Processes are Embedded in Much of the Rest of Psychology

The idea of unconscious mental processes can seem strange, even self-contradictory: How can a thought be a thought if we are not aware of it? The cognitive researcher Ran Hassin has studied this issue (2014).

Hassin reviews a vast range of studies based on "priming" by presenting signals or information subliminally using a tachistoscope, at levels too fast and too faint to be visible consciously. These studies have found strong influences of signals and information of this sort on attitude change, sensory preferences, sensitivity to incongruent stimuli, political preferences, voting, and integration of information (reading of short verbal sentences and ability to do mathematical calculations). Pursuit of goals and various executive functions have also been shown to be affected by priming with stimuli presented tachistoscopically and therefore beyond conscious awareness.

Hasssin concludes:

> You have a lifetime of experiencing conscious events (such as thoughts and motivations) and not experiencing unconscious ones, a combination that intuitively suggests a crucial role for consciousness in many processes. Yet there is a science-based alternative... [the power of unconscious processes] is rendered plausible simply by how little we can consciously do at any given point in time, and it is backed by a lot of research (p. 36).

I think we can conclude from this and other evidence that unconscious processes are not separate from the rest of psychology, they are embedded in it.

An Example: Understanding the Rotherham Disaster

Human trafficking is not limited to the UK; it is active all over the world. Rotherham, however, has some peculiar features: in the length of time it persisted and the length of time that passed before it came to public attention. The large-scale exploitation began as early as 1998 but did not came to light until a court case in 2010.

According to a 2014 special report by Professor Alexis Jay, about 1400 children were sexually exploited over a 16-year period in Rotherham, South Yorkshire. She reported instances of "children who had been doused in petrol and threatened with being set alight, threatened with guns, made to witness violent rapes and threatened that they would be next if they told anyone...The children were raped by multiple perpetrators, trafficked to other towns and cites in the north of England, abducted, beaten, and intimidated." Professor Jay "found that girls as young as 11 had been raped by large numbers of men."

"Pakistani-heritage girls were targeted by taxi drivers and, on occasion, by older men lying in wait outside school gates." The women and girls feared reporting such incidents to the police because it would affect their future marriage prospects. The leadership of the Rotherham Council and the police downplayed the importance and "viewed many of the child victims with contempt." Three reports by front-line social service workers between 2002 and 2006 could not have been clearer in the description of the situation in Rotherham. The first was "effectively suppressed," the author was intimidated, her files stolen from her office. The next two reports were ignored.

"Professor Jay revealed last week that four years of meetings' minutes between children's social care teams, the police and the health service in Rotherham about exploitation issues have also gone missing" (BBC News, 2014a; *Guardian*, 2014; Thornton, 2014).

Many aspects to this situation call for psychodynamically sophisticated research. For example, the first question might be: How did the councilors and police persuade themselves that the situation would never come to light? Is this some sort of *denial*, in clinical terms? Or is it a case of feelings of *impunity*? Or is it a case of *knowing and not knowing at the same time*?

A second question: Stealing files from a researcher's office is bizarre. Years of Council minutes "gone missing?" How could they believe this would not come to light? Is this a *failure of reality testing*?

A third question: Why was this subject *taboo*? We know why the Asian victims (there were white victims, too, as the trafficking developed, but it began with Asian girls) couldn't complain to the police: not only fears of reprisal, but also loss of marital chances. No one in their culture would marry a woman who had been raped, for she is no longer a virgin. A cruel cultural norm and a way of blaming the victim and suppressing women. One wonders if there might be *intense underlying hostility to women* in some sectors of Asian culture; a good topic for clinically informed psychodynamically sophisticated research. We need to look deeper.

But why was the subject taboo for the authorities in Rotherham? We really need to know and therefore we need to look deeper here, too.

A fourth question: The reader will have noticed that a person is missing from every one of these accounts: the fact that there is a customer is never mentioned. This is startling. Why has there been no investigation into the identity and actions of the buyers? Reading the news articles, I feel that *the existence of the customers seems to be under serious repression*—it seems never to have occurred to the journalists or investigators to wonder about, or even to mention, the customers. The girls were being marketed to men who paid to exploit the girls sexually. Surely the customers, almost all of them, understood that the girls they were rented were there under duress, as slaves. Without customers, the whole trafficking scheme would fall to the ground. This is a buyers' market: the customer has the upper hand over the pimps who supply the girls. Where is the customer and who is the customer and what is his mentality, and why is he willing to subsidize slavery?

Some Issues of Social Scientific Inquiry

Falsifiability

The methods explained in this book have as their goal finding things out about irrationality in the political/social world, coming up with assertions about what has been found out, and exposing them to disconfirmation. I see falsifiability, also called "testability" and "disconfirmabilty," as a *technique* used to find out if an assertion is valid. This book concentrates on those social scientific methods of investigation that yield testable assertions *because I think this is especially helpful where irrationality on the world scene is being investigated. This is partly because of the intense skepticism such inquiries arouse in many people.* I do not go so far as to claim that *all* useful methods of social science inquiry seek disconfirmability; some of the anthropological and linguistic and hermeneutic methods, discourse analysis, for example, may not, but those are a topic for a different book.

Even Karl Popper, the theorist of falsifiability, did not require that all components of a theory be testable but he felt that if no component is testable, the theory is without meaning. As I explain in Chapter 4, his views have been criticized by some philosophers of science, such as Paul Feyerabend and Ernest Nagel, as too restrictive, and by my teacher, Thomas Kuhn, as not reflecting how major scientific breakthroughs come about or even how science is usually done. For many years I have been inspired by Abraham Kaplan's conception of the "loose construction" of experimentation: "poking nature with a stick" (1998 [2006]), and in this book I take a far more inclusive interpretation of falsifiability than Popper would.

Technique is not all-powerful. Chapter 2 is devoted to the nature and contribution of empathic understanding in social science research, and Chapter 10 extends that discussion by considering the work of Mannheim, Ellul, Baron-Cohen, Taleb, and Berlinsky on technique versus empathic understanding. It becomes clear that technique has its own limits, and that the kind of crisply articulated proof provided by falsifiability may not always be possible in practice to get in some areas of social inquiry, even though we would like to do so. But we should try. Chapter 7 on narrative analysis, and Chapter 9, on symbolic interactionist collaboration, present qualitative approaches that did result in disconfirmable predictions.

And there are obviously forms of understanding or insight outside the social sciences that do not readily lend themselves to falsifiability. These include art, music, and literature, which give us insights that are sometimes partly inchoate, sometimes partly unspoken, often profound, and deeply freeing, but either peculiarly difficult to disconfirm or perhaps impossible in principle (no amount of ingenuity will work). But these areas are outside the scope of a book on social science research methods.

Subjectivity

Although they sound like opposites, "subjectivity" *and* "objectivity" *are not mutually exclusive.* All research involves interpretation of what to look for and interpretation of what has been found, and this is, by nature, partly subjective, varying with the inquirer or researcher.

In fact, the initial judgment as to whether a political/social event is "highly destructive, self-destructive, or extremely bizarre" (my definition of "the irrational") itself involves judgment and interpretation. Some subjectivity is inescapable.

What is chosen to look for, and how what has been found is conceptualized, will vary with the observer or researcher, and with the culture in which the researcher is embedded. A Japanese, a Frenchman, and an American, each doing an ethnographic study of an inner city (or of a corporation), will see different things; each will contribute a personal and cultural bias, and each will see part of the phenomena and miss part of the phenomena. Many of these differences among the study findings will not be mutually contradictory. *Subjectivity, therefore, can actually increase the amount of insight that can result from* "objective" *(disconfirmable) research.*

But where the differences in interpretation are mutually contradictory, a good answer is to expose the assertions resulting from each study to disconfirmation, as explained in Chapter 4. Even further, before the disconfirmation is attempted, an effort to get a more inclusive interpretation by means of symbolic interactive collaboration, as shown in Chapter 9, could precede and enrich the effort to assess disconfirmability.

Reflexivity

Reflexivity connotes taking into account the effect of the research on the researcher, which then influences the research, which in turn influences the researcher, in an endless cycle.

What I propose in this book meets the criterion of reflexivity. I suggest including the natural history of a study; the open statement of the researcher's initial biases; the account of the researcher's mentality and how it changes during the study; the vicissitudes of the research group; the sometime need for a triple blind to help minimize the researcher's bias; the effect of replication.

As Lynn Chancer and John Andrew point out (2014), transference and counter-transference are factors in reflexivity that are especially important in ethnographic studies. I discuss these in Chapter 6, under the topic of self-disclosure.

Reflexivity is also a basic element in elite and specialized interviewing, which is described in Chapter 10. It begins with a very vague initial question: ("What's it like to be the Head of the Senate Foreign Relations Committee?", or "What's it like to be a tool-and-die maker?"). The interview then proceeds with a free-form statement from the elite interviewee or the specialized interviewee (who is expert in some field or by way of experience). This statement then stirs associations in the interviewer, whose questions stir new associations in the interviewee, whose responses stir new associations and new questions in the interviewer, in a constant cycle.

Reductionism

This accusation refers to transforming a complex social and political and economic situation into a simpler psychological one. Reductionism in psychology itself is an attempt to account for a higher psychological level in terms of what may be perceived as a more basic level, and it is important in a wide array of psychological activities, such as perception, cognition, and neuropsychology, but reductionism is unsuited to the social/political areas we are studying.

The methods I propose here do not involve reductionism, for the following reasons.

Firstly, as I explain in detail in Chapter 4, the psychological dimensions of a political or social event or phenomenon cannot act in a unitary and dominant manner: they are *constrained by the external situation* in largely the same way as the response to a projective test of telling a story to a picture, the Thematic Apperception Test, for example, is constrained by the actual subject of the picture.

Secondly, as I explain in Chapter 4, the psychological component of a political, social, or economic act is an *intervening variable,* intervening between a political cause, such as the slaughter in World War I, and a political effect, the appeasement in the Munich Agreement that gave the Sudetenland, and ultimately Czechoslovakia, to Hitler. The psychological component is *not a cause independent of political causes but instead operates as a member of a sequence of events.*

Thirdly, *a coherence theory of truth,* as explained in Chapter 9, *demands that various components of an explanation fit together rather than operate independently.*

Empathy, Introspection, and Testability

I explain in Chapter 2 that empathy is a basic component of most psychological understanding, and that it depends on introspection, and that it characterizes social scientific inquiry into unconscious factors in political/social events.

Empathy involves looking inward to see one's own reaction to a person or event. This can be shown neurologically, as Chapter 2 explains, and it is related to "mentalization." Empathy and introspection is also called "intraception."

The assertions that emanate from an empathic, introspective analysis, are usually testable. In fact, Chapter 2 includes a set of six experiments by me subjecting the possibility of accurate empathy to empirical test.

In general, empathic insights are falsified by looking at an event outside the observer that should occur on the basis of the insight but did not occur.

N = 1 Studies

In this book I take the view that studies with only one subject (or "participant" in current terminology) can yield important findings and can lead to other studies. In Chapter 6, the study proposed of the Bernard Madoff video is an N = 1 study. In Chapter 8 the study of Zhirinovsky, Le Pen, and Papadopoulos is an N = 3 study, which led to the N = 1 vignette of Nigel Farage. Small samples viewed deeply can be of great value.

What About the Many Different Conceptions of the Unconscious? Do They Affect Testability?

There are many conceptions of what the unconscious is, differing in various ways from Freud's formulation and from each other.

Sigmund Freud viewed the unconscious as a repository of biological drives, primarily sexual but also aggressive. These have a dynamic force, a push for expression and satisfaction, and are kept in check by the force of repression and the activity of the ego, mostly conscious, and the superego, to a major extent unconscious.

The ego psychologists, following the lead of Anna Freud, stress the importance of the ego's many defenses in warding off the direct expression of the unconscious drives.

Stephen Frosh (2010, pp. 7–8), however, views the unconscious as an ever-present deeply disruptive force that constantly prevents the establishment of a true "self."

The object relations theorists view the unconscious not primarily as the repository of representations of biological drives but rather as the representations of interactions that have occurred with the person and important people in the person's early life, a kind of community of interacting people (Frosh, 2002, pp. 17–18).

The political philosopher and psychoanalytic theorist Slavoj Žižek views the unconscious as exhibiting a Lacanian "jouissance," a flooding with unconscious pleasure in "irrational investments in political turmoil," as Frosh (2010, p. 183) points out.

Each of these conceptions of the unconscious, when confronted with a seemingly irrational political/social event, may yield a different interpretation of that event. But what is key is that each of these interpretations is very likely to be testable. Therefore, the variety of conceptions of the unconscious is not a problem for the social science research methods I explain in this book.

For instance, even the interpretation that political turmoil is greeted by some with "jouissance" rather than with apprehensiveness, strikes me as testable, using, for example, scales of anxiety, projective tests, and observations of behavior and body language.

Another testable interpretation: Slavoj Žižek (2010) asserts that in the United States the right-wing forces have stolen the populist appeal from the left wing. A prediction: Tea Party rallies will feature guitar players singing western and country kinds of songs. Result: yes. Another prediction: Music at Tea Party rallies will be reminiscent of the protest music Pete Seeger used to sing at left-wing rallies ("Blowing in the Wind..." and "The Banks are Made of Marble..."). Result: yes. "We're Not Gonna Take It Anymore" was the theme song of Republican leader Paul Ryan until the authors of the song withdrew it.

Testing an interpretation of an event is quite a different matter, however, from testing an entire theory or even testing a component of a theory; those tasks would be infinitely more difficult, but what confronts us is the far easier task of exposing an interpretation of a specific event to disconfirmation. The examples in Chapter 4, and the one at the conclusion of Chapter 9 are examples of what can be done.

What About Introspections About One's Own Inner Psychological Processes? Are They Testable?

Sometimes.

Some introspective processes are about the self and therefore do not have the characteristic of "publicity;" that is, there is nothing external to point to. Can these be a valid form of knowledge or understanding of insight without a predicted external event to point to?

An example is provided by the introspections of Henri Poincaré (1913 [2001]). He describes the processes of his own mathematical discoveries:

> For a fortnight I had been attempting to prove that there could not be any function analogous to what I have since called Fuchsian functions...Every day I sat down at my table and spent an hour or two trying a great number of combinations until I arrived at no result. One night I took some black coffee, contrary to my custom, and was unable to sleep. A host of ideas kept surging in my head, I could almost feel them jostling one another, until two of them coalesced, so to speak, to form a stable combination. When morning came, I had established the existence of one class of Fuchsian functions...
>
> At this moment I left Caen to take part in a geological conference.... Having reached Coutances, we entered an omnibus to go some place or other. At the moment when I put my foot on the step, the idea came to me, without anything in my former thoughts seeming to have paved the way for it, that the transformations I had used to define the Fuchsian functions were identical with those of non-Euclidian geometry. ...

> I turned my attention to the study of some arithmetical questions without any great apparent result. Disgusted with my failure, I went to spend a few days at the seaside and thought of something else. One morning, walking on the bluff, the idea came to me, with just the same characteristics of brevity, suddenness and immediate certainty, that the arithmetic transformations of indefinite ternary quadratic forms were identical with those of non-Euclidian geometry...Most striking at first is this appearance of sudden illumination, a manifest sign of long, unconscious prior work. The role of this unconscious work in mathematical invention appears to me incontestable, and traces of it would be found in other cases where it is less evident (pp. 387–400).

How do I know Poincaré is telling the truth about what happens inside him? Maybe he is trying to fool me? Unlikely, given his stature as a mathematician for the ages, spoken of in the same breath as Archimedes, Newton, Euler, and Gauss.

But could he be mistaken about his own creative processes? Maybe he followed a decision tree, or an algorithm, or a syllogism to get to his revolutionary mathematical insights, and didn't know it? Well, in *The Psychology of Invention in the Mathematical Field* (1944), we have the testimony of Jacques Hadamard, also a world-class mathematician, who recounts similar intrapsychic experiences. He agrees with Poincaré (p. 14), and quotes Gauss:

> Finally, two days ago, I succeeded, not on account of my painful efforts, but by the grace of God. Like a sudden flash of lightning, the riddle happened to be solved. I myself cannot say what was the conducting thread which connected what I previously knew with what made my success possible (p. 15).

But could Hadamard and Gauss be mistaken as well? I suppose given my liberal interpretation of falsification, Hadamard's failure to provide a divergent account could be taken as a failure of disconfirmation.

There is some corollary evidence. A major psychoanalytical inquiry into such matters is the work by Ernst Kris (1952a, 1952b), under the rubric "regression to the preconscious in the service of the ego."

But another method of my subjecting Poincaré's and Hadamard's testimony to disconfirmation is for me to look inward at my own creative processes. Do my major (for me) and original (to me) insights come as a result of a decision tree or as a sudden unexpected insight following work done earlier? The latter, they arrive when I am in the shower in the morning, or preparing for bed in the evening, or when I am talking to someone during the day on another topic, or I am walking along thinking of something else and suddenly I see a new connection. The reader can also look inward at his or her own creative processes to see if they resemble those reported by Poincaré, Hadamard, and Gauss. As David Bakan observed, "Pavlov's dogs are quite dead" but "each scientist has at least one 'dog' he can observe directly" (1967b, p. 98).

In other words, *introspective insights that others relate can sometimes be exposed to disconfirmation by looking at one's own internal experiences to see whether or not something similar can be found.*

Are there introspective experiences that people relate that, in principle, I cannot confirm by looking inward to my own processes, nor by seeking external verification, but which still constitute understanding or insight? (By "in principle" I mean that no amount of ingenuity will suffice.)

Clearly, yes, in the realm of art, music, and literature, but these are beyond the purview of this book. Readers can find a classic guide to these understandings in the realm of poetry in Brooks and Warren (1938 [1976]), and a good modern guide in Marc Polonsky (2001). These are surely understandings and insights but I would reserve the term "knowledge" for the disconfirmable.

Post-modernism, Post-structuralism, and Critical Theory?

What about other modes of analysis, say critical theory, feminist theory, deconstruction, post-modernism, post-structuralism, and Lacanian psychoanalytic theory? What about the writings of Stephen Frosh, Yannis Stavrakakis, Judith Butler, Slavoj Žižek, Jacques Lacan, Jacques Derrida, and Michel Foucault?

Adherents of many of these theories might call the social science methods that are the subject of this book "bourgeois science," or term them "bureaucratic" or "normalizing." Generally speaking, with some exceptions, advocates of these positions argue that modern social science methods and perspectives are overly rational, overly "objective," overly structured, very culture-bound and culture-limited, and serve in a concealed way to organize language and thought to the disadvantage of subordinate social groups, especially women and minorities, and thus constitute a form of subjugation and colonialism. These theories emphasize interpretation rather than verification, reflexivity rather than objectivity, and "meaning rather than cause." They often seem to assume that their insights are untestable, but with this I disagree. The *theories themselves* or the *major components* of their theories may be difficult or impossible to test, but once they are applied to *interpreting the meaning of a political/social event,* that *specific interpretation* is, in my view, falsifiable in Popper's terms.

These are important and influential ideas, rooted in philosophy and language, as well as in psychoanalysis. I believe the reader will find that a strength of many of these perspectives is that they dissect language and concepts to show that they are not universalistic but rather are culture-bound, supporting systems of thought and action that preserve existing social arrangements. Neil McLaughlin (2014) argues that there is a deep connection between the Lacanian perspective and that of sociology: both reject the sharp distinction between the individual and the society. John Andrews (2014), also writing from a Lacanian viewpoint, argues for a deep connection between socioeconomic phenomena, such as foreclosure and the Occupy Our Homes Movement, and unconscious processes.

I think it is fair to say that most of these perspectives are very complex, often paradoxical (as with Lacan and Žižek), and given to metaphor and the use of common words in very unusual senses. As a result, they are far from easy reading and deserve and require their own detailed presentations. Since most proponents of these perspectives would reject the concept of falsifiability of their theories, they are beyond the scope of a book on social science methodology, which inevitably focuses on methods to assess validity and testability. A more intensive consideration of them must be left to the reader, with two exceptions: the contributions of the Frankfort School, and the nature of the overlap of these theories with social science research methods.

The Frankfurt School

An exception to the densely written and sometimes enigmatic writings of the theorists cited above is the work of the "Frankfurt School," which includes Theodor W. Adorno, Herbert Marcuse, and the psychoanalyst Erich Fromm. I think the reader will find these more readily understandable and more closely related to social science research methods. Like the above theorists, they take a "critical theory" approach. In that approach the assumptions and ideology underlying social conditions, and involved in social investigation itself, are examined and questioned, particularly in relation to their function in supporting the existing social structure. Adorno, with the psychoanalyst Else Frenkel-Brunswik and the American social scientists Daniel Levinson and Nevitt Sanford, produced *The Authoritarian Personality* (1950), a landmark empirical study of the ideology of authoritarianism, complete with attitude scales, which has inspired decades of research by legions of researchers.

The methodological approach of the present book is very consistent with the approach of Adorno, who used statements from the speeches of

Adolf Hitler to construct the F (Fascism) Scale in *The Authoritarian Personality*. It is also kindred to the work of Erich Fromm (1941, 1961), who conducted an empirical study of the German working class (as pointed out by Neil McLaughlin (2014).

The implicit message of the Frankfurt School is that something in the social system is wrong, something is amiss, something has gone awry. This *is also the implicit message of modern social science research. Social scientists know where the bodies are buried,* so to speak, they know something has gone wrong (e.g. racism, sexism, absurdly skewed distribution of income and wealth, and threats from climate change), *and in that sense they are at one with the* "critical theorists," although this fact is not openly acknowledged.

If one says, as sociologists do, that social class is the most powerful explanatory variable in the social sciences, one is not making a normalizing statement but rather an implicit critique of the status quo. And documenting that in the United States women earn only 79 percent of what men earn for the same work is not making a normalizing statement: something is amiss, something is awry, something has gone wrong.

The reader will see that most of the examples I analyze in this book have something amiss by definition: "irrational" is defined in terms of the highly destructive, the self-destructive, and the very bizarre.

Other Overlaps of Social Science Research Methods With "Post-modern" Perspectives

Our presentation of social science research methods overlaps with "post-modern" perspectives in three additional ways: firstly, our use of empathy and introspection in our research efforts; secondly, our recognition of "reflexivity," as explained in the previous section; and, thirdly, our attempt to confront and lessen interpretive bias in the researcher, which is roughly analogous to counter-transference in psychoanalytic terms. We seek to confront and limit it by self-disclosure, by providing a natural history of the study, and by detailing the researcher's phenomenology during the study, as explained in Chapter 6, and we also show that counter-transference can be illuminating if understood.

The Chapters

It will be helpful to the reader to have an indication of what the following chapters will present.

Chapter 2: Exploring the Empathic Method

Methods explained: Mentalization, empathy, and introspection

The extensive basis of mentalization and empathy in *clinical experience*, particularly in early child development, and its relation to clinical phenomena such as Asperger's syndrome, is discussed. Then there is a presentation of the *modern neuroscientific research* that puts this area on a scientific basis. This chapter aims to give the reader a clinical and neurological understanding of how one person's thoughts and actions can resonate in another person and be understood by that person.

The chapter also summarizes experiments I conducted, the results of which indicate that, *under certain specific conditions and in certain specific circumstances*, mentalization and empathy can yield accurate and valid inferences on social and cultural matters.

Chapter 3: What to Look for in Psychodynamic Inquiry

Method explained: A research protocol for psychodynamic inquiry into world events

How exactly can clinicians apply and use the mentalization and empathy processes described in Chapter 2? To answer this, Chapter 3 offers a detailed *protocol* useful for psychodynamic studies. A research protocol in the social sciences is a specified set of research procedures that tells the investigator what kinds of data to look for and how those data should be considered and understood. The concrete examples in this chapter will help the reader understand in detail what is involved in the attempt to apply psychodynamic insights to world events.

Chapter 4: Explorations in the Disconfirmation of Psychodynamic Assertions on the World Scene

Methods explained: Popperian disconfirmation of unusual predictions; coping with the inherent difficulties in psychodynamic inference; identity with the inferential procedures of projective testing; psychodynamic processes as intervening variables; multiple indicators and multiple measures

This chapter explores *the procedure of Popperian disconfirmation* as applied to psychodynamic assertions on the world scene. This is a radical approach, using a very strict criterion to assess the validity of psychodynamic assertions. The examples include the trial of Marshal Pétain; the strange reception accorded two escapees from Auschwitz; the mass murder, by physicians, of the retarded and brain damaged in Germany; and the bombing of Beirut. Two solutions to the problem of reductionism are also explained. The importance of replication is illustrated by a short study of urban air traffic overflights.

Chapter 5: Integrating Social Science Concepts and Findings into Psychodynamic Inquiry

Social science concepts whose relevance is explained: alienation, anomie, deindividuation, dehumanization, attitudinal modernity versus traditionalism; stigmatization, deviance, social disorganization, pluralistic ignorance, bystander apathy, obedience to authority, conformity, groupthink, perspective-taking, Verstehen, Gemeinschaft, Gesellschaft, social class, social stratification, and national character

The relation of psychodynamic inquiry to some of the social sciences is not solely one of method. It is also a matter of integrating *substantive social science concepts and research findings* into the planning and interpretation of the research.

This chapter suggests detailed procedures for achieving that integration. Creative use of items from established attitude scales is explained with examples.

Chapter 6: A Panoply of Social Science Methods to Illuminate the Phenomena, Reduce Researcher Bias, and Permit Disconfirmation

Methods explained: Specification of a protocol; systematic and random sampling methods; purposeful sampling; thick description and very extensive verbatim quotations; self-disclosure by the researcher of personal background and possible bias; the natural history of a study; quantitative and qualitative content analysis; multiple raters; validation through symbolic interactionist procedures or the Delphi technique; use of informants in the tradition of urban sociological field work; and Popperian disconfirmation procedures using risky prediction; narrative analysis of Timothy Garton Ash's The File; *and similar personal accounts, memoirs, and oral histories.*

The unconscious motives and fantasies underlying irrational actions are paradoxical: time does not exist, everything is in the present, opposites don't cancel each other out, and there is magical thinking. As a result, the structured methods of the clinically sophisticated social sciences are necessary for drawing valid inferences about these matters. These methods can *illuminate the phenomena*, estimate and *reduce researcher bias*, and subject the researcher's assertions to *disconfirmatory testing*.

Creative use of scales from established instruments like the MMPI (Minnesota Multiphasic Personality Inventory) in the analysis of data is also explained.

Chapter 7: An Adventure in Narrative Analysis: "A Regular Terrible Story"

Method explained: Narrative analysis

This chapter presents a case study of a narrative analysis of a series of scandals in the American media. The chapter begins with a discussion of the nature of narrative analysis: what one looks for, and why. Then the fabricated story series in the *Washington Post*, which got a Pulitzer until discovered, and a repetition at the *New York Times*, are presented and analyzed.

Chapter 8: A Systematic Study of Irreality

Methods explained: Survey sampling, content analysis, thick description, and very extensive verbatim quotation

What does a psychodynamically informed study of world events actually look like? There are many varieties, but to give the reader a more concrete feel for the process, Chapter 8 presents as an example a study of my own concerning world press reports on Vladimir Zhirinovsky, Jean-Marie Le Pen, and Georgios Papadopoulos, focusing on a concept I call *irreality* in political affairs. The chapter includes a detailed exposition of the expansion of the irreal in the present day, in political life (Nigel Farage), on the Internet in many forms, and in modern literature.

Chapter 9: The Munich Crisis Examined: An Experiment in Collaboration in Data Interpretation

Methods explained: Collaboration in the interpretation of data; iterative interaction; the emergence of jointly agreed meanings through the process of symbolic interaction; the use of informants; elite and specialized interviewing; the Delphi technique; content analysis; non-reactive data; control for researcher bias; Popperian disconfirmation

This chapter describes an experiment in collaboration, in response to a psychodynamic inquiry on the mentality of the Czechoslovak leaders, the populace and media, before and during the Munich crisis of September 1938. Three eminent Czech political psychologists, who lived through the Nazi or Communist dictatorships in Czechoslovakia, engaged in scholarly collaboration with clinician and historian David Beisel. I examine their interaction and the extent that through working together a meaningful consensus has been reached. The degree of agreement might also be understood using a coherence theory of truth and McGuire's boundary-setting procedure or by a disconfirmatory study. The chapter concludes with an effort at disconfirmation.

Chapter 10: Methods for Studying Irrationality in Organizations, Institutions, and Social Movements: Overview and a Case Study: Urban Design

Methods explained: Elite and specialized interviewing; use of informants; field work; participation in the social role; participant observation; field experimentation; analysis of the logical sequence; stratified sampling, content analysis, legal research, and in-milieu studies

This chapter sets forth some *generally* useful methods for doing research on irrational elements in organizations, institutions, and social movements. The chapter then considers a case study: urban design and the livability of cities, and special research methods useful for this kind of study.

Chapter 11: Methods for Studying Irrationality in Organizations, Institutions, and Social Movements, and Two Case Studies: Climate Change Denial and Corporate Acquisitiveness

Methods explained: Elite and specialized interviewing; use of informants; field work; participant observation; in-milieu observation; systematic random sampling; purposeful sampling;, content analysis; legal research

This chapter provides two case studies, one of *a social movement, the denial of man-made climate change, and one of an institution, the large Anglo-American publicly traded business corporation*. One case concerns our irrational responses to the reality of climate change and global warming caused in considerable part by human activity. A second topic is the untrammeled acquisitive mentality of some of the large corporations that have come to dominate modern economic life. Each is often very destructive or self-destructive, and very bizarre, suggesting the influence of irrational mental processes outside of conscious awareness. Appropriate research methods for studies like these are explained.

2
Exploring the Empathic Method

If a thing is impossible, it can be done.
Hungarian proverb

This chapter will look at the mental processes involved in doing psychodynamically informed studies of world events. These processes turn out to be deeply rooted in the basic nature of the human mind. A key element in this type of investigation is a process called "empathy."

Terminology

First, let me clarify the terminology: *empathy* has been variously called *mentalization*, or *perspective-taking*, or *having a theory of mind*, and it has been studied under those names. Some researchers prefer one term, others prefer another. The results under the three rubrics have been consistent with each other. Let us begin with the neuroscientific evidence that empathic processes, of the kind needed for psychodynamically informed inquiry do, in fact, exist.

Neurologic Evidence for Empathic Thinking

Neuroscientists have found neurologic bases for empathy. One of these bases is the activity of "mirror neurons," discovered by Giacomo Rizzolatti, a neuroscientist at the University of Parma, in a study of monkeys. In people, these neurons are located in various areas of the brain, including the premotor cortex, the posterior parietal lobe, the superior temporal sulcus, and the insula. Researchers such as Dr. Marco Iacoboni, a neuroscientist at the University of California, Los Angeles (UCLA), and Dr. Christian Keysers, who studies the neural basis of empathy at the University of Groningen in the Netherlands, have found that when we observe another person performing an activity, mirror neurons become activated in the same areas of our brain as in the brain of the person being watched. Sometimes we are aware of having an empathic emotional response with what we are watching or hearing, but sometimes our response is entirely outside of conscious awareness.

Neuroscientific Evidence for Unconscious Mental Processes

Neuroscientists, as we saw above, have found that the emotional excitation associated with the activity of mirror neurons, often occurs outside of conscious awareness. In other words, what we call *empathy* or *mentalization* often occurs at the unconscious level. What other evidence have neuroscientists found for the existence of unconscious mental processes?

Modern brain imaging research appears to indicate that the idea of two systems, conscious and unconscious, has analogs and concomitants in the neurologic structure and functioning of the brain. There is mounting evidence that the concept of unconscious mental processes is helpful in explaining certain neurologic phenomena, and vice versa.

Nobel Laureate Eric Kandel (2007) writes:

> A century after Freud suggested that psychopathology arises from conflict occurring on an unconscious level and that it can be regulated if the source of the conflict is confronted consciously, our imaging studies suggest ways in which such conflicting processes may be mediated in the brain. [This research] validates biologically the Freudian idea that unconscious mental processes are part of the brain's system of information processing (quoted in Kouvelas and Akinosoglou, 2014).

In a Plenary Address to the American Psychological Association (2009), the UCLA neuroscientist Alan Schore quotes the following:

- "UCS [unconditioned stimulus] processing of emotional stimuli activates right and not left hemisphere. The left side [of the brain] is involved with conscious response and the right with the unconscious mind" (Mlot, 1998).
- "We found that the left hemisphere more than the right can mediate conscious elaboration...This result is in line with previous research, that underlined a left-conscious/right-unconscious dichotomy" (Balconi and Lucchiari, 2007).

- "In most people, the verbal, conscious and serial information processing takes place in the left hemisphere, while the unconscious, nonverbal and *emotional* information processing mainly takes place in the right hemisphere" (Larsen, 2003).
- "That explicit and implicit aspects of the self exist is not a particularly novel idea. It is closely related to Freud's partition of the mind into conscious, preconscious (accessible but not currently accessed), and unconscious (inaccessible) levels" (LeDoux, 2002)

A further account of some of these ideas is given in Carhart-Harris and Friston (2010).

Empathy as a Developmental Process: The Concept of Mentalization

In recent years, empathic ability has been conceptualized and studied as "mentalization." Peter Fonagy (in Busch, 2008, p. 1) defines mentalization as

> ... *the capacity to conceive of mental states as explanations of behavior in oneself and others*...We define mentalization as a form of mostly preconscious imaginative mental activity, namely interpreting behavior in terms of intentional mental states (needs, desires, feelings, beliefs, goals, purposes, and reasons). ... Mentalization...had great evolutionary value in helping the organism understand and cope with his world (my emphasis).

In this passage from Busch (2008), "preconscious" refers to thoughts, memories, and feelings that are just outside of awareness but are accessible and can be brought into awareness more easily for some people than others. Ernst Kris (1952a, 1952b) and Heinz Hartmann (Hartmann et al., 1951), in their studies of creativity, found that easy access to preconscious ideas and fantasies is important to the creative process, and Busch is asserting that this access is also essential to the ability to sense how others are thinking and feeling.

How Mentalization Develops

Mentalization is a very deep component of mental development as it arises from *the attachment relationship*: the emotional connection between mother and child, and it helps the infant understand his or her world. Busch observes:

> More generally, the attachment relationship serves as the context within which mentalization can be acquired because in this context the child can relatively safely explore the mind of the other feeling relatively certain that the latter will harbor few if any hostile attachments toward the self (2008, p. 15).

and:

> The capacity to mentalize is a key determinant of self-organization that...is acquired in the context of early attachment relationships. Disturbances of attachment relationships will therefore disrupt the normal emergence [of mentalization] (2008, p. 3).

Mentalization Requires Introspection

Mentalization is importantly related to introspection. The ability to mentalize, that is, to understand how another person thinks and feels, requires the ability to look inside oneself and get access to one's own inner life.

> We should remember that mentalizing pertains to interpreting mental states in both self and others. ... Self-awareness and awareness of the mental states of others are closely related in terms of the brain areas involved (Busch, 2008, p. 9).

Busch is not alone in this view of mentalization and empathy. Theodor Reik (1948) observed that one has to be able to listen to one's own inner life in order to be able to tune in to another person's. Reik was speaking of conducting clinical treatment of a patient, but a similar phenomenon is involved in clinically informed inquiry in the social and political realm. *Doing psychodynamic inquiry validly and accurately involves the ability to understand how another person thinks, and this requires listening for echoes in one's own thoughts.*

Other social scientists have also been concerned with these matters. There is a tradition of discussion, starting at least with Dilthey, or even earlier, of the need to put oneself in the mindset of the people one is studying (Dilthey, 1978). The psychologist David Bakan (1967b) explained introspection as a method of investigation that involves empathy.

Perspective Taking and "Having a Theory of Mind"

Where many researchers use the term "mentalization," or "empathy," other researchers have used the term *having a theory of mind,* for a similar concept. They view it as more heavily biologically rooted than do the clinical researchers, who are concerned with the influence of attachment on mentalization.

Social psychologists have used the term *perspective taking* to describe something akin to what clinicians have called "mentalization." For example, Allison Hall says:

> Perspective taking is the ability to see things from a point of view other than one's own...In describing perspective taking, Moskowitz says: "We must be able to stand in the shoes of others, see the world through their eyes, empathize with what they are feeling, and attempt to think and react to the world in the same way that they think and react to the world." Perspective taking is often referred to as or considered a part of the "theory of mind," a concept introduced in 1978 by researchers Premack and Woodruff who tested chimpanzees to see if they understood that others had a different mind and point of view. Perspective taking, or theory of mind, is considered an important step in the cognitive development of children (2004, pp. 1–2).

When Mentalization Fails: Autism and Asperger's Syndrome

The autism researcher Uta Frith (2008) presents an extended discussion of research on mentalization in children and adults by Baron-Cohen and colleagues at Cambridge University (2000, 2001). She concludes that the failure to have "a theory of mind" is one of the defining characteristics of autism and of Asperger's syndrome. Even more relevant for us, these researchers also examined differences in the tendency to be empathic among people who are in the normal range of psychological functioning.

Some Caveats With Regard to Empathy

But some caveats are necessary in our exploration of this topic. For one thing, "empathy" has become a very widely used term in a variety of contexts in the clinical field, often without a careful definition. Moreover, there are likely to be different kinds of empathy, from street smarts to clinical intuition, to identification, to projective identification, to merger fantasies. And despite the frequency of difficulties with empathy and mentalization in people with Asperger's syndrome, clinicians have found that severely disturbed people sometimes show astonishing bursts of empathy.

Empathizing Versus Systemizing: Differences Among the Professions

In a classic article, Baron-Cohen et al. (1985) argue that people within the normal range vary in their proclivity to form a theory of mind, and that they vary along a dimension called *systemizing* versus *empathizing*.

Nassim Taleb observes:

> According to [Simon Baron-Cohen's] research purely systemizing persons are drawn to engineering and similar occupations (and when they fail, to, say, mathematical economics); empathizing minds are drawn to more social (or literary) professions...Males are overrepresented in the systemizing category; females dominate the other extreme (Taleb, 2010, p. 340).

Is Accurate Empathy Feasible in Scientific Investigation?

We have looked at the neuroscientific evidence for the existence of unconscious mental processes. We have also looked at the neuroscientific evidence for the existence of empathic mental reactions often outside of conscious awareness.

We have seen that clinicians have studied empathy, which they call "mentalization," or "having a theory of mind," in children and its value for adult functioning as well, and the disability faced by persons unable to sense that others have minds and feelings.

We have also noted that social scientists have studied the workings of empathy under the title of "perspective taking."

We have also looked briefly at evidence that people in the various professions tend to differ in their access to, or reliance on, empathic modes of thinking.

So the reality of empathy as a kind of mental functioning, often outside of conscious awareness, is pretty well established from a scientific and clinical point of view. This bodes well for considering empathic understanding as a key element of clinically sophisticated psychodynamically oriented research into social and political problems and events.

In fact, the reality of empathy is so well established by social science and neurologic research studies that measures of empathy have been constructed.

The Measurement of Empathy

Research to measure empathy has a long history and is proceeding apace today. The website www.cultureofempathy.com lists more than a score of measures, both those in questionnaire format and those using recognition of facial expressions in photos.

Here, for example, are some items from the Toronto Empathy Scale (Spreng et al., 2009):

> When someone else is feeling excited, I tend to get excited too
> It upsets me to see someone being treated disrespectfully
> When a friend starts to talk about his/her problems, I try to steer the conversation towards something else (scored in the opposite direction)
> I become irritated when someone cries (scored in the opposite direction)
> I am not really interested in how other people feel (scored in the opposite direction)
> I get a strong urge to help when I see someone who is upset.

Experimental Evidence of Accurate Empathy With Specific Social Groups

Can we go further? *Can we find further evidence that empathic understanding of other social groups can be accurate?*

The philosopher and sociologist of knowledge Abraham Kaplan (1998 [2006]) has defined the experimental method as "poking nature with a stick to see what happens." Experimentation is certainly the most powerful method of settling intellectual disputes in cases where we can find a way to get experimental purchase on the problem.

In certain situations, there are ways of getting experimental evidence on the accuracy of empathy. For example, a series of experiments I have conducted indicate that, under certain circumstances, some people can accurately replicate the thought patterns of certain professional and social groups. I will outline some of these studies here and present them and others in detail in the Appendix.

Essentially, and in summary, I first studied the responses of small numbers of artists (mostly painters and sculptors) and scientists (mostly physicists) on an attitude test called the Intraception/Extraception Scale (I/E; Murray, 1938). This measures a person's tendency to rely on external objective facts (extraception, looking outward) versus being interested in one's own inner life and thought processes and those of others (intraception, looking inward). The extremes might be an engineer and a poet, perhaps.

I found that my two groups of participants differed greatly on the I/E Scale, in the expected direction: the art students were much higher in intraception and the physics students were much higher in extraception.

Next, I asked a group of people, mostly students, who were neither artists of any kind nor scientists of any kind, to take the I/E test, first as an artist would and then as a scientist would. They proved able to duplicate the scores achieved by the actual artists and scientists in the previous experiment, scoring very high in the intraception direction when answering the items as they imagined an artist would, and scoring very high in the extraception direction when answering the items as they imagined a scientist would.

In experiment IIB we consider a somewhat different social and professional group, namely people defined by our society as highly creative and original, from the 1950s and 1960s. Such people were studied by Professors Donald McKinnon and Frank Barron at the Institute for Personality Assessment and Research (IPAR) at the University of California at Berkeley (Barron, 1963). Participants came to IPAR for the studies and stayed a week. The participants for the studies included Pulitzer Prize winners, National Book Award winners, Nobel Laureates, famous architects, and the like. They were systematically compared with a matched group of people from the same professional fields with the same education, who were ordinary competent professionals rather than national or world-class creative professionals. Barron and McKinnon identified a number of traits in which the two groups differed, and were able to find a considerable group of attitude items, which the highly creative participants answered differently from their professional colleagues. One such attitude was dubbed the Barron Originality Test (Barron, 1955).

I was interested to see if ordinary people could answer these attitude questions in the same ways in which the highly creative people studied at the IPAR had done.

The participants in my study were undergraduate students at Harvard and Radcliffe. There were three groups. Participants in group A1 were given the Barron Originality Test and asked to answer it (standard instructions).

Participants in group A2 were given the Barron Originality Test (Barron, 1955), and asked to answer it "as a very creative and original person would."

Each participant in group A3 was given the Barron Originality Test with standard instructions. When he or she had finished, each participant was given the Barron Originality Test a second time, with instructions to answer it "as a very creative and original person would."

The results were that the participants in group A2, with the empathy-based instructions, scored much higher on the Barron Originality Test than did the participants in group A1, which had the standard instructions.

Moreover, the participants in group A3, which had first the standard instructions, and then the empathy-based instructions, scored much higher on the Barron Originality Test with the empathy-based instructions than they had earlier with the standard instructions.

I think these results indicate that when motivated to do so, many people can empathize accurately with a socially defined group, namely persons designated as highly creative and original by our society.

It is important to remember that the changes in scores reported here are not measures of increased creativity of the participants; rather, they are measures of their ability to empathize with the attitudes and visual preferences of another social group.

The next experiments went beyond attitude items and explored visual preferences. I ran a number of related experiments on this topic, but I will describe only one of them in this summary.

The third experiment used tests of *visual preferences* that characterize people socially defined as creative and original.

The Welsh Figure Preference Test consists of 400 black and white abstract line drawings (Barron and Welsh, 1952). The participant in the experiment is asked to indicate whether he "likes" or "dislikes" each of the drawings. A minority of items, about 60 in number, form subscales dubbed the Barron–Welsh (BW) Art scale and the Revised Art (RA) scale.

Judged by their content, these two subscales measure a preference for complex asymmetrical "dynamic" drawings that seem to ask for further organization, and a dislike for simple, symmetrical, balanced, static, and completely organized drawings. The scales were therefore considered measures of "preference for complexity" by their originators (Barron and Welsh, 1952).

Further research gave evidence of impressive validity (Welsh, 1959). These tests can distinguish students in creative writing classes from other students; artists from non-artists; art students rated as high in ability from art students rated as having lower ability; "independents" from "yielders" in the Asch (1956) situation (a measure of a person's tendency to conform to a group consensus that is patently false); Ph.D. candidates rated "original" by faculty from Ph.D. candidates rated "unoriginal," both in the sciences and in other graduate fields; and medical school seniors rated "original" from medical school seniors rated "unoriginal" by the medical school faculty. What is important for us is that these individuals typically scored high on the BW and RA scales. These findings supported the idea that creative people prefer to deal with complexity, and that the BW Art scale and RA scales are measures of preference for complexity.

I used the BW and RA scales in the present experiment as measures of a visual preference presumably associated with creativity, and characterizing creative people. I hoped to show that participants, either psychologically naïve or sophisticated, when asked to answer these scales as a creative person would, can actually do so. If the participants can actually do this, it will imply that people actually can "mentalize," that is, they are able to empathize accurately and validly with a socially defined group, sufficiently well to produce on request the kind of thought processes characteristic of people in that social group.

A strength of the study is that instead of using the BW and RA scales alone, the first 200 items of the Welsh Figure Preference Test were used. Of these, only 30 were items from the BW or RA scales; hence, the 30 relevant items were only 15% of the 200 items the participants were asked to judge. This means that the relevant items were hidden among a much larger group of items, making the task of the participants much more challenging as they had no idea that only a minority of items were relevant.

Group A consisted of five graduate students in psychology at Harvard and Boston University, aged between 20 and 30. It was intended to include people fairly sophisticated in psychology.

Group B consisted of five people and was intended as a group of "lay" people of good intelligence. All were college graduates. Three were working as secretaries, one as a city planner, and one as a graduate student in chemistry. They were selected so that none had any appreciable undergraduate training in psychology nor any special interest in it. None had ever been in psychotherapy or psychoanalysis.

No participant in either group knew that this research pertained to creativity.

The study hypothesis was that the overall group of ten participants would improve their scores after being given role-playing instructions, and that this would be true also for both subgroups of five, group A and group B. There were two administrations of the tests, the first time with standard instructions, and the second time with instructions to "answer it as a very creative and original person would." On the first administration, the participants had no clue that the testing related to creativity; on the second administration they were led to believe that all items pertained to creativity. Under such challenging conditions, could either group improve its scores from the first administration to the second?

The improvement was very large and hence statistically significant, despite the small numbers of participants.

Examination of the test results produced by the participants in each administration revealed that participants in both groups seemed to have an almost uncanny sense of which items pertained to creativity. Very few of the irrelevant items were answered differently in the second (role-playing instruction) administration compared with the first administration.

The number of participants in this study was very small, only ten, so I then conducted three more experiments with larger groups of participants in varying contexts to establish the validity of the findings. All told, there were over 100 participants. I found that the above results were replicated. All six experiments are presented in more detail in the Appendix, and their strengths and weaknesses from a methodological standpoint are also set forth.

These studies provide some experimental evidence that *in certain contexts*, some people actually can "mentalize," that is, they are able to empathize with a socially defined group sufficiently well to produce on request some of the thought processes characteristic of people in that social group.

The Next Chapters

In the next chapters I present a variety of methods from the social sciences to aid the investigation of unconscious phenomena on the world scene. They build on the empathic method and explain how to get and analyze relevant data, and how to assess the scientific validity of the findings.

Chapter 3 will set forth the method I call "specifying a research protocol."

3
What to Look for in Psychodynamic Inquiry

This chapter aims to help the reader to understand *how the psychological processes of empathy and mentalization are actually applied in psychodynamic inquiry.* By setting forth a *protocol*, that is, a specified set of procedures, we can clarify the interpretive process for those skeptical of the enterprise. We can also create a frame of reference for the researcher. What I propose here will be incomplete but others can revise and improve it.

Loewenberg (2002) emphasizes a highly disciplined and sophisticated subjectivity as the path to validity in psychodynamic interpretation. Subjectivity he conceptualizes as counter-transference, the awareness of the feelings the materials examined stir in the researcher and which help the researcher become aware of unconscious themes inherent in the material. Awareness of one's own free associations to the material is important to making psychodynamic inferences, Loewenberg (2002) believes.

In his much loved book, *Listening with the Third Ear*, Theodor Reik (1948) also emphasizes the need to free associate to what is being said in order to understand the underlying meaning. Reik had the courage to use many of his own free associations as examples, making the book much more appealing and convincing. His idea was that to understand another person or group, one needs to become aware of what thoughts and feelings are stirred in one's own mind by what the person or group says or does.

For example, Peter Gay (1985) has suggested "reading entries in private journals as though they were chains of associations," and seeing what they call forth in our own minds.

The essential point being made here by these researchers is that *empathy can gain strength through free association*: what comes to mind as we listen to a speech or read a document or consider a set of external events can help us get a sense of the underlying feelings of a person or a group.

In Chapter 8, the reader will have a chance to see whether his or her free associations to the various political speeches and pronouncements accord with what has come to my own mind about them.

The suggestions of Loewenberg, Reik, and Gay are general recommendations for attentiveness. *But what in particular should we be attentive to?* Specifying that is the task of this chapter. I will try to offer the beginnings of a protocol for psychodynamic research, specifying some things for the inquirer to attend to, specific things that may stir fruitful free associations and thereby foster empathic understanding.

A word of caution is appropriate as we begin to search for paths to sensible inferences. Lots of seemingly reasonable inferences in many fields have been shown to be in error, so a separate issue will be testing psychodynamic inferences for validity. This will be the subject of Chapter 4.

A *protocol* is a set of procedures for a scientific investigation. If we can create a more or less detailed protocol for making sensible inferences about unconscious processes, it is likely to be helpful. Documents like *Mein Kampf*, or the anti-Semitic Nazi Party newspaper *Der Stürmer*, or the bloodthirsty letters of Lenin (Service, 2000) surely contain material from which unconscious processes might be inferred. To create a protocol, this chapter looks first at *barriers* to sensible inferences, then looks at *indications* for inference, that is, psychological phenomena that might elicit sensible inferences, and then suggests *guidelines* for making these inferences.

In parsing psychodynamic inferences into barriers, indications, and guidelines, one is isolating threads from a fabric. From one point of view, a psychodynamic study of a person or a group is all of a piece. Consider Peter Loewenberg's (2002) study of Himmler, or his study of Nazi youth cohorts, or his study of graduate education. A fabric is being woven, and all things about the person or group are relevant. Yet it is possible to separate out threads of assertion from the fabric: for example, the assertion that Himmler was cold and obsessive, isolated from his feelings, or that he had homosexual interests. What the present chapter will address are the conditions under which it is sensible to create those threads of assertion. A justification for examining each thread of the fabric separately is Freud's statement about dream interpretation, as quoted by Loewenberg in *Decoding the Past* (2002): "the work of interpretation is not brought to bear on the dream as a whole but on each portion of the dream's content independently" (p. vi).

The Mask of Rationality

It is important to realize that the various indications of out-of-awareness fantasies I describe below often do not appear by themselves, isolated, like a dream fragment, or like a disorganized verbal production from a person who is actively psychotic. Instead, they are embedded in seemingly rational and logical arguments. In the midst of these arguments these indications of unconscious fantasies may be easily overlooked, but they do strike a strange and disquieting chord, whose sound we can discern by "listening with the third ear." Helping us listen is the task of this chapter.

The politician Joseph Stalin specialized in breaking the spirits of his subordinates: he had the wives of some of his subordinates imprisoned and yet continued to make the subordinates work closely with him on a daily basis, without mentioning the arrests. In one case he had a man's wife brought in from prison to dance on a table at a party.

Joseph Stalin, five feet four inches in height, had a withered arm and a deformed foot. He was violently abused by his drunken father. He endlessly sketched wolves. He changed his last name to the word for "steel." Could these facts foreshadow paranoid fantasies, fantasies of revenge, a terrible fierceness, and cruelty? Or was his behavior totally rational and easily understood in terms of concepts like ambition, cognitive complexity, framing, decision theory, utility maximization, role analysis, reference group theory, or social dominance theory, which eschew concern with unconscious mental processes?

Barriers to Sensible Inference

Projection by the observer

At first blush, a document describing a political or social event or process seems entirely different from the results of a projective test. In the Rorschach Test, the inkblots are largely ambiguous, except for a few obvious forms such as birds or bats. Therefore, few determinants of the response lie in the external reality of the cards. Because the taker of the test is little constrained by the properties of the blot, the responses to the Rorschach Test are taken as indicating processes stemming from the person's inner mental life, rather than from external reality.

But in the speeches and writings and actions of historical figures there are social determinants that might account for the behavior. Critics fear that the inferences about unconscious motives and fantasies from political and social data reveal more about the mental life of the interpreter than of the subject, and that it may be the clinical researcher and not his or her subject who is projecting his or her inner life onto the external world.

The Infinite Reach of Interpretation

No one seems beyond the reach of inferences about unconscious processes. This fact can be unnerving. Living long ago is no protection from psychological analysis. Peter Green's (1991) study of Alexander the Great offers what amounts to an Oedipal interpretation of Alexander's relationship to his mother and to his father, Philip of Macedon. Green posits "ambivalence" and an unconscious rivalry of Alexander with his father. Philip's own reaction to a dream he had about his wife and to a seer's interpretation of it, are also described in terms of unconscious psychological forces (pp. 35–40).

The unconscious meanings of everyday events have also served as grist for the mill of inference of unconscious processes. Fenichel (1945, pp. 211–12) describes the "Cafehaus" syndrome in his discussion of anxiety hysterias: "Certain persons state that they need 'stimulation' or 'distraction' to work at their best. They have neurotic disturbances of concentration. Their work is disturbed by inner tensions which make themselves felt as restlessness. However, they can overcome the disturbing feelings by seeking surroundings that provide external restlessness..." Fenichel notes, "Concerning the sociological role of the so-called Cafehaus in certain parts of Europe (or of the club in other countries)...the following case history may be significant. A patient was an excellent worker in the Cafehaus—and he preferred the noisy ones, with music playing and many people around but he was unable to work in his study at home, where he was alone and everything was quiet...[he] was able to become relaxed and quiet when people were making noise around him."

Fenichel has taken the innocent, if mildly eccentric, habit of working in cafes, coffee houses, and libraries, where there are people around, and has inferred from it the defensive structure of the anxiety hysteric. I'll consider some of the difficulties entailed by this line of interpretation below.

Sometimes an otherwise mundane event practically begs for psychological interpretation. Reportedly, at "EDU," a large university, posters from the administration appeared on bulletin boards showing photos of cheerful, celebratory groups of students, under the caption "The majority of EDU students (2 out of 3) drink responsibly." One might wonder, "Is this is an admission that one third of the students drink irresponsibly?" Apparently this potential implicit message was conveyed outside of conscious awareness.

Counter-transference

We all find that events in the present stir up memories from the past, and people in the present remind us of the past. This is called, in patients, *transference*. The patient sees the therapist in part as like some important person in his past. In the therapist, this is called *counter-transference*, experiencing the patient as though he were some earlier important person, usually a family member, in the therapist's life.

Counter-transference, as Loewenberg (2002) pointed out, can be helpful or even crucial in understand what is going on in the treatment situation or in understanding a psychodynamic phenomenon: How does what is going on make me feel (angry, sad, worried, pleased), and is this a clue as to what is going on?

The difficulty, for therapists and for psychodynamically oriented researchers, comes when the counter-transference feelings are so intense that they disturb the therapist or the researcher. In that case the phenomenon causing the counter-transference is ignored or misinterpreted. Everyone is prone to this, but the more sketchy the clinical training of the researcher, the more misleading the counter-transference is likely to be.

Multiple Frameworks for Interpretation

There are various frameworks for inferring unconscious processes: Sammet (2001) notes that interpretations of political phenomena can be in terms of unconscious drives, or ego psychology, or object relations theory, or self-psychology. Fred Pine (1990) has demonstrated with clinical material that these alternative interpretations can supplement each other. Pine's work with individual patients may be a template for doing parallel interpretations of a document in terms of unconscious processes.

Stigmatizing Deviance

There is a problem of making inferences that may stigmatize innocent social deviance, the unusual in thought and behavior. The research on creativity exemplifies these dangers and is well worth examining here. Studies of Nobel Laureates, Pulitzer Prize winners, and the like concluded that their highly creative subjects were "both crazier and saner" than the rest of us (Barron, 1958). Such individuals have greater access than most of us do to preconscious thinking (Kris, 1952a, 1952b), and so their thinking is more deviant, playful, and imaginative. A recent study summarizes a large number of studies that reach a similar conclusion (Carson, 2011), finding "reduced cognitive filtering" and "cognitive disinhibition" in highly creative individuals, a tendency that it is claimed reaches its zenith in schizophrenia.

A danger in inferring unconscious processes too freely in the realm of creative production is that one may stigmatize the creative as "psychopathological." Fenichel's strictures against the Cafehaus syndrome seem one-sided because working in this environment helps some people feel free to dip further into the preconscious and come up with more imaginative approaches. Jean-Paul Sartre, Simone de Beauvoir, Arthur Schnitzler, Alfred Polgar, and, very recently, J.K. Rowling, wrote in cafes. Nobel Laureate Richard Feynman did much of his physics theorizing on the back of napkins as he sat doodling in bars and night clubs in Los Angeles (Feynman, 1984).

Many creative people are helped by special circumstances that enable them to return to memories and feelings from their early life. Diane Ackerman (1989), in *A Natural History of the Senses*, observes: "the poet Schiller used to keep rotten apples under the lid of his desk and inhale their pungent bouquet when he needed to find the right word. Then he would close the drawer, but the fragrance remained in his head... Amy Lowell, like George Sand, liked to smoke cigars while writing, and in 1915 went so far as to buy 10,000 of her favorite Manila stogies to make sure she could keep her creative fires kindled."Alexandre Dumas, père, wrote his non-fiction on rose-colored paper, his fiction on blue, and his poetry on yellow. Robert Louis Stevenson, Mark Twain, and Truman Capote all used to lie down when they wrote. If this be madness, bring it on.

Ideology and Unconscious Processes

Karl Mannheim (1936) defined ideology as a set of ideas, and an underlying conceptual framework for understanding the world, a basic set of assumptions, and a generalized world view. Ideology also includes a specific set of ideas consonant with a person or group's social status and role. Ideology tends to be reflective of life situation, life experiences, and often self-interest.

Ideology is not always free of unconscious processes. Newspaper reports described the trial of two American tourists, father and son, who were accused of what amounted to blasphemy of Islam. The Islamic court, after some deliberation, found them innocent. The crowd of fundamentalists outside the courthouse, on hearing of the verdict, wept. A psychodynamic inference might be that the mental structure of the individuals and their religious ideology were fused, so that a blow to the ideology threatened their psychological integrity.

This line of interpretation approaches ideological analysis. It consists of relating a person's utterances and behavior to his or her social position. But Max Weber (1921) observed that ideological analysis is not "a cab that one may enter or alight from at will" (quoted in Mannheim, 1936). The tool of ideological analysis can be turned against those who invented it.

But there is no way out. There is no way to avoid having an ideology. Everyone's perspective is related to his or her social position and social role. Mannheim argued that although ideology is inevitable, by becoming aware of it one could attenuate its sway on one's perception of the world. He believed that attaining partial freedom from ideological constraint can be easier for intellectuals because they are so often in marginal social positions. I think it follows that psychodynamic researchers, hopefully as intellectuals, can become aware of some of the ideological influences on their interpretations.

Indications for Inferring Unconscious Processes

The obstacles to sensible inference need to be surmounted through self-awareness by clinically sophisticated researchers. There are many situations where psychodynamic inferences are clearly called for and urgently needed. The following list of irrational behaviors is not complete, only suggestive as to some things that clinically sophisticated researchers should look at.

Self-defeating Behavior

If Richard Nixon had confessed his Watergate error at the beginning, he would have not had to resign. It was the cover-up and not the burglaries that forced his resignation. Had Bill Clinton admitted his sexual indiscretions and apologized to the American public, he would not have been impeached and nearly convicted. Patterns of self-destruction, where a prominent figure persistently does himself in, suggest the presence of unconscious factors.

Vengeance

Vengeance also invites attention to unconscious determinants. Revenge is a sadistic drive rooted in the unconscious. *Mein Kampf* (Hitler, 1923), for example, is organized around revenge. One wonders what childhood experiences could underlie the intense lifelong characterological sadism that Hitler exhibited. And Lenin's letters show that he took great pleasure in slaughtering the kulaks, dwelling on it in detail (Service, 2000). One doubts that this joy can be entirely rational. I have already commented on Stalin.

Paradoxical Behavior

A paradox is a seeming contradiction that can't be easily explained by rational analysis. Something that is unexplainable on rational grounds, which are the grounds we all prefer, makes one wonder if unconscious processes could provide an explanation. Certainly worthy of psychodynamic inferences are anomalous and paradoxical individual actions, such as Deputy Fuhrer Rudolf Hess's flight to England during World War II (Pick, 2012). Hitler's refusal to let the German troops save themselves by withdrawing from Stalingrad is another example of paradoxical and self-defeating behavior.

Bizarre Behavior Over a Considerable Period

Bizarre behavior is another indication for psychodynamic inference. The entire lives of strange individuals can be grist for the psychodynamic mill. The President of Iran has a view of the world discordant with almost everyone else's. Kim Jong-un of North Korea is widely felt to "not have all four wheels on the ground." Pol Pot, who slaughtered four million people, owned a water board for personally torturing people. Hitler was gassed as a corporal during World War I, and as Fuhrer he gassed others: Is there a connection?

A Pattern of Accidents

Avner Falk (2005) infers unconscious forces underlying the fatal accidents Ariel Sharon was responsible for as an officer in the Egyptian and Lebanese military campaigns, and the two accidental deaths in Sharon's own family, one from a car accident and one from a handgun Sharon owned. Falk believes Sharon could readily have prevented them.

Attribution to Others of Negative Characteristics of the Self

Ascribing obvious flaws in the self to others is an instance of the unconscious psychological defense, *projection*. It is derived from the early days of childhood ("my brother did it") and it indicates psychopathology if strongly present in an adult. An example is anti-Semitism, in which Jews are accused of the very traits (greedy, grasping, vulgar, mercenary, clannish) that anti-Semites despise in themselves.

A Sense of Impunity

Impunity is a sense of being so special that one is invulnerable to blame or punishment, and can get away with anything. President George W. Bush's daughters used false IDs in order to be served liquor in Austin, Texas. Given the embarrassment they caused their father, a sitting

President, himself a reformed alcoholic, one might consider inferring a sense of impunity or unconscious hostile wishes toward their parents.

Too Good to be True: Failure of Reality Testing

Occasionally a person's presentation of self, in speeches or writings, goes far beyond the believable, presenting a glorified picture of an idealized person. Later, the achievements and exploits turn out to be fabrications.

Janet Cooke's embellishment of her vita serves as an example. We discuss this in detail in Chapter 7 but let me anticipate a few points here. The reality of Janet Cooke was impressive enough. Benjamin Bradlee, the editor of the *Washington Post,* where she worked, described her: "Janet Cooke is a beautiful black woman with dramatic flair and vitality and an extraordinary talent for writing" (Bradlee, 1995). She had been an outstanding reporter for the *Toledo Blade,* a respected newspaper. Cooke, however, saw fit to embellish her resume by falsely stating that she was a Phi Beta Kappa magna cum laude graduate of Vassar College, had attended the Sorbonne in Paris, and spoke French, Italian, Spanish, and Portuguese (ibid); Maureen Dowd (2003) states that Janet Cooke claimed to have graduated from the Sorbonne and to be a tennis ace into the bargain.

Cooke's article "Jimmy's World," the story of an eight-year-old heroin addict in Washington, DC, won a Pulitzer Prize. Two days after receipt of the Pulitzer, the article was revealed to be a fabrication: there was no Jimmy and the Pulitzer had to be returned. Bradlee states (1995, p. 440): "How come we never checked [her resume when she first applied for a job as reporter]? Simply put, Janet Cooke was too good to be true, and we wanted her too bad."

Obviously, unconscious forces are at work in the production of an inflated self-portrait that must inevitably be shown to be false. One has to wonder at the failure of "reality testing" in Janet Cooke, and in those who hired her. In Chapter 7, I use narrative analysis to try to clarify this perplexing situation.

Morbid Themes

Morbid means "characterized by an abnormal interest in death and disease." James Howard Kunstler (1993) observes that themes of death, decay, and putrescence permeate the Disney World exhibits and tunnels. There are skeletons, coffins, ghosts, ghouls, corpses, and putrescent matter. Kunstler notes,

> A recurring feature in nearly every attraction is the theme of death and mayhem. ... [The] Pirates of the Caribbean are all busy ravishing

> women, pillaging taverns, stabbing, hacking and shooting each other...The "Haunted Mansion" ride is a celebration of organic decay, with shrieking corpses and holographic images of howling lost souls flying around the cobwebbed spaces. The amount of creative energy invested in morbid depictions of violent death is impressive. ... How does this differ from past entertainments directed at children? ... Mainly in this way: Disney pretends so hard to be wholesome (1993, pp. 225–6).

One wonders if the claims of wholesomeness that cloak the death fetish might conceal unconscious depressive and hostile themes in the minds of the creators of Disney World.

Inability to Learn From Experience

This is a kind of ego failure, in which a dreadful error is nonetheless repeated faithfully and in detail. I am not sure if this process has a relation to repetition compulsion, in which a trauma is repeatedly reenacted, apparently in an effort, usually futile to master it: for example, a woman who had an alcoholic father marries an alcoholic.

Strange Echoes of Language

One indication that something strange may going on at the psychodynamic level is an exact current use of language phrases that have a terrible history. No one says, "Let them eat cake!" ("Qu'ils mangent de la brioche!") any more but there are troubling illustrations today.

In Chapter 8 we will see that right-wing French politician Jean-Marie Le Pen has suggested making an "oven load" ("four née") of a Jewish singer he disliked. One fears that the unconscious motives and fantasies of a person like Le Pen may resemble some of those evident in the days of the concentration camp ovens.

Here is another example of the strange echoing of language, drawn from an illustration from a St. Patrick's day article by Timothy Egan in the *New York Times* (2004).

Egan describes the Irish potato famine that killed at least a million Irish; one person in eight died. "At the very same time the Irish were starving to death, rich stores of grain and fat livestock owned by absentee landlords were being shipped out of the country." A Quaker relief agent: "We entered a dark cabin. Stretched in one dark corner, scarcely visible from the smoke and rags that covered them were three children huddled together, lying there because they were too weak to risk, pale and ghastly... perfectly emaciated, eyes sunk, voice gone, and evidently in the last stage of actual starvation."

But in Victorian England, "flush with the pomp and prosperity of the world's largest empire," Sir Charles Trevelyan, in charge of Irish relief, felt it would be wrong to provide the Irish with free food: "Dependence on charity is not to be made an agreeable mode of life." He termed the Irish national character as "defective," and termed them a "selfish, perverse, and turbulent people."

Egan notes that politician Paul Ryan has spoken of "a culture of dependency," arguing that the current American safety net has become a "lazy-day hammock," and so he actually opposes free school lunches for hungry children. Poverty he believes is a result of "laziness," unwillingness to work. The echoing of language about "dependency" and character defects in the context of hunger is eerie and suggests that the unconscious mental life, the fantasies and motives outside of awareness, may be similar in Trevelyan and Ryan.

Guidelines for Psychodynamic Inference

In view of the indications for inference, and taking account of the barriers, what guidelines can be offered?

Attention to Context

Appreciating context isn't so easy for some of us: the family therapist Jay Haley (1973) avers that "psychologists have a trained incapacity to appreciate context." He no doubt refers to our proclivity to reduce human life into variables that can be correlated. But there are a number of aids in appreciating context. For example, the epistemologist C.I. Lewis (1946) speaks of a "coherence theory of truth," in which one evaluates the degree of truth of a statement in terms of the degree to which it coheres, fits into a pattern, with other statements. It needn't be a corollary of other statements but it must form an understandable pattern with them.

William McGuire (1983) has formulated a view of how to do science that he calls "contextualism:" he urges that investigators seek to discover through their research the boundaries within which a proposition holds true rather than attempting to prove it clearly true or false. This approach protects one from making overly sweeping formulations. McGuire's contextualism seems to me to be one way of operationalizing Lewis' coherence theory of truth.

A context-related set of guidelines for interpretation is suggested by Herbert Blumer's (1956) classic work on sociological investigation. Blumer's *symbolic interactionism* implies a full discussion of the researcher's own emotional reactions, preconceptions, and biases, as these are part of the creation of meaning.

Thick Description

"Thick description" consists of describing a social event, process, situation, or document by providing exhaustive information about as many aspects of the material as possible (Geertz, 1973). This has become the modus operandi of sociological fieldwork.

Thick description as applied to psychodynamically sophisticated research would imply the use of a plethora of verbatim quotations, with little effort to avoid redundancy. The idea would be to give the reader of the study a deep understanding of the motives and experiences of the people being studied, by using their actual words.

Thick description helps readers make their own judgment as to whether the researcher's interpretations cohere with the materials presented. In my view, there is an element of disconfirmability here. The readers can compare their own interpretations of the described and quoted materials with those of the researcher, taking into account the expressed biases of the researcher. Operationally, disconfirmability consists of the readers saying, "As we read the materials presented, do we find enough detail and verbatim material to enable us to conclude that the inferences presented by the researcher are faithful to the materials?" This criterion could usefully be applied to psychodynamic inferences. Chapter 6 includes a further discussion of this topic.

The Quest for Disconfirmability

Suppose we consider clinically sophisticated psychodynamically oriented inquiry into world events as a *scientific*, as well as a *hermeneutic* (i.e. based on contextual interpretation of documents), enterprise. What makes an inquiry *scientific* is the possibility of disconfirming the conclusions. A statement for which a disconfirmation cannot be specified has no scientific status, as Karl Popper (1935 [1968, 2002]) has argued. This criterion has also been termed the "falsifiability" of a proposition. If the sine qua non of scientific investigation is disconfirmability, the key question to be asked of an inference in terms of unconscious processes would be, "What predicted evidence if *not* found would disconfirm the inference?" Chapter 4 gives a more complete account of how a disconfirmatory approach might be usefully applied to psychodynamic assertions.

Consensus Among Observers

There can easily be multiple interpreters of unconscious themes in historical documents, providing a correction for idiosyncratic individual biases. In this respect it would also be helpful to have scholars representing more than one psychological school of thought. Failure of consensus among interpreters could be considered a form of disconfirmation. Chapter 9, presenting an application of the symbolic interactionist approach, will give a fuller picture.

Introspective Comparison

Theodor Reik (1948) describes "listening with the third ear," paying attention to one's own feelings and associations that are stirred by the patient's communication. He distinguishes several kinds of attention to unconscious processes *Poised attention* is free-floating attention, the kind of attention where everything is noted equally. *Inward attention* looks within oneself to one's own reactions. *Involuntary attention* is not directed toward selected content but toward obtruding content. *Voluntary attention* narrows consciousness to selected content. Reik is speaking of attention to the utterances and actions of individual patients in the therapeutic situation. The issue is, what associations does the communication stir in the hearer? I suggest that a similar attentive introspective process comes into play in the case of inferring unconscious themes from historical materials. The introspective free-associative method seems especially suitable for primary sources, where we have the person's original words. But what is the scientific validity of introspection?

David Bakan, the statistician and psychologist, has analyzed the probative value of data obtained by introspection. Bakan argues:

> A major criticism that has been leveled against the introspective method is that the data of introspection are not public...That introspective data are not public in this sense is not to be questioned... However, can we not have verification without publicity? Let us consider one of the most acceptable kinds of investigatory procedure from this point of view, the conditioning experiment. There is no way of verifying Pavlov's experiments today by having another observer watch them, since, to say the least, Pavlov's dogs are quite dead. To verify Pavlov's findings we would have to get other dogs... If the criterion of publicity is not met by introspection, it is not really very serious as long as each scientist has, so to speak, at least one "dog" he can observe directly (1967b, p. 98).

Bakan is suggesting *that replicability (in the introspection of each interpreter) can serve as a substitute for publicity.*

Applied to our situation, Bakan's analysis means that each reader of an interpretation of a document or event in terms of unconscious motivation can, by looking at his or her own introspections, tell if he would have interpreted the document or event in a similar way. If other people, also attuned to unconscious processes through experience and training, find that their own introspections do not yield associations coherent with those offered by the researcher, one might conclude that the inferences drawn have suffered a disconfirmation.

Mentalization and empathy, discussed in Chapter 2, provide the basis for introspective comparison.

Associating to Language and Phrasing: Slips, Denials, Questions, Strange Phrases

Whether one takes a scientific or hermeneutic approach to psychodynamic inferences, detailed attention to the specifics of the words and phrases used in the primary sources is essential. Language is subtle and can connote many things at the same time. One looks or listens for *slips of speech* and wonder whether what has slipped out gives a clue as to what may be underneath. One looks or listens also for *strange phrases, or phrases that carry multiple meanings, after the manner of puns*. With free association to these, what multiple meanings echo within the reader or hearer?

It can be fruitful for the researcher to *remove the negation in aggressively stated denials*. Hitler said, after annexing Czechoslovakia: "I have no further territorial ambitions." Could the denial cover up the opposite impulse or intention? Freud argued there is no negation in the unconscious: opposites exist there without canceling each other out. If so, something may be learned by considering excessively emphatic denials.

One can also try *removing question marks*. Freud argued that a question contains a statement: Why bring it up as a question unless you think something might be there?

Highly evocative phrases suggest there may be unconscious fantasies beneath the surface. "Manifest destiny," "the white man's burden," "the wave of the future," "lebensraum," "Judenfresser," "the yellow peril," "the Iron Curtain," "by any means necessary," and "death panels" merit associative interpretation.

Listening for Metaphors

Association to the metaphors people use may provide clues about unconscious fantasies and wishes.

A university was hosting an event. The president of the university was seated in the audience. He was unexpectedly called upon to give a short speech about the university. He said, "If I can't give a short extemporaneous speech about the university, I should be taken out and shot." Interesting metaphor. Listen for metaphors.

Vladimir Putin, President of Russia, and former head of the Soviet secret police, said, speaking of the asylum request of Edward Snowden, "I myself would prefer not to deal with these issues. It's like giving a baby pig a haircut—there's a lot of squealing but there's little wool" (Hermant, 2013).

In Chapter 9 we will examine certain more glaring examples of suggestive metaphors. For example, during the Munich crisis, in the period leading up to World War II, European leaders spoke of Czechoslovakia as a newborn infant who might not survive, and described the Sudetenland as an appendix that might have to be cut out.

Use Concepts From Legal Theory

A number of concepts from American legal theory may be helpful to the psychodynamically sophisticated researcher in analyzing materials and presenting conclusions. Among these are the following.

Reasonably foreseeable consequences

In the American legal system a person is held by the courts to have intended the "reasonably foreseeable consequences" of his or her actions. For example, if a person makes a contract, let us say to supply certain goods at a certain time, and does not do so, he is responsible for any damages suffered by the other person as a result of the goods not being delivered on time, if those damages were reasonably foreseeable by the person breaking the contract. A relevant phrase is "he knew or should have known" (American Law Institute, 1981).

The concept of being held responsible for the reasonably foreseeable consequences of one's actions is also a mainstay of tort law: the negligent person is held responsible for all damages caused that were reasonably foreseeable from his actions (Best and James, 2007).

Some psychodynamically sophisticated researchers are quite aware of this. David Beisel, in *The Suicidal Embrace* (2003), notes that if a person sees in advance what the consequences of his action will be, then in some sense he intended it. This idea he applies to the actions of political leaders. It seems to me that one can go a step further: if the consequences the action will have are obvious, the political leader can be taken to have intended them.

Res ipsa loquitur

Literally, "the thing itself speaks." This concept is used in American tort law, the law of personal injury. For example, if a driver has an automobile accident while on a cell phone, being on the cell phone speaks for itself and the person is held to have been negligent (Harper, 1945; Hodgson and Lewthwaite, 2007).

There are applications for psychodynamic studies: Pol Pot owned a personal water board. One needs no further information to infer sadistic needs.

Due diligence

A trustee of a property on behalf of another person is subject to the requirement of *due diligence*. This is defined as "such a measure of prudence, activity, or assiduity, as is properly to be expected from, and ordinarily exercised by, a reasonable and prudent man under the particular circumstances" (Garner, 2009). This applies not only to the trustee of an estate, but also to other persons whom the law considers to be a relation of trust, for example investment managers for individual investors. Due diligence means taking adequate pains to investigate matters thoroughly before making a decision on someone else's behalf. In the case of managers who referred clients to Bernie Madoff and received a fee for doing so, most clearly failed to exercise due diligence, and the law is therefore holding them responsible for the losses.

Although the psychologically sophisticated psychodynamically oriented researcher is far from being in a legal relationship of trust, I think it would clarify matters and help dispel skepticism if researchers described the scope of their efforts to gather the relevant data so as to demonstrate due diligence. Usually they let the reader infer this from the footnotes and references, but I think it would be wise to discuss the matter directly in addition. There may be a portion of the relevant literature that could not be examined because access was not granted, or because the researcher was not fluent in the original language and had to read it in translation or not at all. It would help the reader if this were stated outright so the reader could take it into account in interpreting the account.

Reprise: Listening to the Data

I have argued that when considering the various indications that unconscious processes may be at work, we need *empathic understanding* based on free association to the phenomena. What an indication signifies, if anything, depends on our free association to it.

The idea of immersing oneself in the data and associating to it has roots in the social sciences, as well as in clinical work. The pioneering social ecologist Charles H. Cooley emphasized "sympathetic introspection" in understanding social phenomena; the cultural anthropologist Clifford Geertz (1973) urged "thick description" of the phenomena; and the social anthropologist Rosalie Wax (1971 [1985]) stressed the importance of listening and looking without being dependent on preconceived theory. This kind of approach is also explicit in the field work of the "Chicago School" of urban sociology, pioneered by Ernest W. Burgess (1926), Robert E. Park (Park et al., 1925), and Louis Wirth (1928, 1964), and carried out by their colleagues and successors, most notably by William Foote Whyte (1943), Jane Jacobs (1961 [1993]), Herbert Gans (1962), and William H. Whyte (2009). It is implicit in the studies of city life by the urban planner Jan Gehl (Gehl, 1971, 2010; Gehl and Svarre, 2013). In Chapters 5 and 6 we will consider in detail the connections of psychodynamically oriented inquiry with the social sciences.

Thinking of political and historical phenomena in terms of "data" is helpful because it reminds us that theory is inevitably involved even in the beginning stages of inquiry. "Data" is itself a theoretical construct: we have to define what we consider as data and what we exclude. In immersing ourselves in the "data" we are choosing what to look at. That is a theoretical choice and is unavoidable: we have to choose what to count as data. An example may help: in Chapter 8 the reader will see that the "data" I chose to consider are certain sets of articles in the world press. All these choices embody an implicit theory about what is important and should count as data. So there really is no way to avoid imposing some kind of theory on the events being studied, and I have argued that having no theory is also a theory. In the present chapter I have suggested some things that might be considered as data, and presented some of my own associations to specific examples.

Putting the Data Together: A Factor Analytic Analogy

An analogy to factor analytic studies will help explain how the clinician can evaluate the various inferences that spring from the suggestions and indications I have set forth above. Factor analysis is a way of looking at data to see if there are underlying trends of some sort. Quantification and statistical testing are involved in factor analysis but it is the logic itself that will help us here (for an example of factor analysis of quantified data, see Meyers et al., 1977).

Let us take a hypothetical example. Suppose we find a number of indications of unconscious processes in the materials (speeches, writings, actions) of a political leader or group that we look at. These indications would be of the kinds described earlier in this chapter. And suppose we find that each indication could suggest more than one kind of unconscious fantasy, idea, feeling or motive. We can array them as follows:

Indication 1 could signify themes of anxiety or of depression
Indication 2 could signify revenge themes or depression
Indication 3 could signify paranoid suspicion or anxiety
Indication 4 could signify manipulativeness or depression
Indication 5 could signify emotional withdrawal or depression
Indication 6 could signify sociopathy or anxiety

And so forth. More examples could be given.

We would need many more indications in order to do a formal quantified statistical factor analysis. However, we can also look at our data from a less formal point of view, as recommended by John Tukey (1977); if we had only Indication 1 we would be hard put to tell if the political figure or group was expressing anxiety or depression. If we had only Indication 2 we would be hard put to tell whether the political figure or group was manifesting paranoid suspicion or anxiety. But with the six indicators, we can say the underlying themes are primarily depression and anxiety; other themes seem subsidiary. *There is no reason a psychodynamic researcher could not array his or her data in a tabular form like this and consider what inferences seem likely.*

Of course, if we had a great deal of quantified data and could approach this statistically we might be able to express quantitatively the degree of probability that there are two "principal factors" at work here, anxiety and depression, with other themes, such as paranoia or revenge, playing a lesser role.

Moving Forward

We have considered *barriers* to sensible inferences, *indications* that such inferences might be called for, and *guidelines* for making these inferences by means of associative processes. I hope that these perspectives will make psychodynamic inquiry on the world scene more understandable to the reader and perhaps even contribute to the perspectives of the researcher.

Later in the book we can look at an example of a psychodynamically oriented study. Chapter 8 presents a study I did of similarities in the world press articles of three prominent dictatorial figures. As part of the context, I draw parallels to themes in world literature. The chapter also illustrates three of the social scientific methods I suggest for clinically sophisticated inquiry: *sampling, content analysis,* and *thick description using extensive verbatim quotations.*

> *You can observe a lot by looking.*
>
> Yogi Berra, New York Yankees catcher and, later, manager

4
Explorations in the Disconfirmation of Psychodynamic Assertions on the World Scene

In this chapter we will consider a number of salient methodological issues, including Popperian disconfirmation of risky predictions; the creation of meaning through symbolic interactionism; the inherent difficulties in psychodynamic inference; similarity to the inferential procedures of projective testing; psychodynamic processes as intervening variables; multiple operationism, and replication. These are all involved in the effort to disconfirm assertions about unconscious processes on the political–social scene.

It is traditional to consider the mentality of leaders, and the populace, and the media according to motivational categories such as "ambition," "pride," or "hostility," or "conflict avoidance," or cognitive categories, such as "framing," "information processing," or "cognitive complexity." Psychodynamic inquiry focuses instead on motives and ideations and fantasies outside of conscious awareness. In this way it seeks to provide a new perspective, *supplementing rather than displacing other perspectives*, in an insightful way.

Psychodynamic Inference and Projective Testing

Psychodynamically informed researchers assert that the utterances and actions of political figures, the media, and the general populace, on the world stage, although constrained by the demands of external reality, also contain elements expressing unconscious wishes, fears, and fantasies. They seek to uncover these unconscious elements through an empathic and introspective process based on the human capacity for mentalization, as described in Chapter 2, and deepened by their clinical training and clinical experience. In fact, their belief that they infer unconscious processes with some accuracy is based on their clinical experience with patients, where they continually encounter expressions of unconscious wishes.

In their psychodiagnostic work, clinicians often make use of projective testing. It is not generally realized that the logic of the inference made from the results of projective testing is very similar to the logic that is used in drawing psychodynamic inferences from the words and actions of political leaders, the populace, and from media accounts.

From the point of view of logical inference, the environment of political leaders is somewhat analogous to the situation of a person responding to a projective test. There are crucial elements representing the external realities the person has to deal with, but there is also room, and even necessity, for a political leader to respond to the situation based on themes from his own internal psychic life.

An example that may be helpful is the Thematic Apperception Test, devised by Henry Murray at Harvard (1938). A series of 10 to 20 pictures, in the form of line drawings, each on a separate card 8 × 10-inch white card, is presented to the person, who is asked to tell a story about each card. Each picture contains some definite elements, say a drawing of an elderly woman looking over a younger woman's shoulder, or a drawing of a young man turning his eyes away from a young woman who is lying on a bed. These elements constrain the story to a major extent but there is a great deal of room for the person to fill in the story with his own ideation, which comes from inside the person and is not intrinsic to the picture.

For example, is the older woman supportive of the younger woman, or is she critical? Or does the older woman represent in the young woman's mind what the young woman will one day become? Or is the older woman remembering the days of her youth?

In the second picture, is the young woman ill and is the young man expressing grief? Or have they just had sexual relations and he is feeling regret of remorse? Or is he reluctantly leaving her to meet his responsibilities elsewhere? Many other story themes are possible for each picture depending on the person's inner life.

Clinicians who inquire into the world scene assert that leaders and political groups are reacting, in part, to very real external forces and constraints, such as economic, military, diplomatic, and natural resource issues, and partly in terms of their unconscious needs and fantasies. They ask: Would everyone have reacted to their particular external circumstances as did Woodrow Wilson? Or Hitler? Or Chamberlain? Or Churchill? Or Raoul Wallenberg, the Swedish diplomat who rescued so many people from the Holocaust? Or Ratko Mladic, who carried out the siege of Sarajevo and the Srebrenica massacre?

But do the external constraints of the world political situation far exceed those of the ambiguous projective test? Only in some cases and for some people. Some became collaborators of despotic regimes and some became Raoul Wallenbergs.

External constraints, including economic, political, and military factors, *are taken into account* in psychodynamic studies of world events. They use a logic of inference analogous to that used in projective testing, which also takes external constraints into account. Consequently, the criticism of this type of inference as "reductionist" is unwarranted.

Psychodynamic Inference and Intervening Variables

It is important to realize that fantasies and motives outside of conscious awareness often have the character of intervening variables. The following explanation draws on Morris Rosenberg's brilliant and classic book, *The Logic of Survey Analysis* (1969).

Consider a causal sequence: A leads to B, which leads to C. An example is the carnage and mass deaths caused in the trenches of World War I. This, the independent variable, leads to C: the capitulation at Munich. But the causation occurs to a large extent through intervening variable B, the horror that leaders, the populace, and the media felt at those deaths, and their fear at precipitating another slaughter. This, the intervening variable, then led to the dependent variable in this causal sequence, the capitulation of British and other European leaders at Munich (the Czech leaders were not permitted to attend the Munich Conference!). The intervening variable, in this case feelings of depression, grieving for the casualties, and terror at the prospect of a repetition gets its causative power from the independent variable, which it *transmits* to the dependent variable. A similar explanation applies to the failure to resist Hitler's reoccupation of the Rhineland in 1936.

Notice that the situation is complex: the horror at the causalities in World War I affected most European leaders in the way it affected Neville Chamberlain. But the horror at the casualties, and the terror at the prospect of a repetition, affected Winston Churchill in a very different way, leading him to urge immediate rearmament and taking a hard line against Hitler as early as possible.

A key thing to understand about intervening variables is that they get their causative power because they transmit the causative force of the preceding independent variable. Clinically profound feelings and fantasies (the European leaders during the Munich crisis suffered from depression and despair, and had psychosomatic symptoms) do not usually stand alone as causes, they usually transmit causation. And causal sequences extend much farther than only three variables.

Therefore, it is not a question of whether psychodynamic variables explain as much of the capitulation at Munich as are explained by powerful economic and sociological variables, such as the slaughter and carnage in World War I, and the economic disasters that followed it. Psychodynamic variables are in the chain of causation, not competing influences.

Let's consider an example from an entirely different realm. The *New York Times* reports on several studies of the results of an unintended "natural experiment," when "in 1996, the Eastern Band of Cherokee Indians in North Carolina's Great Smoky Mountains opened a casino. ... The tribe elected to distribute a proportion of the profits equally among its 8000 members" (Velasquez-Manoff, 2014) Several long-term follow-up studies by social scientists showed a remarkable decrease in behavioral problems among the poorest children but not among the already well-off children. Minor crimes committed by Cherokee children declined, high school graduation rates improved, and there were fewer substance abuse and psychiatric problems in adulthood. Interviews with both parents and children disclosed that the money, "which amounted to between one third and one quarter of the poor families' income at one point, seemed to improve parenting quality by reducing the intense stress of poverty on the parents."

Here we see again a causal chain: change in an environmental variable (provision of badly needed income) leads to deep psychological effects (reduction of intense emotional stress and anxiety in the parents), which lead to environmental consequences (better parenting), which lead to more environmental effects (reduction in school dropouts, crime, and lessened substance abuse and fewer psychiatric problems in the children). In this sequence, the psychological variable, the reduced emotional stress and anxiety, and lessened feelings of despair and failure in the parents, serves as an intervening variable in this causal sequence.

Where psychodynamic factors are treated as intervening variables rather than stand-alone influences, the criticism that psychodynamic interpretations are necessarily "reductionist" is unwarranted.

What Psychodynamic Researchers Consider

Clinically informed researchers do consider the influence of childhood experience on the adult personality, as with Vladimir Zhirinovsky, an inquiry that seems absurd to many readers. But both Hitler and Stalin were badly beaten by their fathers as children. They also take into account matters such as threats to the stability of the personality, as with cartoons of Mohammad as experienced in Islamic nations; projection of unwanted aspects of the self onto others, as in anti-Semitism; and magical thinking, the belief that merely thinking a thought can cause things to occur in the external world, for example the idea that one "race," through its beliefs, can pollute the blood of another "race," as with Nazi ideology. The search for unconscious processes makes psychodynamic inquiry different in important respects from other forms of inquiry. For example, unconscious guilt is invoked to explain Marshal Pétain's failure to mount a serious defense of his actions during his trial for treason at the end of World War II (Szaluta, 1980). Pétain didn't actually verbalize that he was wrong in setting up the Vichy government, and in a letter to his wife he questions whether he really did deserve trial and conviction. Yet his defense at the trial was tepid.

Special Difficulties Posed for Inference by the Nature of Unconscious Processes

Psychodynamic inferences refer to unconscious processes, unconscious motivations, and unconscious fantasies. But unconscious mental life is peculiarly difficult to observe. Further, there is a kind of semantic contradiction in speaking of mental processes outside of conscious awareness. We are accustomed to using the term "thoughts" or "feelings" or "mental processes" to mean things going on in our minds of which we are aware. The idea that we are not aware of all that we are thinking seems strange to us.

Another puzzling feature is that in unconscious thoughts and fantasies and memories, there is no distinction between past and present. Traumas from the past are experienced as happening now. (This does become obvious even to outside observers, in post-traumatic stress disorder, in the depressions and suicides of successful people, and in lifelong reactions to the loss of a parent in childhood.)

Moreover, unconscious processes are deemed to be not subject to ordinary logic, such as the law of contradiction: opposites don't cancel each other out. For example, in psychodynamic theory, love and hatred for the same person can coexist in the unconscious without negating each other; each remains in full force, resulting in deeply ambivalent feelings. And it is possible, according to these theories, to know and not know, at the same time, as with the daughter of an alcoholic father, who, despite having been warned by her mother, unknowingly marries another alcoholic.

The theory of "reaction formation" also poses problems for psychodynamic interpretation. An overly sweet disposition may be authentic or it may be a saccharine sweetness, serving to keep its opposite, anger or rage or hatred, out of the person's conscious awareness. Similarly, feelings of hatred may be a reaction formation against forbidden love, as in the persecution of homosexuals.

Understandably, these characteristics pose considerable difficulties for psychodynamic formulations. Critics argue that they have no definable meaning because they are too paradoxical and protean to permit contradiction. Any contradictory data, critics say, can be explained away. And it is generally accepted that any statement for which one cannot think what a disconfirming observation would look like is probably devoid of meaning. "It cannot even be wrong."

Is Disconfirmability an Answer?

One way to dispel these doubts would be to use the criterion proposed by the logician and philosopher Karl Popper (1935 [1968, 2002]). We can ask whether psychodynamic formulations admit of disproof, or whether any evidence that seems disconfirmatory will be dismissed as irrelevant, as happens with astrology, horoscopes, and tea-leaf reading. According to Popper, not every component of a theory must be disconfirmable but a theory with *no* disconfirmable components cannot be scientifically valid. If a theory is right, Popper says, a particular predicted observable event should occur. If it doesn't occur, the theory is not right. Exposing a theory to disconfirmation by means of the non-occurrence of predicted events is a major criterion (not the only criterion) of the scientific method, and I think that *in many instances* it can be usefully applied to psychodynamic inquiry. The predictions, according to Popper, must be *risky*, that is, the events predicted must be unlikely to occur unless the theory is correct.

Some philosophers of science, such as Ernst Nagel (1967) find the Popperian disconfirmation procedure too stringent even for the physical sciences. Nagel argues that there can be some doubt as to whether the predicted outcome is closely enough related to the theory being tested to constitute a disconfirmation if not found. Thomas Kuhn (one of my teachers) and Paul Feyerabend have also criticized the criterion of falsifiability as too restrictive. Kuhn pointed out (1962 [1996]) that important scientific theories are not easily discarded in the face of disconfirming evidence, and argued that to some extent this reluctance is wise. Yet I feel that the special difficulties posed by psychodynamic inference makes a disconfirmatory approach advisable *if at all possible.*

Because psychodynamic inquiries into world events are public, and in print, unlike clinical treatment interpretations, which are ordinarily private, they are available to all observers who wish to test them by generating risky predictions. Most of these assertions about world events are therefore open to falsification if the predicted external events do not occur. We need to take advantage of this.

I believe that what we need to do is to try to generate "risky predictions" from psychodynamic assertions and then observe whether the predicted events occur or not. There are three possibilities under this procedure. A lack of occurrence would tend to disconfirm the theory. If the predicted event does occur, it is a failure to disconfirm, and so strengthens the theory. If we find that, owing to vagueness, ambivalence, or self-contradiction in the assertions, we can't generate risky predictions from them, then we have to consider them untestable and hence perhaps lacking in meaning.

Again, it is important that the predictions be *risky:* the events predicted must be *unlikely* to occur unless the theory is correct. An example from physical science is the bending of starlight as it passes close to the sun, which is observable during a solar eclipse. This was predicted by Einstein's theory of relativity and by no other theory.

Disconfirmation is hardly unknown in historical inquiry. The eminent philosopher and political scientist Jon Elster points out that there can be empirical disconfirmation of a particular historical assertion by the discovery of a new document or a new archeological site (quoted in Taleb, 2010, p. 309). What I believe is new, however, is the proposal that *psychodynamic* assertions about world events be *systematically* exposed to disconfirmation through the failure of predicted events to occur.

Advantages of the Disconfirmatory Approach Given the Nature of Unconscious Processes

Because of the enigmatic and perplexing nature of unconscious processes, and the difficulty of observing them, even critics who admit their reality have doubted that they can be identified in historical studies. I contend that the discipline of specifying what would constitute a disconfirmation would set boundaries to the discourse: if the events predicted in advance are not, in fact, found, the theory will be considered to be erroneous.

The explanatory and persuasive power of the disconfirmation criterion arises because a logical consequence of the theory, predicted in advance of the empirical inquiry (in the physical sciences, usually an experiment), has been found not to occur. This procedure endeavors to remove the element of "capitalizing on chance," that is, sifting all available potentially relevant instances, and selecting only evidence favoring the hypothesis.

A much less demanding criterion, what might be called "the weight of the evidence," is ordinarily applied to historical conclusions, and also to scientific contexts where experimentation is impossible or where there are many studies to be reconciled. Why apply a stricter criterion to psychodynamic formulations? We have seen several reasons: the impossibility of directly observing unconscious processes; the semantic problem with thoughts that are, by definition, outside of awareness; and difficulties arising from violations of the law of contradiction. To lessen the possibility of error, I propose that a more severe criterion be invoked insofar as circumstances permit.

Bridging the Credibility Gap

Credibility to a highly skeptical audience is also a major advantage of a disconfirmatory approach. Many people greet the idea of unconscious mental processes with intense skepticism and even with outright rejection. With skepticism rife, a high standard of proof is needed in order to be persuasive, and I suggest one somewhat akin to the standards of science, so far as is reasonably possible.

Limitations of the Disconfirmatory Approach

Some historians define their work as a *narrative enterprise*, with the historian seeking to tell as complete a story as possible about a specific event or sequence of events, rather than seeking to identify general lawful relationships, and hence having nothing to do with science. I contend that psychodynamic formulations, going so far beyond the observable data of historians, are theoretical structures, not simply detailed interwoven narratives, and so need a stronger criterion of validity.

Yet it would be going too far to apply the standards of chemistry and physics algorithmically to psychodynamic statements. Physical laws, like Einstein's equation $E = MC^2$ relating matter and energy, with the speed of light as a constant, have the character of being absolutely true under the conditions stated in the law. The phlogiston theory has the character of being absolutely false under stated conditions; there is no phlogiston. But in psychodynamic inquiry, there are no "critical experiments" like the Michelson–Morley experiment that demolished the theory of the "ether," or the Lee and Yang experiment showing that parity is not conserved in weak interactions. Psychodynamic formulations have the character of being more true, or less true, as opposed to being absolutely true or absolutely false. This is the case because unconscious phenomena have multiple determinants, and because the logic of the unconscious is not rational: opposites can coexist, love and hate do not cancel each other out. Therefore, a theoretical formulation about an unconscious process cannot be absolutely true or absolutely false.

Fuzzy Logic and Multiple Predictions

We are therefore in the realm of "fuzzy logic," where truth is a matter of degree. Fuzzy logic is complex mathematically and is still controversial among some mathematicians. Martin Gardner (1999, p. 158) explains it this way: "A fuzzy set is one with fuzzy boundaries. Members are graded by finite degrees, with incremental transitions between them. For example, heights of persons can be broken down into such fuzzy adjectives as very tall, tall, medium, short, and very short. ... True and false are replaced by degrees of truth and falseness. ... Although reasoning with fuzzy is precise, all its conclusions are fuzzy." It has been suggested that fuzzy logic could just as well be called "set theory with degrees of membership." Probability of membership is not involved in fuzzy set theory, just degrees of membership, Gardner explains. As members of the fuzzy set of true psychodynamic formulations, some psychodynamic formulations are very true, some are rather true, and others are hardly true at all. Very few are 100% true, like the equation $E = MC^2$, or 100% false, like the phlogiston theory or the ether theory.

A "fuzzy truth value" is indeed what we might expect from the characteristics of the human personality. As a psychodynamic theory is very unlikely to be 100% right or 100% wrong, it follows that finding a single predicted event not to occur will usually not suffice to disprove the theory but will rather serve only to diminish the truth value somewhat. How many instances of non-occurrence of predicted events are necessary to persuade us to consider the theory as having little truth? Here, reasonable people may justly differ. Two instances may be too few, as there is the danger that the two will be too closely related to each other and hence almost redundant. I therefore suggest the *specification of several diverse instances*, of predicted events that if not found would serve as disconfirmations. This procedure would imply that the theory is scientific in the sense of vulnerable to disconfirmation. It is of course regrettable that in this field exact numbers cannot be assigned to the appropriate number of predicted events, nor to the exact degree of truth to be assigned to a theory that survives these disconfirmations.

In the social realm, several theories may predict the same event. It would be ideal to choose an event that is predicted only by the theory under consideration, but in social inquiry this is usually impossible. Multiple predictions are needed, such that *as a group* they are predicted only by the theory under consideration and would not be expected otherwise: the prediction must be *risky*.

After you, Alphonse!

These predictions must be for *events that are logical consequences of the theory and have not yet happened, or else to specific data not yet examined by anyone,* to avoid the objection that the data have been sifted to find supportive instances. But usually the clinically sophisticated researcher simply adduces evidence in favor of his or her formulations but does not specify predictions. Perhaps the requirement to specify disconfirmations will one day become part of the norm for researchers in this field. That is my hope in writing this chapter. In the meantime, the task of specifying predicted events must rest with the reader. Readers, in effect acting as a scientific peer review group, may allow themselves to choose any event that is a logical consequence of the theory and whose outcome is not known to them, regardless of whether it has already occurred.

The Social Construction of Predictions

Consider what this means in terms of the sociology of knowledge: the reader is helping create the meaning of the researcher's formulation, which now becomes more of a socially created construct. W.I. Thomas formulated the *social constructivist* view (Thomas and Thomas, 1928): in the social world meanings are constructed by individuals from their experience rather than pre-existing as a given. The *symbolic interactionists* go further: they are at pains to inform us that meanings and indeed our pictures of reality are formed as a result of interactions among people. In the symbolic interactionist view (Mead, 1934; Berger and Luckman, 1966; Blumer, 1969), shared meanings gradually evolve from a series of such interactions, which can sometimes involve the negotiation of meanings. In the procedures I suggest, the meaning of the clinical researcher's formulation is elaborated and deepened by the reader's specification of predicted events. The reader, by predicting events that if not found would serve as disconfirmations, is carrying out an essential part of the psychodynamic inquiry.

Multiple Operationism

Notice that I am advocating multiple predictions. Using multiple risky predictions gives multiple measures of the predictive adequacy of a psychodynamic assertion.

This approach to disconfirmation is consistent with *multiple operationism*, a well-established procedure in the social sciences. Multiple measures of a concept or assertion are important because operational definition, sometimes workable in the physical sciences (voltage can be measured by a galvanometer), is usually unsuited to the social sciences. Most operations (necessary procedures for measurement) in the psychological and social realm have specific limitations. For example, projective tests like the Rorschach or the Thematic Apperception Test, paper and pencil checklists like the Minnesota Multiphasic Personality Inventory, personal interviews, and ratings by one's friends, get at different parts of the personality. Each tells us part of the story but presents an incomplete picture if used alone. Using several measures or, in our case, several predicted outcomes, gives a broader, more stable result, less biased by the peculiarities of a particular measure.

Confronting the Beast

Let's consider some psychodynamic formulations to see what the disconfirmatory approach would entail in the realm of world events. This will not be an easy quest. This will require examining painful subjects: material is kept out of consciousness not because it is pleasant but because it is highly unpleasant. The examples we will look at include Marshal Pétain's trial for treason, the theme of suicidal ideation in the betrayal of Czechoslovakia at Munich, the origins of the gas chamber system in German mental hospitals, a neglected account of a heroic escape from Auschwitz, and the bombing of Beirut, as a source of concern over unpredictable catastrophic events. These are all painful topics. But perhaps confronting the beast is a path toward freedom.

The Trial of Marshal Pétain

In two classic articles, the historian Jacques Szaluta (1978, 1980) formulated an interpretation of Marshal Philippe Pétain's personality, based on a study of Pétain's childhood, adulthood, military leadership, and his conduct at his trial for treason. One might ask how the hero of the great French victory at Verdun could be characterized in those articles as passive aggressive and masochistic. Szaluta responds:

> In line with his personality, he ultimately sought martyrdom. During his trial for treason in 1945, he initially made a statement to the High Court repudiating the right of the court to try him. Afterward, he did not speak again in his own defense. However, his attorney, Jacques Isorni did defend him. Well after the war, in 1947, when he was in prison, Pétain did speak to a group of French parliamentarians who were investigating the causes of the defeat of France in World War II. When Pétain spoke to them, during this interview, he did not show regret for his actions, for his collaboration during the Vichy regime. However, he accepted his sentence, which had been reduced from capital punishment to life imprisonment, because of his advanced age, with alacrity. He said that he had no complaints about being in prison. In effect, on an unconscious level, he admitted that he was guilty, of heading a reactionary regime which ultimately caused a civil war in France. ... Pétain gave ample evidence that he wanted to sacrifice himself, to be a martyr, and that he wanted to be punished. Fundamentally, Pétain acted in a masochistic manner (personal communication).

Szaluta points out that even Pétain's great military victory at Verdun in World War I came because he was so much less aggressive than the other French generals.

Szaluta's work is careful and scholarly. Nonetheless, there are alternative hypotheses to explain Pétain's strange passivity at his trial for treason: as Pétain was 91 years old at the time, one would not expect him to be as spritely as a younger man. Another possibility, as political psychologist Peter Suedfeld suggests, is that Pétain's behavior simply shows *situational* depression: he was after all imprisoned and facing a death sentence for treason after a lifetime of public leadership, in a trial that he would experience as "victor's justice."

On the face of it, these are simpler and more obvious explanations for his withdrawn passive demeanor and conduct at his trial. But Szaluta proposed instead an explanation based on a lifetime passive-aggressive orientation by Pétain.

I have argued earlier in this chapter that previously undiscovered or unanalyzed data sources can be used for Popperian disconfirmation. The prediction is that these sources must exhibit certain characteristics, or the theory cannot be true. For example, for a reader in 1978 and 1980, the time of Szaluta's first articles on Pétain, could hypothesize as follows:

> If previously undiscovered or unavailable correspondence or diaries or personal statements from Pétain are found or made available, they must show marked hostile passive-aggressive themes of masochism and martyrdom.

If these themes are not found prominently, Szaluta's hypothesis about masochistic and passive-aggressive personality trends in Marshall Pétain cannot be right.

After I wrote the above, I became aware of an additional article, previously published but unknown to me. Nearly ten years after the original two articles by Szaluta, Pétain's attorney, Jacques Isorni, granted Professor Szaluta access to Pétain's voluminous unpublished letters to his lover and wife, Annie, written over many years of his lifetime. Szaluta then published a new article in 1990 analyzing the letters and quoting them at length, verbatim. In these letters, the hostile, passive-aggressive themes of martyrdom are strikingly evident, astonishing in their intensity. I believe any reader of these letters would find this to be so. Indeed, readers can conduct their own adventure in Popperian disconfirmation by consulting the 1990 article. The extensive verbatim quotations in the article make a Popperian disconfirmation test possible. These quotations are powerful in showing the martyrdom theme. For example, Pétain said, as he assumed leadership of the Vichy regime in 1940: "I make to France the gift of my person to alleviate her suffering."

This is not to say that Pétain's advanced age explains nothing, or that situational depression played no part in his demeanor at his trial. They seem obviously relevant. But Pétain's personality was also an important factor, and the Popperian disconfirmation procedure illuminates this.

I believe we can fairly conclude that Szaluta's formulation can be considered to have survived this particular attempt at disconfirmation. Finding predicted events that if not found would have been disconfirmations lends credibility to a theory.

Psychodynamic Inquiry and the Munich Agreement

In *The Suicidal Embrace*, David Beisel (2003) portrays the unconscious fantasies of European leaders in their statements about Czechoslovakia during the Munich era. The theoretical formulation to be considered is that there were death wishes toward Czechoslovakia from British and French leaders, and that these wishes were mirrored by suicidal ideation by Czech leaders. Here are some predictable events that come to mind to test the validity of this theory:

- British and French political leaders and statesmen made public or private statements derogating the importance of the Czech nation and minimizing the need for it to survive
- British and French political leaders and statesmen expressed doubts publicly or privately about Czech political leadership
- Czech political leaders and statesmen complained publicly or privately that the Czech nation had always been doomed.

In Chapter 9 we will discover a rather different test of Beisel's assertions about the Czechoslovak mentality during the period immediately preceding the Munich Agreement of 1938. This opportunity occurred adventitiously during a related effort and I will present it in its own context, in Chapter 9.

Psychodynamic Inquiry and the Holocaust: Ruth Linn

The next example is both painful and controversial; it concerns Ruth Linn's focus on the lack of attention given to the extraordinary heroism of two Jewish youths, who, despite incredible difficulties and great risk, succeeded in escaping from Auschwitz. Ruth Linn, Dean of the Faculty of Education at the University of Haifa, in her book *Escaping Auschwitz: A Culture of Forgetting* (2004), documents that information about what was happening at Auschwitz was provided to the Hungarian Jewish leaders (the "Judenrat" in Budapest) in late April or very early May 1944 by two escapees from Auschwitz, Rudolf Vrba and Alfred Wetzler. After escaping, the two youths had somehow made their way across occupied Europe from Auschwitz to Budapest, eluding Europe-wide Gestapo and SS surveillance and pursuit, in order to warn that Auschwitz was not agricultural resettlement, it was mass murder upon arrival.

Their information, which included a 32-page report plus maps of Auschwitz, was not acted upon and people were not warned. According to Linn's account, the failure to act was first dismissed and then forgotten for many decades by Israelis in general and Israeli historians in particular. Linn argues that there was first avoidance, then suppression, and then unconsciously motivated forgetting. She asserts that by first disregarding and then repressing the memory of the revelations, the collective feelings of guilt among the Jewish and Israeli communities about the Hungarian Jewish leaders' failure to take action to warn Hungarian Jews on the basis of the revelations by Vrba and Wetzler, could also be forgotten.

Beginning on 15 May 1944, two weeks after the 32-page Vrba–Wetzler report had been transmitted to the Judenrat, and continuing over a period of the next eight weeks, about 437,000 Jews boarded the trains for Auschwitz, unwarned by their leaders, thinking they were headed for agricultural resettlement. All were gassed immediately on arrival. Elements of the Holocaust, like the heroic resistance in the last days of the Warsaw ghetto, could be emphasized in Israeli historiography of the Holocaust, Linn asserts. The quiet boarding of the deportation trains to Auschwitz by 437,000 unwarned Hungarian Jews could receive lesser emphasis.

So much for Linn's assertions. While I am implicitly in agreement with her critique of the Judenrat's failure to warn, of course I wasn't there and didn't have to make these terrible decisions. I also recognize that any formulation that implies that any group or subgroup of the victims of the Holocaust may have acted in any way counter-productively, is an intensely painful idea. But our task here is not to judge the issue, it is only to see if Linn's formulations can hold up to the scrutiny of the Popperian disconfirmation procedure.

Can we subject Linn's theories to the criterion of disconfirmation? Is there unconsciously motivated forgetting by Israeli scholars of the Holocaust? How about subsequent generations of scholars?

I suggest as examples of predictions from Linn's theory:

- upon publication of Linn's book, Israeli scholars will write vehemently critical reviews
- Linn's efforts to obtain an honorary degree for Rudolf Vrba from Haifa University will arouse strenuous opposition from the faculty there
- the interval between publication of Linn's book in 1994, and the inclusion of references to Vrba and Wetzler and to the failure to warn, in new editions of textbooks in Israeli schools, will exceed one decade (*a quantitative prediction*)

- the interval between the publication of Vrba's book on his escape from Auschwitz, in English, and its publication in Hebrew, will exceed three decades (*a quantitative prediction*).

Psychodynamic Inquiry and the Holocaust: Rael Strous

Other psychodynamic formulations related to the Holocaust almost cry out for verification. Rael Strous (2006), an Israeli psychiatrist who has taught ethics at Harvard Medical School, asserts that in psychiatric hospitals in the Third Reich, the foundations and even the details of the Holocaust were developed and tried out by means of the "eugenic" murder, in basement gas chambers, of over 100,000 mental patients, often children, who were severely mentally disabled. Implicit in the evidence Strous presents is the theory that many of the parents involved had strong unconscious death wishes toward their severely and hopelessly mentally disabled children. Can we assess the validity of this theoretical formulation through the method I propose? Here are some suggestions for predictable events that are logical consequences of Strous' formulation:

- many parents quickly accepted the offer of a supposed possible cure that was stated to have a 50% chance of being fatal
- only a minority of parents elected to come to the hospital and pick up their mentally disabled child and take the child to live at home rather than expose the child to the eugenic treatment with its described 50% risk of fatality.

As we look at these examples, it becomes obvious that it is possible for a reader to specify predictable events that are logical consequences of the theoretical formulation. Readers will vary in what they suggest but, taken together, their suggestions provide a way of validating the clinically sophisticated researcher's formulations, and of elaborating and deepening their meaning.

The clinically sophisticated psychodynamically oriented researcher may choose, wisely in some cases, to dismiss some of the predictions as irrelevant, but a dismissal of them all calls into question the validity and even the meaningfulness of the theory.

My Own Test of Linn's Assertions

Let us consider a more extended example of how the proposed approach may prove of value in assessing psychodynamically oriented research. Ruth Linn emphasizes the short shrift given to Vrba and Wetzler's superbly heroic escape from Auschwitz, undertaken largely to warn the Hungarian Jews who were planned to be the next group to be annihilated. She contrasts it with the acclaim accorded Hannah Szenes, a Jewish heroine of the Holocaust resistance whose brave efforts failed entirely. As Linn puts it (2004, p. 91), "Szenes is one of the most commemorated Holocaust symbols in Israel...although her mission was a complete failure. Vrba and Wetzler's fundamental contribution to saving the Budapest Jews is not made clear, whereas Szenes failure to save even one single Jew is not discussed." Linn believes the disinterest in the exploits and accomplishments of Verba and Wetzler stems from an unwillingness of modern Israeli historians to call attention to the failure of the Budapest Judenrat to warn the Jews of Budapest.

This really is a complex and painful comparison, in my view. Yoel Palgi's book, *Into the Inferno: The Memoir of a Jewish Paratrooper Behind Nazi Lines* (2002), makes it very clear that Hannah Szenes was indeed a truly heroic figure and deserving of the recognition she received as an inspiration to others, although, as Linn points out, she was unsuccessful in saving anyone. The issue for Linn is the motivated ignoring of the extraordinary heroic escape and greatly more important effort of Rudolf Verba and Alfred Wetzler, which, despite at first being dismissed by the Judenrat, was ultimately successful in saving the lives of about 200,000 of the 640,000 remaining Jews in Budapest.

This theory by Linn was very much in my mind when I came upon *The Holocaust Chronicle* (Hogan and Aretha, 2003), a vast foundation-subsidized scholarly compendium published in the United States, one of the most complete and moving chronicles of the Holocaust. I decided to put Linn's theories to a severe test: I predicted that the Vrba–Wetzler report would be briefer than the discussion of Hannah Szenes. (A quantitative prediction in this case.) If this was not found to be the case, it would be a clear disconfirmation of Linn's theory. Here indeed was a quantitative test: number of words; and a qualitative one as well: amount of emphasis given.

Upon examination, I found, on the lower right-hand corner of page 521 in typeface several sizes smaller than the rest of the text: "April 10, 1944: Two Slovakian Jews, Alfred Wetzler, age 26, and Rudolf Vrba, age 19, escape from Auschwitz. The pair will provide the Allies with the first eyewitness accounts of the 'Final Solution' as well as a warning about the Nazi's intention to exterminate Hungarian Jewry." Forty-six words, in fine print in an obscure corner of a 765-page volume. It is stated that Vrba and Wetzler's warning was transmitted to the Allies (it was much later, nevertheless saving most of the remaining 200,000 Hungarian Jews through pressure on the Hungarian dictator Admiral Horthy by the Allies) but there is no mention that the Budapest Judenrat failed to warn the 437,000 Hungarian Jews who boarded the trains from 15 May to 9 July, when Horthy stopped the boarding as a result of pressure by the Allies.

On page 529, in a prominent position, appears a photograph of Hannah Szenes, sitting in a chair in her home in Budapest, with the following text in larger font:

> Hannah Szenes relaxes in her native Budapest, Hungary, before the war. Very gifted, Hannah excelled in her studies before immigrating to Palestine, where she joined a kibbutz. Her diaries and poems reflect a love of life exceeded only by her fierce commitment to the Jewish people. One of a daring band of parachutists sent into Yugoslavia to rescue Allied pilots and further Jewish resistance, she was captured after crossing into Hungary. Tortured, she refused to reveal radio codes. Her poem, "Blessed is the Match," became an emblem of her own heroic self-sacrifice. It included the line, "Blessed is the match consumed in kindling flame."

Here are 104 words and a photograph, in large font and in a prominent position in the text.

Consider what this simple instance means. Failing to find more than a comparatively tiny reference to Vrba and Wetzler's report in this huge compendium book provides only a small piece of supporting evidence for Linn's thesis that their work and their role was first suppressed consciously and then slipped out of Israeli memory for decades. A piece of evidence, come upon haphazardly, or even encountered in a thorough sifting of sources, carries only a limited weight. But finding a *predicted* event has considerably greater importance for two reasons: (1) it is derived logically from the theory, which limits the field of relevant evidence; and (2) since it is predicted, the element of "capitalizing on chance," that is, selecting only evidence favoring the hypothesis, is removed. Consequently, had the *predicted* event, a much shorter write-up on Vrba and Wetzler and their report than on Szenes, not been observed it would have struck a substantial blow to Linn's theory that the work of Vrba and Wetzler has slipped from memory. Such is the greater power of Popper's criterion. It is therefore a more exacting criterion than the "weight of the evidence," which is used in historical works and in ethnographies and field studies, and also in many natural scientific contexts, particularly where there are many studies to be considered, or where experimentation is not feasible.

Nassim Nicholas Taleb Tests a Psychodynamic Assertion

Another exposure of a psychodynamic assertion to disconfirmation is provided, perhaps unwittingly, by the redoubtable Nassim Nicholas Taleb, a Wall Street trader, statistician, and polymath. He is the author of two intriguing books, *Fooled by Randomness* (2005) and *The Black Swan* (2010), which deal with our tendency to underestimate the importance of crucial rare events. Taleb is skeptical about psychodynamic factors, as about much else in the current Zeitgeist. Nonetheless, in one of his fascinating inquiries, he unknowingly provides an elegant test of a psychodynamic assertion.

Taleb, a Lebanese (a "Levantine" in his own eloquent parlance), in his childhood and early adolescence lived through the disastrous Beirut civil war, spending much of the time crouched in his basement reading omnivorously while the bombs burst around him and neighboring buildings crashed to the ground. When he spoke years later at an international conference, a psychologically minded conferee suggested that Taleb's intense concern with sudden disastrous unpredicted events might stem from his experiences as a youth hiding in his basement during the long civil war. Taleb disputed this putative instance of unconscious motivation and unconscious fantasy. To refute it he found a total of 36 Levantines who lived through the Beirut war, and who were also Wall Street traders—trading of all sorts has long been a feature of Mediterranean cultures—and found he was the only one of the 36 who espoused any theory about the overwhelming importance of rare events in the financial markets.

Taleb's exposure of an assertion to disconfirmation involved quantitative data. So did the example from the Israeli pantheon of Holocaust heroes and heroines. Where quantitative outcomes are predicted in order to subject the psychodynamic assertion to the possibility of disconfirmation, tests of statistical significance can be applied if random samples have been drawn. But in two of the examples given—the Taleb case and the profoundly disturbing monograph on the Holocaust—the universe of cases appears to have been included, so tests of statistical significance are not needed nor appropriate.

I think we can fairly conclude that the disconfirmatory logic formulated by Karl Popper can help us assess the probative value of psychodynamic inquiries into the near-madness that surrounds us.

The Power of Replication

Broadly speaking, replication is the effort to repeat a study. *Replication and disconfirmation are deeply related concepts.* In a replication the assertion that the study can be repeated with similar results is exposed to disconfirmation, as a repetition entails the possibility that the results will be different when repeated.

Replication in the Physical Sciences

Replication is a protean concept with different meanings in different spheres of investigation. For example, in the physical sciences, replication has several meanings. One meaning is using the exact same procedures and instruments to see if the exact same results are obtained. Physics furnishes an example. A 1989 experiment by Martin Fleischmann and Stanley Pons appeared to have obtained nuclear fusion at room temperature, the so-called "cold fusion" study (Fleischmann and Pons, 1989; Huizenga, 1993; Taubes, 1993). This held promise of almost unlimited energy from small amounts of matter. When attempted replications by other researchers failed, the Fleischmann–Pons study was discredited. These replications attempted to repeat the study exactly, as results are determined by physical laws. Finally, an investigation by the National Academy of Science found measurement errors in the original study.

Astronomy furnishes a second meaning of replication in the physical sciences. The rate of expansion of the universe is called the *Hubble Constant*. Its precise value has been debated for over 80 years (Carnegie Science, 2009). As the Hubble Constant is an important factor in estimating the age of the universe, so study after study has attempted to fix the value precisely, using related but not identical methods to gather and analyze data. Through this type of replication scientists have been able to narrow greatly the possible range of estimated values of the Hubble constant.

Replication in the Social Sciences

In the social sciences a researcher who has found something of interest in his or her data may try to replicate the study as exactly as possible. Even if the original differences were found to be statistically significant and therefore unlikely to have occurred by chance variations in the samples studied, the researcher will want to establish a greater base of data showing the results.

It is more usual, however, for the researcher to repeat the study, using a somewhat different population, for example, a different social group, or a different location. The aim would be to assess the generality of the phenomenon beyond the original laboratory or research site. This kind of replication seeks to establish the degree to which the original results can be expected to hold true over samples of different populations, or in different locations, or at different times. Sometimes the researcher will vary the original instruments, or vary the study procedures, to see if the findings are limited to a particular measure or a particular instrument, or to a particular research procedure or research setting.

Replication to Establish the Generality of a Study's Findings

Let me give a couple of examples from studies in an area I find of great interest, the psychology of urban life. The famous "horn-honking study" was a field experiment conducted by two graduate students at Stanford University to fulfill a seminar requirement (Doob and Gross, 1968). They drove a car up to a red light in the nearby upscale town of Palo Alto, and when the light changed to green, waited ten seconds before proceeding through the intersection. They measured the latency and frequency of the horn honking by cars in the queue at the light. They used at different times an old jalopy, owned by one of the students, and a new car, which they had rented for the experiment. They also used a variety of intersections in Palo Alto. They found that honking started much sooner, and was more frequent and more insistent with the jalopy than with the new car. The jalopy was, in fact, rammed once. This was one of the earliest studies of what has come to be called "road rage." To assess the stability and generality of the study findings, other researchers repeated it, not just in Palo Alto, but in other cities and with systematic differences in the research procedures. They found, for example, that the phenomenon held true across a wide variety of locales, but subject to certain variations. For example, if the experimenters' vehicle had a gun rack in the back, honking started much later and there were fewer honks.

Another famous field experiment concerned the effect of perceived social status on jay-walking at urban intersections (Lefkowitz et al., 1955). When the researcher's confederate was very well dressed, more people followed him as he jay-walked across the urban intersections than when he was dressed in shabby clothing. This study has also been repeated in various locales, showing the generality of the influence of social class perceptions on public behavior.

In replication in the social sciences, many small studies are preferable to one large study, as pointed out by Lee Cronbach (1981), because they are robust over different researchers, and over variations in design and in locale. In the social sciences, a study finding is considered more robust if in the replications, the measuring instruments, and the locales differ somewhat but similar results are nevertheless found.

Replication to Broaden a Concept

If a study endeavors to test or establish a very general theory, then a replication that applies it in a very different substantive context can greatly strengthen the theory and deepen our understanding of the concept.

Let's consider an example from urban studies. Donald Appleyard and Mark Lintell's study (1972) was (incredibly) the first to investigate the impact of urban traffic on the quality of life in residential city streets. They chose three, one-block long, adjacent parallel streets in San Francisco. One street they chose had a low amount of auto traffic, one had a moderate amount, and one had a high amount, as measured by actual vehicle counts per hour. Questionnaire-based interviews with systematically chosen residents on each of the three streets showed major differences in feelings of pedestrian safety, in the presence or absence of friendship patterns across the street, in subjective reactions to noise, in efforts to shut out the traffic sounds within residences, in feelings of stress or contentment, and in measured decibel levels. The study drew its conclusions about the results of auto traffic.

Much later, to test the generality of the impact of traffic on residential well-being, a graduate student, Mary Meyer, and I used the Appleyard–Lintell questionnaire, modified slightly, to study the effects of commercial aircraft flights over residential areas within 15 miles of the large Cincinnati Northern Kentucky airport (Meyer, 1994). We selected three areas: one had low overflights many times a day, another had a moderate frequency of overflights, and one had a comparatively low frequency of overflights, and at higher altitudes. Decibel measures confirmed our choice of high, moderate, and low overflight areas. Our findings paralleled those of Appleyard and Lintell: the usability of the residences, the amount of time spent outdoors in one's front- and backyards, the ability to hear telephone conversations, and overall residential satisfaction, differed markedly in the three areas. The study therefore, besides its unexpected practical use in helping residents negotiate with the airport authorities, served to extend the meaning of the concept "traffic."

It seems to me that replication could also deepen and broaden some of the concepts involved in understanding irrationality on the world scene. Replication would contribute not only to establishing the validity of particular studies, but also to enriching the conceptual base of these studies, something I will argue, in Chapter 5, is necessary.

There is Another Path

Chapter 9 sets forth a remarkable collaboration among experts and informants in assessing a major psychodynamic study. We will focus again on the Czech mentality during the Munich crisis, which we discussed above in terms of Popperian disconfirmation, but this time we will look at it from an entirely different perspective. I think the reader will find that the method involved in the collaboration represents a valuable complement to Popperian disconfirmation. Chapter 9 will also seek to give the reader a further understanding of psychologically informed psychodynamically sophisticated research.

5
Integrating Social Science Concepts and Findings into Psychodynamic Inquiry

The reader will note that I have been urging that psychodynamically informed studies of world events that seek to take unconscious processes into account, need to use the *methodology* of the social sciences. For example, presenting a protocol of what to look for, as described in Chapter 3, makes the research procedure more understandable to the researcher and to the reader. A Popperian criterion for predicted consequences of assertions, described in Chapter 4, makes validation or invalidation possible. We will see in Chapter 8 that survey and content analysis methods, and thick description, can help in choosing and interpreting data. Chapter 9 will explore a collegial interactive procedure that would permit the creation of deeper meaning through a symbolic interactive process.

But more is involved than linking psychodynamic insight to social science *methods*. It is also a matter of integrating *substantive* social science concepts and research findings into the planning and interpretation of the research. That is the subject of the present chapter. Here we will look at a variety of substantive (rather than methodological) social science concepts that I feel are particularly germane to understanding unconscious processes on the political–social scene.

Here is how I have organized this chapter. Firstly, I will discuss a way of looking at the *meaning* of research findings. Secondly, I will present a *procedure* for *integrating* these kinds of concepts with depth psychological research. Thirdly, I will *array* many of the relevant social scientific concepts. Fourthly, I will consider three of them in more *detail*. Finally, I will conclude with a couple of brief *examples*.

What Does a Research Finding Mean?

There are a number of ways to consider the *meaning* of a research finding. What does it predict? What does it exclude? What are its causes? What are its consequences? What are its correlates?

But the meaning that is relevant for us here is *of what sets is it a member? That is, of what social science concepts is our psychodynamic finding an instance?* This is what we shall explore in this chapter. But first, a discussion of what "integration" means and how integration is to be accomplished.

A Procedure for Integration

There are six steps to integrating social science concepts and findings into the findings of research that delves into unconscious mental processes on the world scene.

1. Immerse oneself in the relevant social science concepts. This means finding and reading the relevant theory and research literature.
2. Next, one must systematically relate one's findings to those concepts. This is a matter of doing theory oneself. This is tough for most people, even most researchers.
3. Deepen one's understanding of the concept by looking at how it is measured, that is, by examining the relevant attitude scales.
4. Choose the most striking and significant items from the attitude scales and quote them verbatim in one's own research write-up.
5. Examine in detail one's own research data, finding and quoting verbatim statements by the people being studied that parallel those items from the attitude scales.
6. Explore one's data to see if any actions by the political figure (or a group or a media source) seem to exemplify these concepts and parallel these items from the attitude scales.

An Array of Some Key Concepts

Studies that consider unconscious processes are deeply connected to the social sciences generally, and many social psychological concepts have components that are outside of conscious awareness—they are saturated with references to unconscious processes. And when social psychologists and sociologists discuss mentality, they are often willing to consider the effect of mental states that are at least partly outside of conscious awareness.

Here are some social scientific concepts of particular interest for our efforts. Where possible I have tried to choose very early works on these concepts, seminal works influential on later efforts. The concepts of special importance to our investigative efforts outlined in this book include the following: *alienation* (Simmel,1950; Ray, 1982), *anomie* (Durkheim, 1897 [1997]; Srole, 1956), *pluralistic ignorance* and *bystander apathy* (Latane and Darley, 1969), *conformity* (Kelman, 1958), *dogmatism* (Rokeach, 1954) *dehumanization* (Montagu and Matson,1983; Zimbardo, 2007) *mass psychology, collective behavior, and deindividuation* (Le Bon,1896; Tarde, 1903; Zimbardo, 2007), *obedience to authority* (Milgram, 1974;), *prejudice* (Allport, 1954; Pettigrew, 1980; Staub, 1989), *stigmatization* (Goffman, 1963), and *cognitive complexity* (Tetlock, 2006; Suedfeld and Jhangiani, 2009; Suedfeld, 2010). And the concept of *Verstehen*—a partly intuitive understanding of social rules (Wax, R., 1971 [1985], Wax, M., 1967)—can provide a sociological and anthropological context for the clinical researcher's emphasis on empathy.

Three of the Most Important Concepts

Let's look now in some detail at three salient social scientific concepts: national character, social disorganization, and social class.

National Character

National character, a well-accepted area of study within sociology and within social psychology, often deals with matters of clinical significance. It seems to me therefore that psychodynamically sophisticated studies would be strengthened by buttressing their assertions with evidence from studies of national character. National character often has deep roots in unconscious processes. Gerda Lederer has pointed out that in German families in the first half of the twentieth century it was believed that the child's love for the parents must be based on fear of the parents: "Liebe ist Furcht" (Love is Fear) And the mother's love for her infant was disparaged by the term "Affenliebe," as in the expression "Mutterliebe ist Affenliebe" meaning the primitive love of monkey mothers (Lederer, personal communication).

In *The Suicidal Embrace* (Beisel, 2003), and elsewhere, are presented examples of widespread national psychodynamics. Beisel, for example, points out that Hitler was beaten as a child, and that German children generally were harshly disciplined; Stalin was beaten as a child, and this was standard practice in Russia and Georgia at that time; Neville Chamberlain was abandoned as a child and then subjected to the sadomasochistic environment of the English public school, as was much of the British leadership. French infants from the upper classes were sent away to rural wet nurses for their first year of life. These are not trivial matters. These events leave marks, and the person emits from the unconscious some subtle indications of the damage done. For example, Stalin obsessively doodled snarling wolves and naked men.

A recent example of the deep connection between psychodynamic phenomena and national character is Peter Loewenberg's (2009) elegant study of the concept of "face" in Chinese culture and its impact on self-esteem and self-concept. Loewenberg says a Chinese national anthem includes the words: "Jump up! Jump up! We are not a subject people!"

The national character literature *per se* has a long and respected history, often grounded in massive in-depth interviews studies resulting in quantitative indicators and attitude scales, as well as portraits of individuals. For example, consider some classic studies: Alex Inkeles and David Smith's *Becoming Modern* (1974), and Daniel Lerner's *The Passing of Traditional Society* (1958). Inkeles and Smith developed a measure of *overall individual modernity.* Lerner created a quantitative index of individual *modernity*, and Joseph Kahl (1968) created another early measure of *modernism*, as did Harrison Gough (1976a, 1976b). I believe that psychologically sophisticated psychodynamically oriented investigators of political–social events could benefit from *looking at the items* in these scales. This is highly reputable research. Alex Inkeles was at Harvard, Daniel Lerner was at M.I.T., Daniel Levinson was at Harvard and then at Yale, Nevitt Sanford and Harrison Gough were at Berkeley, Joseph Kahl was at Cornell, and Peter Loewenberg is at UCLA. Nothing peripheral about any of them.

Despite this impressive tradition of sociological research, some researchers have been skeptical of "national character," dismissing it as an overgeneralization and an oversimplification. In my view, "national character" has been much too quickly dismissed by critics. The concept of a national character does not imply that everyone in that culture or subculture shares those characteristics, or even that a majority do, only that unusually large numbers of people in that culture or subculture share them. This is, after all, a *quantitative assertion* and one that can be tested quantitatively, as Alex Inkeles, Joseph Kahl, and Harrison Gough have done.

Obviously, modern nations embrace or at least comprise a variety of subcultures. Modern France, with its immigrant population from North Africa, is more than one culture, and so there is no longer a single "national character." Germany, with its immigrants from Turkey, includes more than one culture. Italy, England, and Scandinavia, with their immigration from elsewhere in the European Union, aren't single cultures either, and so each nation does not have a single national character. But within those nations, there are distinct subcultures and they can be studied.

Terminology may contribute to the skepticism. Perhaps "national character" should more accurately be called "cultural predispositions among demographic subgroups."

Confirming National Character Statistically

Cultural predispositions are particularly salient among expatriates because they stand out from the larger culture. These differences can be *confirmed quantitatively.* A few small examples will be illustrative but obviously will not be in themselves conclusive.

Consider a salient case of cultural predispositions among demographic subgroups: Asian American students. As of the 2010 U.S. Census, Asian Americans constitute only 5.6 percent of the population of the United States. But Asian Americans formed 19.9 percent of the students admitted to Harvard College in 2013 (and 40% of the 24 outstanding students elected to Phi Beta Kappa in their Junior year). Other elite universities, particularly those pre-eminent in science or technology, are reputed to have shown similar results.

Another small but telling example of cultural predispositions among demographic subgroups can be drawn from the New York City school system. Asian Americans make up only 14 percent of New York City's public school students, but in 2012 they constituted 72 percent of the student body of Manhattan's Stuyvesant High School (Spencer, 2012). This science and mathematics-oriented public high school admits the 800 applicants scoring highest on its entrance exam, who constitute the top 3.5 percent of the approximately 29,000 students who take the test each year. Success at Stuyvesant is widely viewed as a route to M.I.T., Cal Tech, Stanford, and Harvard, so there are private preparatory courses for the fearsome "Stuyvesant Test" all over New York City, and as far away as Hong Kong and Singapore. In 2013 "The successful applicants included 9 black students, 24 Latinos, 177 whites and 620 Asian–Americans" (Sowell, 2013) .

As Jerome Krase (an expert on race and ethnicity in New York City) observed about the Asian students, "The children hold the honor of the family in their hands. If they succeed, the family succeeds" (quoted in Spencer, 2012). Therefore, the pressure on them to exert scholastic effort is much greater.

Two examples do not constitute proof of a cultural predisposition of a demographic subgroup; rather, they illustrate the kind of quantitative data that are relevant to establishing an assertion of this sort.

Connecting psychodynamic findings to *quantitatively established cultural predispositions* is one way of relating clinically sophisticated inquiry to the social sciences. We have seen that another path to establishing this relationship is to *look at the actual items in the various scales* that have been developed by social scientists in various fields.

A key concept for the understanding of social phenonena is *Verstehen,* a German word used in social anthropology to mean the intuitive understanding of the social rules, actions, and social meanings of another culture. This intuitive understanding is based not only on observation, but also on an empathic process.

Social Disorganization

Depth psychological investigations of individuals and groups can benefit from the social science literature on *social disorganization.*

From a sociological point of view, social disorganization includes unemployment, social isolation, social deviance, crime, delinquency, divorce, alcoholism, suicide, sexual abuse of children, family and marital violence, homelessness, drug use, mendicancy, street crime and prostitution, displacement of the extended family by the nuclear family, and displacement of the nuclear family by the one-parent or no-parent family. Factor analytic studies show that these are related statistically: they intercorrelate significantly, and fall on a general factor that demographic factor analysts have termed "social disorganization" (Sweetser, 1965; Meyers et al., 1977).

From a social psychological point of view, the analogues of social disorganization include the following:

- *Alienation* refers to a sense of being outside the social system and feeling deeply distrustful and suspicious of social institutions, including politicians, the police, schools, churches, and the election system. It includes a belief that no one and no institution has their interests at heart, and that, in fact, all are out to do them in.
- *Anomie* refers to a sense of not knowing what social rules or moral standards apply to their life situation, a sense of having no inner or outer compass to guide them as to what is proper, permissible, and moral behavior. A sense of rootlessness. Emile Durkheim found that certain kinds of anomie were significantly correlated with suicide.

- *Pluralistic ignorance* is a situation, often an emergency, where no member of the group knows what the others are thinking or why they are behaving as they do. This ignorance paralyzes action by each member. Owing to pluralistic ignorance, a person who needs help in an emergency is actually more likely to be helped if only one person is present, or if the members of the group present are friends or relatives of each other and so can ascertain each other's thinking.
- *Deindividuation* is a person's sense of loss of individual identity, replaced by a sense of merger with a group, as, for example, in a riot or lynching or other mob situation. The individual under such a situation loses a sense of responsibility for his or her actions, and is capable of participation in atrocities while identified with the group.
- *Stigmatization* is a situation where a person or group is marked by another group as different, alien, and evil. Stigmatization is deeply involved in prejudice and often is a prelude to violence.

The social psychological syndromes I have described above have obvious analogues in psychodynamic theory. Examples are the concepts of anxiety, depression, compulsive reenactment of a trauma, sense of abandonment, disruption of attachment relationships, flat affect (emotional unresponsiveness), unconscious enabling of deviant behavior in others, self-destructive behavior, and, of course, projection.

And *irredentism,* a concept from political science, describes the endless yearning for lost territory, as in the Italia Irredenta movement and the current Israeli–Palestinian conflict. Irredentism has an obvious analogue in psychodynamic theory: the endless yearning for a lost person. An example is a child's lifelong longing for a parent lost in childhood, or a parent's longing for a lost child.

Social Class and Psychodynamic Inquiry

The most powerful predictive variable in the social sciences is *social class.* It is usually assessed by combining measures of an individual's income, education, and occupation, but other measures are also used. Social class membership predicts a huge variety of important things about an individual, such as voting preferences, cultural and intellectual interests, home furnishings, hobbies, choice of vacation venues and activities, geographic mobility, home ownership, child-rearing practices, dietary preferences, television watching habits, choice of college, and more.

Social class is therefore one of the primary interests of sociologists and of some social psychologists. But not enough connection has been made between psychodynamically oriented studies, and the sociology or social psychology of social class. I believe that psychological portraits of world leaders should be placed in the context of the characteristics of the social class from which they emerged or which they achieved. This applies to studies of almost any world leader: Bismarck, Stalin, Hitler, Napoleon, Churchill, Roosevelt, Nixon, Clinton, Bush, Obama.

The use of the social class context, as with the national character context and the social disorganization context, will make the psychodynamic research findings deeper, and more understandable to the reader and so more credible. Besides the benefits of increasing explanatory power, there are benefits in communication and credibility.

Empathy and Perspective-taking

Even the *validity* of inquiry into unconscious mental processes itself can be strengthened by explicating its relationship to well-established social science concepts. For example, as we saw in Chapter 2, psychodynamically oriented researchers claim that "empathy" is a legitimate component of their research methods. That claim would be greatly bolstered if placed in the context of the social psychological research on "perspective-taking" (Hall, 2004).

An Example of the Relationship of Psychodynamic Investigation to Social Science Concepts

Suppose, for example, a political figure is found to have a personality and unconscious mental life similar to that of Hermann Hesse's character, Steppenwolf: confused, fearful, caught up in fantasies that he has difficulty telling from reality, distrustful, intensely lonely, and isolated. (These inferences might be drawn from the kinds of data suggested in Chapters 3 through 9.) At least two social scientific concepts come readily to mind for this example: *alienation,* and *anomie* (normlessness).

Firstly, there is a rich social science literature to be consulted on these concepts in relation to the plight of modern man. Secondly, there exist several well-established and well-researched attitude scales on *alienation* and several on *anomie*. The researcher must examine his or her own findings to see if verbatim quotations echo any of these items, and also if any actions by the political figure (or media) seem to exemplify these concepts. Let's consider some illustrative items from some widely used scales measuring these concepts. The items can be compared with verbal data and with actions, from the persons, groups, or medium the psychodynamic researcher is studying.

As we noted earlier, *alienation* refers to a feeling of isolation from society and from close personal relationships, distrust of others, and rejection of the prevailing culture. Here are some items from the widely used Margins of Society Alienation Scale (Travis, 1993):

> I feel all alone these days
> I often feel discriminated against
> My whole world feels like it is falling apart.
> I'll never find the right person to care enough about me.

Anomie, as we noted above, refers to a feeling of normlessness, uncertainty about how life should be lived, and not knowing what rules apply. Here are a few illustrative items from Leo Srole's widely used Anomia Scale (1956):

> These days a person doesn't know whom he can count on
> Nowadays a person has to live pretty much for today and let tomorrow take care of itself
> It's hardly fair to bring a child into the world with the way things look for the future

Travis (1993) has published a version of the Anomia Scale with the intent of improving on the Srole version.

Psychodynamically based research findings will be enriched by examining measures of the relevant social science concepts and looking for parallels in the data from the research.

Another Example

A political figure, a social group, or even a media source may be found by psychodynamic inquiry (perhaps including some of the indicators suggested in Chapter 3) to be rigid and constrained in thought and action, with an obsessive–compulsive personality orientation rooted in feelings and fantasies outside of conscious awareness, but to the person or groups involved, it all would seem rational. Neville Chamberlain, with his tightly furled umbrella, comes to mind.

Relevant scales might include *anxiety, ethnocentrism, dogmatism, parsimony, localism, class consciousness, and social dominance.*

Here, for example, are some items from the Neuliep and McCroskey's Ethnocentrism Scale (1965):

> Most other cultures are backward compared to my culture
> Most people in other cultures just don't know what's good for them
> People in other cultures could learn a lot from people in my culture

How can these items be related to the inner mental life of Chamberlain, or that of the British people, at that point in time?

Well, for example, we will see Chapter 9 that "the British repeatedly spoke of Czechoslovakia (and other smaller countries) as 'wretched little places...half the size of Yorkshire...snuffling little countries, and funny little people.'"

Dogmatism refers to the tendency to be rigid in one's belief and attitudes and to reject emphatically alternative views. It was first measured by Milton Rokeach (1954), but there have been improvements since then. Here are some illustrative items from Troldahl and Powell's Dogmatism Scale (1965):

> My blood boils whenever a person stubbornly refuses to admit he's wrong
> Most people just don't know what's good for them
> There are two kinds of people in this world: those who are for the truth and those who are against the truth
> Of all the different philosophies which exist in this world there probably is only one which is correct

Social dominance is the belief that some particular groups should dominate or be in ascendance over other groups. A great deal of research has been done on this concept, and some researchers view it as better conceptually, and better psychometrically (better measured) than the related concept of *authoritarianism*. Here are some items from the Social Dominance Scale (Pratto et al., 1994):

> Some groups of people are simply not the equals of others
> Some people are just more deserving than others
> Inferior groups should stay in their place

Collaboration

This chapter proposes a broad collaboration between social scientists and psychodynamically oriented researchers, professions that have often kept somewhat apart. If social scientists take some of the initiative in this collaboration, both groups will benefit. A good example is the work of three Czech political psychologists with the clinical researcher David Beisel, which will be presented in Chapter 9. These days, most research is collaborative anyway, usually *within* a given discipline. But why not collaborate *across disciplines* and get additional purchase on some of the problems confronting us?

Crossing the Boundary with Literature

Literary works can be very relevant to psychodynamic studies. We saw in Chapter 1 that the poet Czeslaw Milosz provided insight into "the captive mind." In Chapter 8 the works of Kafka, Orwell, Ionesco, and Pirandello illuminate the meaning of "irreality." There are other examples: *The Dwarf*, by Par Lagerkvist (1944), gives insight into alienation and the impulse to martyrdom; Herman Hesse's *Steppenwolf* (1927 [2002]) describes dissociation, alienation, and anomie.

Placing a psychodynamically oriented study in the context of social science research findings and concepts gives the reader an understanding of the *generality* of the phenomena found in the study. Placing the study in the context of literary themes and analogues is quite different: it gives the reader a better *intuitive understanding* of what the psychodynamic study has found.

Given the cultural differences between Europe and the United States, we can expect that the recommendation to include literary references in research studies will seem obvious in Europe and outré in the United States. There are marked differences in the social sciences in many respects in the two areas, as a comparison of professional journals easily reveals.

One may even say that the entire field of psychodynamic inquiry into world events has a European sensibility. But the problems it addresses are important to everyone. In subsequent chapters we will turn to some particularly challenging problems.

> *Tambovsky volk tebe tovarisch* ("You are not my comrade, the wolf of the steppes is your only comrade").
>
> Russian proverb, said by guards to prisoners in the Siberian gulags

6
A Panoply of Social Science Methods to Illuminate the Phenomena, Reduce Researcher Bias, and Permit Disconfirmation

There is a great variety of social science methods that will be helpful in our quest, and I have chosen some of the most interesting and important for our purposes. In this chapter we will discuss the specification of a protocol; systematic and random sampling methods; thick description and extensive verbatim quotations; self-disclosure by the researcher of personal background and possible bias; quantitative and qualitative content analysis; multiple raters; validation through symbolic interactionist procedures or by means of the Delphi technique; use of informants in the tradition of urban sociological field work; narrative analysis; and Popperian disconfirmation procedures using risky predictions.

Why Clinically Sophisticated Social Science Research Methods are Needed

The unconscious motives and fantasies underlying irrational actions are paradoxical: time does not exist, everything is in the present, opposites don't cancel each other out, and there is magical thinking. As a result, the structured methods of the clinically sophisticated psychodynamically oriented social sciences are necessary for drawing valid inferences about these matters. These methods can *illuminate the phenomena,* estimate and *reduce researcher bias,* and subject the researcher's assertions to *disconfirmatory testing.*

The Limitations of Traditional Historical Methods

Historical and journalistic studies of world events usually deal only with the conscious level, where they have made great contributions. There are many works of history that are widely considered to be substantially correct and deeply informative: Tony Judt's *Post War* (2005);

Siddhartha Mukherjee's *Emperor of All Maladies* (2011); Sir Peter Hall's *Cities in Civilization* (1998); Peter Gay's *Modernism* (2010); Drew Faust's *Mothers of Invention: Women of the Slaveholding South in the American Civil War* (1996); Sidney Fay's *The Origins of the World War* (1928); David Hogan and David Aretha's *The Holocaust Chronicle* (2003); and William L. Langer's *European Alliances and Alignments* (1931), to name just a few.

But where profoundly irrational actions, stemming from unconscious motives and fantasies, are involved, the traditional methods of history are sometimes not sufficient to reach agreement. Examples we will discuss in this chapter include the Gopal/Ferguson controversy over neo-colonialism; the motivations for the Dresden fire-bombing; and the exploration of the Stasi files.

Many factors limit the usefulness of the traditional methods of history *in situations where unconscious motivations and fantasies are likely to be importantly involved.* The limiting factors include the lack of methods for assessing and controlling for researcher bias in problem conceptualization and data interpretation, the lack of psychodynamic understanding, the distortions caused by counter-transference, the absence of a natural history of the study, the reliance on common sense psychology, the absence of a protocol, the lack of attention to systematic sampling, the aversion to inferential statistics, and the absence of formal procedures for disconfirmation.

Let's first look at the evidence for my contention that where motivations and fantasies outside of conscious awareness are likely to be involved, historical methods are frequently unable to agree on an answer, much less test it for validity.

Empire or Empiricism?

Consider the case of Niall Ferguson, the Tisch Professor of History and Ziegler Professor of Business Administration at Harvard, author of eight major books and hundreds of scholarly articles, and author of a long historical series on public television. Ferguson is certainly a well-known historian, but his very positive view of the accomplishments and responsibilities of empire have elicited this evaluation from Dr. Priyamavada Gopal, who teaches post-colonial studies at Cambridge University, where she is Dean of Churchill College:

> "Neocon ideologue" rewriting history "driven by the messianic fantasies of the American right...Colonialism—a tale of slavery, plunder, war, corruption, land grabbing, famines, exploitation, indentured labor, impoverishment, massacres, genocide and forced

> resettlements—is being rewritten into a benign developmental mission (quoted in Tassel, 2007, p. 36).

In fact, Niall Ferguson describes himself as "a fully paid-up member of the neo-imperialist gang" (quoted in Bromwich, 2011).

Here we have two historians, Gopal and Ferguson, from two elite universities, and two wildly different accounts, and a sharp controversy with allegations of biased historical analysis. To assess and lessen bias, I think social science methods are helpful.

Two "Parfit Gentil Knights"

Let us look at another instance where unconscious processes in both researchers and subject arouse biases that make agreement impossible. Consider the very different accounts of World War II given by two British historians, both knighted for their historical work. Sir Basil Liddell Hart wrote the well-respected *History of the Second World War* (1970). Liddell Hart had been a captain in the British Army in World War I, and was subsequently a military journalist for *The Spectator* and other British newspapers. He became recognized as the leading military historian of his time. His *History of the Second World War* focuses on military strategy and tactics only. Liddell Hart was an early advocate of the importance of tank warfare, which was unfortunately ignored by the British and but read in translation by the German military leadership.

For a sharply skeptical view of Liddell Hart, see Mearsheimer (1988), who criticizes Liddell Hart for self-promotion, and for advising Chamberlain against organizing military intervention in Continental Europe, arguing that Britain should take a defensive stance only, and, if need be, conduct warfare in Europe through air power rather than by means of large land armies, in order to avoid catastrophic battlefield casualties like those seen in World War I. But Mearsheimer does note that Liddell Hart did advocate strong air defenses for England. Generally speaking, the rhetoric can be fierce in this area of historical inquiry.

So, in recent years Liddell Hart has become much more controversial. But it seems possible that Liddell Hart may actually have been correct in his belief that England alone could not win a land war against Germany, which had much shorter and entirely land-based supply lines, a somewhat larger industrial base, and a considerably larger population to provide troops. With the landing of many thousands of American troops (along with the British), beginning on D-Day, 6 June 1944, and continuing thereafter, a victory in a land war against Germany become more achievable, especially since two-thirds of the German troops were on the Eastern Front. In fact, some historians have concluded that the Red Army was the single biggest factor in the defeat of Germany in World War II.

Sir Martin Gilbert, another respected historian, was the official biographer of Winston Churchill. Among his works is a huge and well respected scholarly book, *The Second World War: A Complete History* (1989), covering all aspects, military and civilian, and documented with thousands of references. Many consider it the best one-volume history of World War II. He deals with all aspects of the war, especially its impact on civilians, which Liddell Hart ignores. Gilbert is also a recognized authority on the Nazi program of extermination of the Jews, and his book, *The Holocaust* (1986), is a classic.

Gilbert's perspective and personal background are very different from those of the military historian B.H. Liddell Hart, whose work was respected by the German generals. They had his books translated into German and they followed his advice on tank warfare, while the British did not until very late. After the war, the generals were glad to talk to him while in internment camps in Britain. Liddell Hart's book on what they said is called "The Other Side of the Hill" in the UK edition (1948), and "The German Generals Speak" (1948 [1971]) in the abridged American edition. Liddell Hart also edited Rommel's memoirs. After the war he served for a while as a military advisor to the Israeli government, counseling them, correctly I believe, that Israel needed to keep the Golan Heights in order to be militarily defensible. In recent years, as noted, Liddell Hart has been criticized for "self-promotion" in advancing his ideas on military strategy.

Personal and social background influence one's historical writing in a major way, and Liddell's and Gilbert's histories of World War II demonstrate that. A few examples among many from those two books follow.

Guderian's Responsibility

Gilbert states that Heinz Guderian, the chief of the Panzer Divisions, circulated a memo from Hitler urging that civilians be treated harshly. But Liddell Hart argues that Guderian accompanied the memo with one of his own reminding soldiers that they must behave professionally.

Dunkirk

The two historians also give very different explanations for the puzzling fact that the British were allowed to, or were able to, evacuate their troops at Dunkirk (although they were forced to leave their weapons behind). Liddell Hart argues that Hitler gave a command to delay the

German advance since he was ambivalent about wiping out the army of a nation with whom he thought he could negotiate peace. Liddell Hart cites instances of German commanders being refused permission to advance in the last few days before Dunkirk. Gilbert, however, argues that it was logistically impossible to advance and that the British troops escaped because the German army was unable to stop them from doing so. Two historians, two very different accounts, each account argued vehemently.

Dresden

Dresden was a medieval gem and was widely considered not a military town. There are very divergent accounts of the purpose of the 1945 fire-bombing of Dresden. Gilbert states that "On the night of February 13 [1945]...245 British bombers struck at the city of Dresden, followed three and a half hours later by 529 more. Their purpose was to destroy the city's railway marshalling yards" (1989, p. 640). No mention is made of why the central city had to be fire-bombed to disable the railroad yards. Gilbert reports that "On the morning of February 15, less than 36 hours after the first British bombers had flown over Dresden, a second wave of two hundred American bombers attacked the still-burning city, on the assumption that still more havoc could be caused if an attack were made while fire-fighting equipment and personnel were at work in the streets, and could themselves be hit" (1989, p. 641). Gilbert quotes a reaction—"...we were in heaven..."—by a Jewish slave laborer from some miles away who saw the flames of the burning city in the distance and realized that he would soon be free, as German resistance disintegrated (ibid). By Gilbert's estimate, more than 60,000 people were killed, though he says the havoc was so great that the exact number will never be known.

Liddell Hart, however, states that the Dresden fire-bombing was

> the deliberate revival of "terrorisation," as a prime aim...On January 27, 1945, [Air Marshall Sir Arthur] Harris was given instructions to carry out such blows, second in priority to oil targets and ahead of communications and other objectives. As a consequence, the distant city of Dresden was subjected to a devastating attack in mid-February—with the deliberate intention of wreaking havoc among the civil population and refugees—striking at the city center, not the factories or railways" (1970, pp. 609–10).

Gilbert notes, in two places (1989, 1999), that Air Marshall Harris, then at the Air Ministry in London, drew inspiration for the fire-bombing raids on Hamburg and Dresden from the devastating fire-bombing of

Coventry by the Luftwaffe. The many fires resulting from the bombing had linked together and created a firestorm that could not be put out, destroying 60,000 of the 75,000 buildings in the town. "A new verb entered the German language: *Koventrieren*—'to Coventrate,' or raze to the ground" (1999, p. 352). This was then applied by the Germans to Rotterdam and Warsaw, among others.

Gilbert states, "At the Air Ministry in London, Air Marshall Harris, who was eventually to be made head of the Bomber Command, later observed that the German raid on Coventry had taught the British the 'principle' of starting 'so many fires at one time' that no fire-fighting services could get them under control" (1989, p. 142). To me, it is not a very large step to infer from this that Dresden might have been a reprisal for Coventry.

Gilbert's quotation of Air Marshall Arthur Harris' reaction to the Coventry bombing prompts us to look a bit further into the words of Harris, when he became Commander in Chief of the RAF Bomber Command in 1942. Harris rejected the previous commitment to the "precision bombing" of specific targets crucial to German industry such as ball bearing factories. Instead, he pioneered "area bombing:" the saturation bombing of areas with dense civilian populations. He issued a directive calling for bombing "focused on the morale of the enemy civil population and in particular of the industrial workers" (Keegan, 1999, pp. 230–1). Harris argued that these bombings would "break German civilian morale," and he promised to "scourge the Third Reich from end to end." And "In his broadcast in German, he told enemy civilians to expect air raids 'every night and every day, rain, blow or snow.'" About 600,000 civilians were killed in these raids (Sutherland and Sutherland, 2010, pp. 118, 125, 232–3).

These words increase the likelihood that creating terror was a major purpose of the Dresden bombing. When we reflect that most of Coventry, and 37% of London, had been destroyed by the Luftwaffe in the Blitz, with great loss of civilian life, we can wonder whether a revenge motive might have also been involved. Destroying the morale of enemy factory workers might be considered a military goal, but Dresden was not a factory or industrial center.

Two More Views on Dresden

A third historian did not try to resolve the disagreement between Liddell and Gilbert but made some suggestive comments. The eminent European historian Norman Davies cites estimates of the death toll from the Dresden fire-bombing to be between 120,00 and 150,000 from one source, and 135,000 from another source. (The reader will notice that these totals exceed the death toll at Hiroshima or Nagasaki.) As for the motives for the bombing, Davies begins by remarking that the Old Market Square, the center of the city of Dresden, was the aim point for the attack: He states:

> at 10 PM on the evening of…Tuesday 13 February, 1945 Dresden's Old City was illuminated by a phosphorescent Primary Flare dropped by a high-flying pathfinder plane of 83 Squadron RAF. The Altmarkt had been selected as the base point of the Target Area of the most destructive bombing raid in Europe's history (Davies, 1998, p 414).

Historian Frederick Taylor, author of *Dresden: Tuesday, Feb. 13, 1945* (2004) estimates the death toll to be 25,000, much less than previous estimates. In an interview with *Der Spiegel* (2009), Taylor discusses

> memoranda written by the British Air Marshal Charles Portal, Chief of the Air Staff. In the first, Portal argued for a new rationale, based on a hugely increased bomber force, which would carry out not just precision bombing but also indiscriminate "area bombing" by night of all German cities with populations exceeding 100,000. Portal thought that the resulting damage to the German war effort and civilian morale would lead to victory within six months. A second memorandum a year later made a similar argument.

But,

> by late 1944 Portal had changed his mind, and unsuccessfully tried to persuade Royal Air Force Marshal Arthur "Bomber" Harris, to scale down attacks on German cities. "I [Taylor] remain unconvinced that maximizing civilian casualties—rather than winning the war by whatever means necessary—was their chief objective. … The Dresden attack was directly linked to the conduct of the war elsewhere—in this case on the Eastern Front. In Feb. 1945, Dresden was a major transport and communication hub less than 120 miles from the advancing Russians. The aim of the bombing was quite deliberately to destroy the center of the city, thereby making the movement of German soldiers and civilians impossible. This was, in fact, a clear-cut case where maximum destruction was the central aim of the attack. There can be no question that the presence of many refugees was factored into the Allies' calculations. A Feb. 1, 1945 memorandum

> specifically noted the huge tide of refugees passing through the eastern German cities as a "plus point," chillingly adding that attacking these cities would "result in establishing a state of chaos in some or all of these areas."

Frederick Taylor concluded that there was a military purpose. But his defense of the fire-bombing can be interpreted as consistent with Liddell Hart's view that it had a "terrorization" purpose as well. Even Martin Gilbert's discussion of the second wave of fire-bombing can be interpreted that way. And the words of Arthur Harris about area bombing do not put our minds at ease about Dresden.

Rational discussion of the purpose, or purposes, of the fire-bombing is made even more difficult by the neo-Nazi rallies in Dresden each year on the anniversary of the fire-bombing.

I find it difficult to draw firm conclusions about the motives for the fire-bombing. On the one hand, Martin Gilbert is a major historian of modern Europe and I find it hard to simply dismiss his views. On the other hand, I find it even more difficult to get away from the implications of those memoranda by British Air Marshall Charles Portal and the words of Commander Arthur Harris.

In any case, what we have here are four major modern European historians giving very different pictures of a crucial highly emotionally laden event, redolent with intense feelings and fantasies outside of awareness: the obliteration of a medieval town by massive bombing of civilians.

Implications for Psychodynamic Inquiry

Historians do recognize the difficulty of coming to agreement on certain topics. Pieter Geyl (1948) said, "History is an argument without end." But as Paul Doolan (2009) notes "He ends the book on an optimistic note: 'The argument goes on.'"

Voltaire felt historians give biased accounts: "History is a bag of tricks we play upon the dead." Lynn Whyte Jr. argued that the past is too complex for historians to interpret correctly: "Voltaire to the contrary, history is a bag of tricks which the dead have played upon historians."

Limitations of the Traditional Historical Method in the Depth Psychodynamic Realm: An Example

A study of very high quality that just about everyone considers substantially correct is Oxford historian Timothy Garton Ash's (1997a,

1997b) examination of the files the Stasi (the East German State Security Service) had kept on him when he was a young student in East Germany. Yet this study illustrates the limitations of the historical method when confronted with human interactions in which unconscious thoughts, feelings, and fantasies likely play an important part.

Ash had lived in East Berlin, the capital of the East German Republic (German Democratic Republic), from July 1978 to October 1980, writing his doctoral thesis about Berlin under Hitler. Fifteen years later he returned to East Berlin to examine his Stasi files as a historian. His first surprise was to learn that he had been designated the code name "Romeo."

In 1990, after the fall of the German Democratic Republic, the Gauk Authority had been set up to give people access to their files. As described by Ash, the extraordinarily high level of organization, attention to detail, and obsessive thoroughness of the Stasi files, even on the most ordinary people, boggles the mind. There are an astounding 111 miles of files in all, meticulously organized and analyzed by the Stasi. Records show that there were over 200,000 informers or people otherwise associated with the Stasi, plus 90,000 full-time Stasi employees. Dossiers were created on fully one-sixth of the East German population. As Ash notes, people were informed on, or actually denounced, to the Stasi, by all kinds of people: a barber or hairdresser or grocer by a customer; a family by their housekeeper, shopkeepers, people sitting nearby at a restaurant, friends, business and professional associates, anyone, even relatives. One peace activist was informed on for many years by her husband.

On his return to Germany, after seeing his Stasi files, Ash began interviewing the people who had spied on him. He was astonished at the identity of some of these people. He interviewed them in an inquiring, puzzled, non-accusatory way. They gave all kinds of excuses, evasions, and apologies for their behavior, and rationalizations about the necessity of their role in the communist German Democratic Republic, and the difficult positions in which they found themselves. Ash, confronted with all these intense feelings, exculpatory statements, and administrative complexities clearly states that he cannot give a satisfactory explanation of what he has discovered. As he says,

> What is it that makes one person a Stauffenberg and another a Speer? Twenty years on, I am little closer to an answer. A clear value system or faith? Reason and experience? Sheer physical strength or weakness? Firm roots in a family, community, or nation? There is no

> simple rule, no single explanation. But as those who worked for the secret police talked with me about their lives I feel again and again that the key lies in their childhood. I think for example that Major Risse was saved as a human being by his mother's love...But what touches me most, as a father, is the part of the fathers...Sometimes—quite often in fact—the Stasi comes as a substitute father (1997a, pp. 253–4).

This is as far as Ash can go, a tentative common sense explanation, simple and sweeping, and not accompanied by a thorough and scholarly exposition of the psychodynamic forces involved and the data substantiating this interpretation. One can hardly blame Ash for being puzzled or for grasping at a simple explanation but, unfortunately, it is too vague to tell us much about why one person is a Stauffenberg and one a Speer, or why one person agreed to spy and another avoided it.

Ash's work shows the contribution that historical inquiry can make, but it is also shows its limitations. Psychodynamic sophistication and social science methods are needed to investigate hidden motives and unconscious mental processes effectively. The required methods include as ways to disclose, estimate, and lessen researcher bias in the formulation of the problem, and in the selection and interpretation of data. We also need to seek ways to subject the researcher's inferences and assertions to potential disconfirmation, although this is not always easy. And we need new concepts of what should be considered relevant "data" and how these may be best understood. Narrative analysis is an approach to conceptualizing data that has grown in influence in recent years. It will be helpful to look at the Ash account in the light of this technique. (A more detailed example of narrative analysis will be presented in Chapter 7.)

Narrative Analysis as a Technique

If we now analyze Ash's account as a narrative, according to the standard framework explained in Chapter 7, some insights appear. Ash is the protagonist, the story of his doings in East Berlin as a student have as an audience the Stasi, the story of his investigation has as an audience readers interested in political events. There is a beginning to the story, his first years in Berlin; a middle, his return to look at his Stasi files and his interviewing of some of the people who spied on him.

But there is no ending: as he says, he is unable to resolve why some people are spies and some are like Claus von Stauffenberg, who attempted to assassinate Hitler. And there are missing characters: people who were asked to report on him and refused. These are not mentioned in the Stasi files but if they could be found he might come to understand more why some refused to spy.

Ash describes the Nazi courts where people accused by their neighbors, their hairdressers, almost anyone who had contact with them, were tried and—when found guilty—executed. The theme of the story is the use of "reporting" to the Stasi to enforce political control of the populace.

But I think there is an another theme, implied by what Ash found, but not explicitly stated in his account. Consider the enormous magnitude of the Stasi files, the great percentage of the populace reporting on each other, the vast number of Stasi officials, a far greater percentage than the Gestapo had, as Ash documents. It seems to me that spying was also a manifestation of a bureaucracy that functioned for the purpose of functioning, spying for the sake of spying, an end in itself, a kind of obsessive–compulsive inquiry, and an evil malevolent version of Herman Hesse's "bead game" (Hesse, 1943 [1975]).

Self-disclosure as a Technique

I recommend a degree of self-disclosure as a general procedure in psychodynamic studies of world events. It represents a way of constraining ideological bias, by forcing the author to become more aware of it, and by helping the reader to take it into account. Stating one's background, both personal and intellectual, and one's emotional reaction to the data one is considering, also helps the reader understand more deeply what the researcher is saying.

Open discussion of bias and emotional reactions to the data and to the research process is typical in anthropological studies, for example the work of Rosalie Wax (1971 [1985]). They are typical also in sociological field studies in the tradition of "The Chicago School" of urban field work. Examples abound, starting with the pioneering work of Ernest Burgess (1926) and Robert E. Park (Park et al., 1925), and the landmark study by W.I. Thomas and Florian Znaniecki (1919–1920). Also in this tradition are studies by Louis Wirth (1928), Frederick Thrasher (1927), William F. Whyte (1943 [1993]), Jane Jacobs (1961 [1993]), Joseph Howell (1992), and Herbert Gans (1962). These are all qualitative studies. Their practitioners argue that self-disclosure helps the reader in taking bias into account, since objective measures of what they are studying are often unavailable. Even more importantly, they argue, their emotional reactions to what they are studying are themselves data. They are in effect themselves measuring instruments. But the latter is exactly what the clinician claims. All the more reason, then, for *the researcher to fully disclose his or her personal background, intellectual perspective, and emotional reaction to the data and to the research process.* This background has shaped and deepened the inquiry, and, if disclosed, will help the reader understand the study more deeply and also get an idea of what insights might have been missed by the researcher. From a psychoanalytic point of view, what is being discussed here is called "counter-transference," that is, the effect the subject of the study has on the researcher based on the researcher's own personal history. Self-disclosure is one way of attempting to take into account distortions in understanding caused by counter-transference, or at least to disclose to the reader their possibility. And as in the clinical situation, counter-transference can also contain information: like the clinician, the researcher's personal background may sensitize him or her to aspects of the situation that others would miss.

Random Sampling as a Technique

One approach, that I will consider in more detail in the Chapter 8 study of three authoritarian leaders, Zhirinovsky, Le Pen, and Papadopoulos, is to *use objective procedures to obtain textual data.* But instead of taking a small sample of the population of texts of interest to us, we decided to take the entire relevant population of texts as our sample. In our case this meant all articles or speeches by defined persons on a certain topic in a certain time period. As is desirable, criteria for sampling were developed by persons other than the researchers. The sampling or population selection was carried out by computer programs. It was our hope that these procedures would give the reader some confidence that the data were not being selected in an obviously biased way.

From these data, I made interpretative statements about what I called "irreality," documented with *thick description* (metaphorically, description laid on with a trowel), including *very extensive verbatim quotations.* I hoped that the reader could then make a judgment as to whether, based on these data, the assertions about *irreality* I offered are credible.

Sample Size Considered

As I noted, Dr. Christine Gerety and I took 100% samples, getting every item in the population, which is a bit unusual. Ordinarily in social scientific studies, sampling does not include the entire population of data of interest because there are too many units in this population. But if a truly *random* sample is taken, in which each item has a known chance of being selected, it can be shown mathematically that the sample (of appropriate size) will tend to be a very good reflection of the entire population of interest, whether that population be articles, individuals, groups, institutions, widgets, or whatever. Among the huge advantages of random sampling are that it is cost- and time-saving compared to getting the entire population. If it is impossible to reach everyone in the population of interest, a random sample that does reach everyone in the sample plan may well be a more accurate reflection of the population than is a flawed sample of the whole population. That is why many studies by the U.S. Census use sampling. An interesting feature of random sampling of large populations is that the accuracy of the estimates of the population characteristics based on a sample is determined mathematically predominantly by the absolute sample size, not by what percentage of the population it constitutes. As the population of interest gets larger, the sample size needed rises, but more slowly.

Other Paths to Sampling

Random sampling provides the assurance that if the sample is large enough, it is highly likely to represent accurately all variables in the sampled population. Random sampling rebuts the possibility that the instances or documents studied were "cherry picked" intentionally or else were inadvertently chosen by the investigator to support the study hypotheses.

Having said that, I must interject some words of qualification. Sampling is frequently taught in a rigid and doctrinaire way, in which non-random methods of sampling are disparaged and discarded. This is unfortunate.

In his compendium, *Qualitative Research and Evaluation Methods* (2014), Michael Quinn Patton has a chapter on "purposeful sampling methods," in which members of small groups of particular interest or importance to the study hypothesis are chosen by specific criteria without using random sampling. These methods include extreme or deviant case sampling, sampling of information-rich cases, maximum variation sampling, homogeneous sampling, critical case sampling (defined later in this chapter), and "snowball" or chain sampling (defined immediately below). Generally speaking, critical cases or homogenous cases or information-rich or deviant or extreme cases are chosen opportunistically as they are encountered. Since they are usually scarce and don't constitute a defined population they cannot be randomly sampled; the investigator uses as many as he or she can find.

As a graduate student I found purposeful sampling to be fruitful. I took part in a study designed by Professor Samuel Stouffer, one of the originators of quantitative highly structured survey analysis (*The American Soldier*, 1949). This study used simple "snowball sampling" to identify the power structure in the town of Pittsfield, Massachusetts. In this method each interviewee suggests some other people to whom the interviewer should talk. This method is used widely by political scientists, sociologists, and anthropologists in community leadership studies.

In a community study in Massachusetts, *Citizen Participation in Mental Health* (Dorwart and Meyers, 1981), generously reviewed in the *New England Journal of Medicine* as "a model for researchers," the investigators not only interviewed the presidents of each of the 39 state-sanctioned community mental health boards, but also interviewed a purposeful sample of community leaders deemed to be information-rich sources.

Purposeful sampling has seemed particularly appropriate to investigators of the livability of cities. A landmark study by Donald Appleyard and Mark Lintell (1972) used purposeful sampling to investigate the effect of automobile traffic on the quality of urban residential life. A street with high auto traffic, a parallel street with medium auto traffic, and a parallel street with low auto traffic were compared in terms of interaction among residents, response to noise and pollution, sense of safety and comfort, and use of space within their dwellings. Residents of each street were chosen for interviews by a quota sampling method, which, unlike random sampling, does not permit ready analysis of statistical significance. Yet the study has been replicated with similar results in the rest of San Francisco, and in other cities as well.

The seminal books of the architect and urban planner Jan Gehl, *Life Between Buildings* (2011), and *Cities for People* (2010), set forth his use of quantitative measures and qualitative assessments of urban livability. There is a total absence in Gehl's work of any kind of random sampling of cities, or of the places within cities he chose for intensive study. All his sampling has been purposeful, based on judgments as to what areas were critical cases, contained the most data, or were most extreme or most typical or had the most practical importance. Gehl has been for 50 years the most creative and influential person in his field. His books have been translated into 15 languages, and he has made successful interventions in Copenhagen, Stockholm, Rotterdam, London, Amman, Muscat, Melbourne, Sidney, San Francisco, Seattle, and New York. Gehl's research methods are explained in Chapter 10, based on his book with Brigitte Svarre, *How to Study Public Life* (2013).

Random Versus Purposeful Sampling for Psychodynamic Inquiry of World Events

I have argued earlier that random sampling is particularly valuable for psychodynamic studies of world events because of its tendency to rule out biased selection of samples. Two kinds of random sampling are especially helpful here. One is *stratified random sampling*; that is, random sampling of cases within various strata such as military ranks or social classes. The other variety is *cluster sampling*; that is, random sampling of cases that cluster together by location. We will examine Martina Klicperova-Baker's study of Czech poetry in Chapter 9. I think that if that study were to be extended, one could randomly sample poems within a group of anthologies of Czech poetry, a kind of cluster sampling.

But where it is not feasible to draw a random sample, purposeful sampling methods do have value for psychodynamically oriented investigators. Sometimes the underlying population to be sampled cannot be clearly demarcated, or there is administrative resistance to a random sampling process or there are insurmountable practical difficulties in carrying it out. If purposeful sampling is used, the rationale and the procedures involved should be spelled out by the researcher. To this idea we now turn.

Specification of the Sampling Design

Gehl's work deals with large and small environmental features and places that can be seen and touched and felt, and where salient instances are obvious. Psychodynamic studies, by contrast, deal with unconscious processes in leaders, the populace, and the media rather than the built environment. It is therefore particularly important that the study procedures, especially sampling, either random or purposeful, are clearly specified and faithfully carried out so the study can be replicated by others. Replication lends strength to a study, unless a particular methodological artifact is present in the initial study and in all the replications. This is unlikely given the variations usually found in replications, variations that can actually strengthen the robustness of the set of studies. In almost all cases, specifying study methods clearly enough to permit replication will strengthen clinically sophisticated investigations in the political–social arena.

Retrospective Description of Sampling Procedures

Even where researchers decline to select a sampling procedure in advance to guide their work, it would always help them to look at their data selection retrospectively in these terms. They should at least tell the reader what kind of sample they actually used, that is, what realms of data they actually examined and how systematic that examination was. This procedure would both reduce bias and help the reader estimate what kinds of biases are likely to remain.

Describing the Chain of Inquiry

Rather than working from a sampling plan, what very often happens in studies is that one document, or one source, leads the researcher to another, and that leads to still others, a kind of inquiry that researchers characterize as "detective work." This seems logically parallel to snowball sampling, in which one interviewee suggests others to be interviewed and those suggest still others. In either case, the researcher should inform the reader of the chain of inquiry that developed and that he or she followed, so that its probative value can be evaluated by the reader.

The Natural History of a Study

Researchers can supplement the retrospective look at the sampling procedure, and the explication of the chain of inquiry, with a third element, what sociologists have called "the natural history of a study" (Hughes, 1971). The investigators can describe the vicissitudes the research team experienced in doing the study. These would include obstacles they encountered, compromises they had to make, and improvements in the research plan owing to the emergence of new information. A natural history of the study would give the reader a much better idea of the methodological strengths, limitations, and originality of the study.

Interaction of Research Methods

As we examine the various research methods, I should alert the reader to the danger of drawing overly sharp dichotomies between research methods. For example, "critical cases," that is, cases drawn purposefully with particular importance for the theory involved, make excellent candidates for a Popperian test of disconfirmability of the kind outlined in Chapter 4. And in Chapter 9 we will look at a test of disconfirmability that used content analysis, and that appeared suddenly from within a symbolic interactionist research framework. The various approaches I espouse here are neither mutually contradictory nor mutually exclusive. They do, however, stem from somewhat different epistemological premises as to what constitutes social knowledge and how it can be attained.

Thick Description

The sociologist Clifford Geertz coined the term *thick description* (in *The Interpretation of Cultures*, 1973) to describe a process that helps the researcher understand the meaning of an act within a culture or subculture. Thick description is a broadly helpful technique, which, like self-disclosure, was widely used in studies from the "Chicago School" of urban research, and its successors (Park, Burgess, Wirth, Gans, and the others mentioned earlier), and in anthropological studies in other cultures. Chapter 8 will illustrate *thick description* by using world press profiles of Zhirinovsky, Le Pen, and Papadopoulos.

I view thick description as having three main components. The first is heavily detailed description, providing exhaustive and even seemingly redundant information about as many aspects of the material as possible rather than merely providing just enough description to get one's point across. Descriptive overkill is the key concept here and it has been the modus operandi of many case studies by fieldwork sociologists.

The second component of thick description is a plethora of verbatim quotations, with little effort to avoid redundancy. The idea here is to give the reader of the study a deeper understanding of the motives and experiences of the people being studied, and to provide information in the actual words of the person or people being studied, rather than only formulated in the investigator's words.

A third component is a discussion of the researcher's own emotional reactions, preconceptions and biases, including relevant personal background, in regard to the materials being studied. I have discussed one aspect of this earlier in this chapter under the rubric of "self-disclosure."

All three components help readers make their own judgment of whether the researcher's interpretations cohere with the materials presented. In my view, the element of disconfirmability consists in the readers' comparing in their own minds their interpretations of the described and quoted materials with those of the researcher, allowing, if necessary, for the expressed biases of the researcher. Operationally, disconfirmability consists of the readers saying, "As we read the materials presented, we find enough detail and verbatim material to enable us to conclude that the interpretation presented by the researcher is faithful to the materials." This application also extends to interpretations that ascribe unconscious content to verbal materials.

It is important to remember that thick description gives only incomplete protection against bias if important materials have been omitted. One example may suffice to make the point. Some biographical formulations describing the life of Winston Churchill omit one or both of the following troubling elements: Churchill's order that the able-bodied be given preference over the wounded in the evacuation of Dunkirk, and his refusal to warn Coventry of the impending saturation air raid that destroyed it (so as to preserve the secret that the British cryptanalysts had cracked the most important German codes). Without the knowledge of these instances, the reader gains an insufficient appreciation of the extent of Churchill's tough-mindedness. Similarly, even with thick description, if there are important omitted materials, disconfirmability of the interpretations is impaired.

Specification of a Protocol as a Research Technique

This has been elaborated in Chapter 3. I argued that referring to a protocol gives a reader an understanding of the clinical researcher's assumptions and procedures in making inferences. The underlying systematic basis for interpretation becomes clearer, and the reader can more knowledgeably accept or reject the protocol as a reasonable way of proceeding.

Content Analysis in Psychodynamic Studies on the World Scene

Content analysis consists of seeking to identify themes in messages or communications of any kind. It can be done purely qualitatively, in which case it becomes textual analysis of the kinds familiar in the humanities. Or the textual analysis can be supported by quantitative methods, by counting instances of particular words or expressions.

Qualitative analysis can build upon a quantitative content analytical study. For example, in Chapter 8 the reader will find a qualitative study I did of journalistic profiles of three authoritarian leaders: Vladimir Zhirinovsky, Jean-Marie Le Pen, and Georgios Papadopoulos. This was a re-analysis of a quantitative study done with Dr. Christine Gerety.

If one knows what to look for, content analysis can be a useful tool for psychodynamically sophisticated research. We will see in Chapter 9 the very creative use Martina Klicperova-Baker has found for content analysis of Czech poems for themes of energy, resistance, or, on the contrary, sacrifice and suicide. Klicperova-Baker's work shows what content analysis can do in the hands of an empathic reader.

What Content Analysis Might Miss

As an example of what some content analyses might miss, let us consider certain phrases in Hitler's speeches (as reported by in Beisel, 2003). On page 18, Beisel mentions that Hitler stated, "We have lanced the Jewish abscess." On page 19, in a different context, he quotes Hitler's statement that "The Polish Corridor...is like a strip of flesh cut from our body...a national wound that bleeds continuously and will continue to bleed until the land is returned to us." He does not mention a connection between the two statements, both of which refer to painful skin afflictions. There is no mention also of the fact that Hitler's mother died of fungating breast cancer, which broke through the skin and caused terrible bleeding wounds (Orac, 2008).

Her physician, Dr. Bloch, a Jew, sent her for a radical mastectomy, which did not succeed in stopping the cancer.

As the open wounds worsened, Dr. Bloch chose local wound care with daily applications of iodoform-embedded gauze to the fungating chest wound. These treatments were terribly painful and went on for six weeks prior to Klara Hitler's death on 21 December 1907, as described by Macleod (2005):

> The caring and conscientious Dr Bloch was by now visiting daily to apply iodoform directly to the fungating chest wound. Mrs. Hitler was reported as bearing these stinging treatments well over the subsequent 6 weeks to her death. Her son agonized over every moment of her suffering. ... Dr Bloch later recalled that he had "never seen anyone as prostrate with grief" as Adolf Hitler (2005, pp. 413).

Rudolf Binion (1976) has suggested that this experience was a probable root of Hitler's vicious anti-Semitism. I think that as a teenager he may well have unconsciously experienced it as a Jewish doctor torturing his mother, although, as Binion states, as Fuhrer he took no reprisals against Dr. Bloch personally. While a student in Vienna, Hitler sent Dr. Bloch some hand-painted picture postcards (Orac, 2006), and, when in power, Hitler personally intervened to get Dr. Bloch a passport and visa so he could leave Austria after the Anschluss.

Nevertheless, I would suggest a connection between this terrible experience and Hitler's demand that some of the train cars taking victims to the concentration camps be lined with lye, so that they would have horrible skin burns along the way. And, as a corporal in the German army in World War I, Hitler was invalided as a result of being severely gassed, a method he later used for extermination in the concentration camps.

But there is discordant evidence: as we saw, during the Hitler regime, there was no retaliation against Dr. Bloch. A Popperian prediction of retaliation against Bloch personally would have found a disconfirmatory result. And the surgeon David Gorski, writing under the pen name

"Orac," (2006) has sharply disputed Binion's conclusions about the effects of the surgery Hitler's mother had, so we cannot be sure of the link between Hitler's mother's death and his anti-Semitism.

Other Methods from the Social Sciences

Arraying Cases for Comparative Study

A separate kind of inquiry might take a dimension of social psychological or sociological interest, and consider systematically the similarities and differences of a set of people who are deemed to be high in this dimension. Such a study would be comparative, consider several people, and look for elements they hold in common that could help explain why they fell on this dimension, and also why they thought and acted in similar ways. In such a comparative study, psychodynamic and social scientific concepts would be involved, and a formal study design would add to the scientific validity and credibility of the findings.

Studying Impunity

Let us look at an example where the arraying of cases for comparative study would be helpful. This example is provided by the dimension of *impunity,* a depth psychological concept that has attracted more attention recently owing to a number of egregious instances that have arisen. A sense of impunity designates the feeling that one can get way with things without being found out and punished. What do people with a strong sense of impunity have in common? Is it personality organization, social class background, membership in a subculture that countenances activities like theirs, collusion by colleagues and employees, narcissistic needs that make them susceptible to unwarranted praise, grandiose aspirations? Is there a marked failure of reality testing, or is it an unconscious need to fail and be punished? Is there enabling by others? Is there support from implicit subcultural norms ("Everybody does it." "What happens in Vegas stays in Vegas.")

Recent exemplars who appear have shown a blatant sense of impunity include Dominique Strauss-Kahn, then the President of the International Monetary Fund; Silvio Berlusconi, then Premier of Italy; Andrew Weiner, first a Congressman and then a candidate for Mayor of New York; Eliot Spitzer, then Governor of New York; and John Edwards, then a US Senator and a candidate for the President of the United States.

This area bristles with actions and speech tinged with unconscious meanings, that must be listened for with clinically sophisticated understanding, as we saw in Chapter 3. In the cases of Weiner, Spitzer,

Edwards, and Strauss-Kahn, were there unconscious self-destructive elements, a recognition that eventually they would be caught? Or were there fantasies instead that they were all powerful and would never be caught?

All the persons I have listed above are men (is this a coincidence?) and all their alleged transgressions have been sexual. As a second part of the study, suppose we systematically compare these people with a set of people also showing a marked sense of impunity but whose transgressions were primarily financial rather than sexual. Bernard Madoff comes immediately to mind. Others can be found, for example among hedge fund operators who have been indicted for fraud or defalcation. To what extent did their transgressions involve *collusion* by other persons and organizations? For example, Goldman Sachs, the financial firm, was the custodian for Madoff of the funds he obtained through his Ponzi scheme. Were there *subcultural norms* at Goldman Sachs that involved turning a blind eye to suspicious activities?.

Questions like these can be addressed by established methods of *systematic comparative study* drawn from the social sciences, using *substantive concepts* drawn from the social sciences. Studies conducted in this manner would enrich clinically sophisticated inquiry and give it added scientific validity and also credibility.

Chapter 8, which arrays several right-wing authoritarian leaders (Vladimir Zhirinovsky, Jean-Marie Le Pen, and Georgios Papadopoulos) along a dimension of irreal utterances, is only a small example of what can be done by employing clinically sophisticated inquiry, psychodynamic perspectives, and methods and concepts drawn from the social sciences.

Arraying Researchers to Study a Single Case

Arraying cases for systematic comparative and contrasting examination by a research team is only one of scores of applicable methods from the social sciences that would enrich psychodynamic inquiry.

For example, the mirror image of the arraying of cases for comparative study by a single researcher, is the studying of a single rich instance of data by an array of researchers working independently, whose findings could then be compared. An obvious instance of rich data from a single individual would be Lenin's letters, which have come to light relatively recently. We have mentioned the letters of Marshal Pétain. Autobiographies are another rich source; Vaclav Havel's autobiography (1991, 1992) comes to mind for those interested in the Czech Republic.

The modern realm of video recording makes other kinds of data also easily available. Consider the appeal of an analysis of a video recording, by an array of clinically sophisticated observers acting independently, whose findings and interpretations could then be compared.

Here is an example. The William Alanson White Institute on East 82nd street in Manhattan has a meeting room on the top floor where the Philoctetes Foundation, a part of the Psychoanalytic Institute, sponsors forums on a wide variety of topics for the general public. On 20 October 2007 they presented a forum entitled "The Future of the Stock Market." There was an audience of about 30, seated in a circle around the six participants, each of whom spoke at some length during the two-hour forum. The most prolix was a man by the name of Bernard Madoff, who proved to be exceptionally knowledgeable, down to earth, and charming in an avuncular way. At the very time he was speaking, he had already stolen, by means of a Ponzi scheme, the entire endowment of the Philoctetes Foundation, which was sponsoring the Forum. In 2008, when the fraud came to light, the Philoctetes Foundation closed its doors, terminated the journal it sponsored, ended the forums, and dissolved. Remarkable, seeing the personality of a thief chatting amiably with unsuspecting people he had already victimized. A contribution to the growing field of the psychology of fraud.

This is surely an opportunity for a systematic study of Madoff's personality, based on the video tape, carried out by a set of clinical researchers, acting independently, whose results could be compared. Special attention would be paid to indications of motives and fantasies outside of conscious awareness. It would take clinically trained researcher only a few hours to study the video carefully and report on his or her conclusions about the ways, if any, Madoff's underlying exploitative orientation was expressed in the video. It would also be a valuable contribution to the social psychological theory of fraud (see William Alanson White Institute, 2007). This video is now available only through the William Alanson White Institute itself; Madoff's fraud killed the entire Philoctetes program.

How could the findings of the various clinicians be systematically arrayed in order to determine if there was consensus of any kind? As a first step, the discursive paragraphs provided by the clinician could be compared. This would be a fascinating inquiry since not only would it likely reveal aspects of Madoff's personality and functioning, it also would be a rare opportunity to see if psychodynamically oriented researchers give similar pictures of an instance or whether they diverge markedly. If the latter, it implies that psychodynamic studies on the social and political scene need to be replicated in order to discover the role of idiosyncratic interpretation.

To assess the degree of agreement among the clinicians in the Madoff instance, tabular comparisons of the interpretative paragraphs produced by the psychodynamically trained observers could be created by outside judges. These tabulations could show the variety of themes elicited, and the degree of agreement or disagreement among the researchers.

Another approach would be to use iterative written interactions among the researchers, which we describe in Chapter 9, to see if a jointly agreed upon meaning emerges, as suggested by the theories of symbolic interactionism.

Instrumenting Psychodynamic Inquiry of World Events

A dramatically different approach drawn from the other social sciences could also be used in this instance: *the replication of psychodynamic analyses measured by inter-rater reliability*. This would be a way of quantitatively comparing their discursive conclusions to determine the extent to which they were in agreement. In this effort, we might use the scales of the Minnesota Multiphasic Personality Inventory (MMPI) as rating scales. The MMPI 2 has ten clinical scales (Framingham, 2011), including depression, hysteria, paranoia, psychopathic deviate, hypomania, schizophrenia, hypochondriasis, masculinity–femininity, and social introversion.

We could show each psychodynamically sophisticated researcher who viewed the Madoff video, or who read the Vaclav Havel autobiography or the Lenin letters, the items involved in each scale, and explain how they were derived. The MMPI also provides descriptions of the characteristics of the kinds of people who have scored high on each scale in the past. Each clinician, having completed the study, would, in addition to providing discursive written paragraphs of interpretation, be asked to rate the political or economic figure on each scale, assigning a score of high or low on each scale based on the results of his or her response. This procedure would generate ten numbers, one for each scale, for each clinician. The resulting matrix of these numbers could be analyzed to produce a number expressing the overall degree of agreement among the clinicians.

This design is a highly unusual use of the MMPI scales, not originally contemplated by the researchers who designed the instrument. The MMPI consists of 550 items that are ordinarily answered on an agree versus disagree basis by the patient in a clinical assessment situation. But the method I propose here, using the MMPI as a rating scale by clinicians, has several major advantages for our purposes. For one thing, the MMPI has far more quantitative data to support it than any other psychodynamic test. And each scale consists *only* of only items answered *differently* by a given group (depressives, delinquents, schizophrenics, etc.) than by other groups, so in that sense we do know what each scale means in practical terms. Moreover, the procedure we have described permits quantitative estimates of the degree of agreement. Ratings by any clinician can be correlated with the ratings of any other clinician, by a coefficient of correlation, a statistic called Spearman's rho. A statistic called Kendall's *W* gives an overall measure of the degree of agreement among all the clinicians who undertook the task.

The above method for estimating degree of agreement is sharply defined enough so it is repeatable on the same data, similar data, or very different data, and with any willing clinicians. It could be used to compare the responses of clinicians to a series of speeches, or to an autobiography, or to extensive personal letters. And enthusiasts for the Delphi Technique, to be discussed in Chapter 9, might want to seek a convergence of the ratings through successive interactions among the clinicians, a procedure made easier by the quantitative nature of the ratings.

In all these procedures, and many others that could be devised, the psychodynamic insights and use of empathy by the clinical researchers, as described in Chapters 2 and 3, will be essential, and would be amplified and broadened by the methods and concepts of the social sciences.

As a parallel to these studies, one could consult the published literature on Madoff and his firm to see if it echoes or conflicts or enriches the conclusions of the quantitative and empathic studies. For example, a recent discussion by Stewart (2011) chronicles the confusion and fecklessness that enabled the Securities and Exchange Commission (SEC) to avoid finding out about Madoff's Ponzi scheme during the several years of sporadic and inconclusive investigations before Madoff turned himself in. In psychodynamic terms, the SEC both *knew and didn't know* what Madoff was up to. This blindfolded situation could have been the result of partisan political and ideological constraints within the SEC. One thinks also of David Bakan's concept of the mystery–mastery conflict we discussed in Chapter 1.

The great majority of investors in Madoff's firm seem to have been completely deceived; often they were individual investors or charitable institutions that lacked sophistication about investing, and when the collapse of Madoff's firm came, many lost everything.

But one wonders whether *knowing and not knowing*, and the wish not to find out, characterized *some* investors. Madoff was nicknamed "the Jewish T-bill," because of the profits he made every single year, an anomaly among investment firms and something that aroused suspicion in a some potential investors.

Madoff's auditor was not a large accounting firm but rather a single person who was an old friend and whom Madoff took skiing in Switzerland. People would have found this out if they had made even a cursory inquiry but apparently the form of denial called "knowing and not knowing" was a factor impeding such an inquiry.

A Concordance Among Methods

A set of connections among research methods has emerged from our efforts to improve the methodology and conceptualization of psychodynamic inquiry into world events. These research methods are often taught separately, and applied separately, as though there were no deep relations between them. But in the present context—and likely elsewhere—there are, and these connections may be fruitful.

For example, a promising connection soon became evident: as summarized in Chapter 2, and described further in the Appendix, the experimental method can be applied to the study of empathic understanding.

The theme of Chapter 4 was the value of Popperian disconfirmation procedures in the social sciences. These procedures use a model of inference based on the logic of experimentation. When used in clinically sophisticated psychodynamically informed studies of world events, they turn out to be intimately connected to symbolic interactionism in the creation of meaning: people have to reach agreement on what a disconfirming instance would be.

And we have seen in the present chapter, purposeful sampling, which is usually considered an ultimate in subjectivity, can be used to guide and strengthen Popperian disconfirmation, usually considered an ultimate in objectivity. To purposeful sampling can be added methods that examine qualitatively or estimate quantitatively the degree of agreement among judges.

In Chapter 8 we will see that statistical sampling, computer-driven content analysis, and thick description can be used together in psychodynamic inquiry. The use of sampling combined with thick description has also been used in field studies.

In Chapter 9 we will look at another confluence of methods. The study used a symbolic interactionist perspective in an extended collaboration to evaluate psychodynamic inferences of the Munich crisis. Self-disclosure formed an essential part of this collaboration. Also striking was the logical parallel to the Delphi technique, which is ordinarily used quantitatively. And, surprisingly, the collaboration resulted in an experiment seeking a Popperian disconfirmation, using sampling and content analysis.

I believe it will become evident to the reader from these examples that a confluence of methods tends to enrich and enliven research. The interactions among them are complex and can call for flexibility and originality in the researcher. The next chapter sets forth in detail one approach to narrative analysis, which is mainly qualitative but which nonetheless in this case results in a testable prediction.

> *With sufficient thrust a pig will fly perfectly.*
>
> Anonymous

7
An Adventure in Narrative Analysis: "A Regular Terrible Story"

As the Major-General ruefully admitted in a delightful scene in Gilbert and Sullivan's "The Pirates of Penzance" (Act 1, Final Scene) he was not an orphan at all, not "orfen," not ever. But in pretending to be an orphan he had saved his life by telling a "regular terrible story" to the pirates (Gilbert and Sullivan, 1994).

Narrative Analysis

This chapter presents a case study of a narrative analysis of a series of scandals in the American media. My purpose is to give the reader a sense of what is involved in carrying out narrative analysis, and what can be learned from a psychodynamic and social scientific point of view.

Narrative analysis as a research method can be described as a way of construing an account as a "story," which therefore has an author, a beginning, a middle, an end, a plot line, a set of characters, a protagonist, sometimes an antagonist, a social and cultural setting, an intended audience, a time frame, certain linguistic conventions, a medium in which it is presented (for example, a novel, a play, a movie, a newspaper or magazine article, a video, an Internet program), and sometimes a critic or critics. The analyst of a narrative asks questions about many or all of these components. A number of other approaches to narrative analysis have been formulated (see, e.g., Lieblich et al., 1998), but I will consider the most basic and widely used version here.

Journalistic Reports

Journalistic reports (as opposed to opinion pieces), are usually built on story-telling. Reporters in daily newspapers and weekly journals are able to draw in readers by framing their report as a series of stories about individuals experiencing the phenomena—layoffs, sudden fame, urban violence—the reporter is writing about. Some theorists have suggested that people come to understand the personal and social world around them more by means of narrative, that is, stories, than by means of the exposition of abstract categories.

But suppose the story is false, a "regular terrible story." How do people cope? A large question. Let us consider two illustrative cases from the public media. It appears that when the story is false, the media have a terrible time coping, for reasons inherent in the story-telling mode itself. To see why this is, let us look first at a famous false story concocted by a journalist, and a series of attempts to understand and report the fraudulent story accurately. The metaphor of an endless hall of mirrors, endlessly reflecting the same flawed attempt to come to terms with the fraud, is one that I feel captures a great deal of the meaning of this particular event. In looking at this sequence, we will try to infer why untrue stories seem so difficult to cope with, at least in media organizations.

The Story of Jimmy

Janet Cooke's beautifully written article, "Jimmy's World," which appeared on the front page of the Sunday edition of the *Washington Post* on 28 September 1980, tells the story of Jimmy, an 8-year-old heroin addict (Cooke, 1980). There was an intense specificity, what I call *particularity,* in Cooke's riveting article that caught everyone's attention: "Jimmy...a precious little boy with sandy hair, velvety brown eyes and needle marks freckling the smooth skin of his thin brown arms" (quoted from the Cooke article by Remnick (1996)). "The needle slides into the boy's soft skin like a straw into the center of a freshly baked cake. Liquid ebbs out of the syringe, replaced by bright red blood. The blood is then reinjected into the child" (quoted from the Cooke article by Bradlee (1995)). Cooke, and the *Post* itself, received a Pulitzer on the basis of this story. It then turned out that Jimmy didn't exist and that Cooke's educational credentials had also been concocted. The Pulitzer had to be returned, to the immense embarrassment of the *Post.*

Levels of Story-telling and the Hall of Mirrors

In this extraordinary saga, there actually are four levels of story-telling, quite a rare situation and one that begs for examination.

Cooke's story of Jimmy forms a first level of story-telling, in this instance a fabricated life story of a little boy.

A second level of story-telling is a story about a story: it consists of a chapter in the autobiography of Benjamin Bradlee (1995), editor of the *Washington Post.* He tells the story of how the fraud was detected and his interview with Janet as the deception fell apart. He devotes a lot of attention to giving his view of Cooke's mentality as it resulted in the bogus story.

A third level of story-telling is provided by the profile of Bradlee by David Remnick (1996), himself a Pulitzer Prize-winning journalist, retelling the story of Cooke and retelling the story of Ben Bradlee's confrontation with her. A fourth level consists of the interview of Remnick by Orville Schell, the Dean of the School of Journalism at Berkeley, in which Remnick, as the new editor of the *New Yorker,* was questioned about his profile of Bradlee (Schell, 2002). Schell then tries to recast the stories in his own terms.

One thinks of a "hall of mirrors" in terms of the original, at Versailles, in which a series of reflections, and reflections of reflections, stretch out ad infinitum. A series of levels of story-telling can be thought of in this way, in which each successive reported tells a story about all the preceding stories. One would hope that the understanding of the original phenomenon would steadily improve as successive stories modified the preceding stories.

Benjamin Bradlee's Account of the Janet Cooke Case

Benjamin Bradlee was, at the time, Editor-in-Chief of the *Washington Post.* Bradlee's chapter in his autobiography, *A Good Life* (1995), is titled starkly, "Janet Cooke." It details the devastation the faked story caused to the *Post's* reputation, and the factors internal to the *Post* that caused the supervisory editors to be taken unaware by the fraud and to dismiss the doubts of one of the editors, Vivian Aspin-Brownlee, and of another reporter, Courtland Milloy, about Cooke (although none had expressed doubts specifically about her story). Bradlee tells also of the *Post's* response when it became aware of the fakery, the appointment of William Green, an unflinching ombudsman who could neither be edited nor fired. A particularly poignant part of the account, drawn from Green's lengthy analysis, describes the interview with Cooke in which David Maraniss, evidently one of the more compassionate of the editorial staff, persuaded her to own up to the fraud.

Bradlee's story of his own interview with Cooke when her false resume was detected, and it had become obvious that "Jimmy's World" was a concoction also, indicated that the interview was an angry one, with Bradlee cognizant of the immense damage she had done to the credibility of the *Post* and to the free press generally when the Pulitzer prize "Jimmy's World" won, on 13 April 1981, had to be returned.

Bradlee's effort to protect the press was, understandably enough, the lens through which he could view Cooke. Bradlee described his efforts to cope with the disaster as "damage control," something he had learned in his somewhat heroic stint as a destroyer officer during World War II. An apt metaphor, and, as we shall see, fully in line with Remnick's (1996) picaresque characterization of Bradlee.

The *Post* dealt with the disaster honestly and forthrightly, and Bradlee was quietly ironical about the sanctimonious protestations of other papers that it couldn't happen there. Time has proven these false. Bradlee lists a number of precautions editors should take against fraud, based on his experience with the Cooke catastrophe. These include zeal in checking "all information in a resume, specifically including degree verification"(1995, p. 450). Bradlee urges that all the references of a job candidate should be checked. As an ongoing task of supervision, it is an editor's job to double-check "stories that you want to be true"(1995, p. 448), and to keep a lookout for other reporters and editors who have some reservations. While this is sage advice, earned by sore experience, it is a bit like advising a homeowner how to avoid break-ins but not discussing the reasons for the crime rate.

Bradlee describes the measures to avoid fraud from the point of view of editorial policy and of the need to increase editorial vigilance, rather than from the point of view of developing within the editorial staff insight into the social forces that create fabrication and that leave editors vulnerable to being deceived. He lists a few other fabrications that had appeared in the press, but he seems to believe that sufficient diligence on the part of editors would have surely prevented them. The idea that major fabrications might not be totally preventable seems not to have crossed Bradlee's mind, nor David Remnick's, as we shall see below.

Largely missing in Bradlee's account was recognition of the extent to which "Jimmy's World" was consistent with existing knowledge of a widespread social phenomenon (early addiction to hard drugs). Given the social and economic and cultural conditions in the ghetto in Washington, DC, something very like this could have happened, or if not to an 8-year-old, then a 10- or 12-year-old Jimmy, and people knew it. It was for this very reason, the verisimilitude of the events Cooke described, that it was believed.

According to David Remnick, and Benjamin Bradlee, Marion Barry, Mayor of the District of Columbia, claimed the District government knew about Jimmy and was taking steps to help him. According to Bradlee, there were reports that Dr. Alyce Gullattee, the director of Howard University's Institute for Substance Abuse, also knew of Jimmy and his family.

The widespread prevalence of early drug addiction reportedly made Barry, according to Remnick and Bradlee, and, according to Bradlee, Dr. Gullattee, willing to assert its specific truth in the case of Jimmy. The story of Jimmy was easily believable, given what people knew, or thought they knew, about conditions in the ghettos of Washington, DC. A "general truth," we define as a phenomenon of which people are so widely aware that a court might properly feel entitled to "take judicial notice" of it. A general truth about early drug addiction was clearly a social structural factor in allowing the specific falsity of Cooke's article on Jimmy to be believed.

A second social structural factor in producing the Cooke catastrophe was the fact that the liberal press's laudable and appropriate interest in hiring minority reporters had become so intense that it had the effect of causing editors generally to not want to look into the reality of the candidates' credentials. Inadequate supervision of reporters was a third factor. A final factor was the evident complete lack of mentoring of young and somewhat naïve, though talented, reporters, with the result that they lacked awareness of the full implications of their actions.

Disconfirmable Predictions?

As these broad social factors continued in operation, a repetition, perhaps on an even larger scale, was in the cards. The reader will note that despite being a qualitative narrative study, this chapter yields some disconfirmable propositions along the lines proposed in Chapter 4. Specifically, it can be predicted that there will be a repetition of this kind of fabrication in a similar situation: a liberal newspaper or magazine and a young person from a cultural out-group who had received insufficient mentoring and supervision.

The Key Role of Audiences

A key element in this narrative analysis is the importance of the explicit and implicit *audiences* in a narrative. The first audience of concern to us was the *Washington Post* itself, which eagerly awaited a person with Cooke's abilities and credentials, and treated her as a special person after she arrived to work there. The second implicit audience of note were the readers of the *Post* who were amenable to this kind of narrative. As the series of stories of Jimmy were published, they became the explicit audience for whom the studies were crafted. The politicians of the District of Columbia were an unexpected but crucial third audience: they reportedly reacted by claiming that they knew about Jimmy and were already helping him. A fourth and totally unexpected audience, at least at the beginning, were the committee members who award the Pulitzer Prizes each year. As we look at the narrative from this perspective it becomes clearer that an important force eliciting a fabrication like this was the set of audiences. Less important perhaps than Cooke's ambitions, but important nonetheless.

David Remnick's Profile of Benjamin Bradlee

Remnick's portrayal of Benjamin Bradlee appears in a chapter in *The Devil Problem*, entitled "Last of the Red Hots" (1996, pp. 319–37). It begins with a memorable epigram to the effect that Bradlee's autobiography, *A Good Life* (1995), "gives the lie to Socrates' idea that the unexamined life is not worth living." The portrayal is based not only on Bradlee's book, but also on Remnick' personal knowledge of Bradlee as his editor. Remnick, a young intern at the *Washington Post* soon after the Cooke catastrophe, was, at that time, and subsequently, impressed with the adventurous and picaresque quality of Bradlee, shown, for example, in his war record and the fact that women were strongly attracted to him. Remnick calls Bradlee "the very model of the devil-may-care WASP," and "the editor-knight of Watergate," and notes that "Jason Robards played the editor's role with uncanny brio in *All the President's Men*."

Remnick's account emphasizes the forthright and stalwart manner in which Bradlee dealt with the Cooke catastrophe. He is sympathetic to the resultant plight of this turbulent young woman, and understanding of the motives that led the *Post* to neglect to check her vita and references, to supervise her adequately, and to communicate among the editors the concern some of the other reporters felt about the veracity of her reporting. Remnick fully appreciates the damage done to journalism. But he doesn't confront the generality of the social forces that made the *Post* so anxious to hire Cooke, an African American woman whose clippings showed her to have unquestionable talent as a writer—so anxious that they failed to check her resume and references.

Remnick quotes Bradlee: "[Janet's Cooke's letter of application] stood out because she produced clips that showed she could write like a dream; she had top-drawer college credentials, and she was black. The answer to a modern editor's dream." This statement by Bradlee approaches the idea that any editor would react this way (a talented black woman reporter, a Phi Beta Kappa graduate of a top women's college: wonderful!) but doesn't get to the point of implying that it will therefore likely happen again given the forces acting on editors and newspapers.

Remnick sidles up to the idea, too, pointing out that Cooke's resume ("Vassar College, *magna cum laude,* speaks two foreign languages fluently, etc.") was no less a pipe job than "Jimmy's World." His statement implies that pipe jobs happen repeatedly, but Remnick instead luxuriates in recounting the specifics. This reveling in the specific is what Remnick himself, quoting Bob Woodward, calls looking for "holy shit stories." Remnick notes that Bradlee "waved aside...the doubts of some of his own staff and submitted Jimmy's World for the big prize." He goes on to explain "Bradlee had too much faith in his sense of the authentic ever to question that fraud might appear in his midst...'To me, the story reeked of the sights and sounds and smells that editors love to give their readers,' Bradlee writes."

The blunder by the *Post* is thus treated almost as a sui generis, as an inexcusable oversight rather than a predictable outcome. This blind spot exists in part because journalists mostly are attuned to the details of a specific happening rather than to social psychological forces. They need to appeal to their readership, which is interested in hearing about people, not about forces, and they need to write compellingly, which means specifically and descriptively, and not in analytic generalities. Journalists have something of the poetic in their souls, which means the specific not the cognitive. The very fact that an article is called a "story" shows the insistence on the specific, an insistence that makes the writing sing, but not necessarily the right song. The reader is left to infer the general principles from the glowing descriptions of the specific. Sometimes this inference fails.

Remnick, like Bradlee before him, mentions frauds that had happened before at other notable papers, including the *New York Times Magazine,* but he appears to see the Cooke fraud as an individual transgression rather than a social regularity, and particularly so because it was the only fabrication to win a Pulitzer.

Orville Schell's Interview With David Remnick

In an interview with Remnick at Berkeley, Orville Schell, Dean of the School of Journalism at the University of California at Berkeley, questions Remnick about the values and plans that are guiding his newly assumed editorship of the *New Yorker*. In that context he asks Remnick about his profile of Bradlee:

> Q: You wrote a wonderful profile of Ben Bradlee and in it you expressed the opinion that he was a "dangerous" editor. Are you going to be a dangerous editor?
> A: Oh, I hope so. What I meant by dangerous editor is that he edited not just with his brain. There was vitality in his editing. I don't mean because he was extraordinarily handsome and a great presence in the newsroom—which is no small thing, a kind of presence one doesn't hope to imitate—but he had guts and not stupid guts, ill-considered guts, because any idiot can say "publish!" But to know when, is really an amazing thing (Schell, 2002).

Here the focus is his portrait of Bradlee, and particularly on Bradlee's courage to tell the truth and his leadership ability. Bradlee's loyalty to the tenets of journalism, that is, to tell the truth and to cover important events, Bradlee's picaresque courage and Bradlee's judgment about when to take risks, as with publishing Bob Woodward and Carl Bernstein's stories exposing the Watergate scandal, caught the focus of Remnick's attention. This is certainly understandable, especially since Remnick himself was on the way to editing the *New Yorker*, where reportage, though not an exclusive concern, would be vitally important, and where courage and good judgment would be crucial. It seems never to have occurred to Schell to ask Remnick how he planned to avoid a future Janet Cooke catastrophe, or how journalism could cope with the social factors causing newspapers to first take major risks in hiring a Cooke and then providing inadequate supervision and no mentoring. We are left with the probability that Schell and Remnick both thought the Cooke affair was the result of bad judgment in an individual instance. The social forces leading to failure to check resumes and references, and provide supervision and mentoring, are not confronted.

Janet Cooke's Own Story?

For 15 years after the 1981 debacle, Janet Cooke gave no interviews to the press. Then, in 1996, Mike Sager, a journalist and apparently a close friend of Cooke, published in the popular press an account he describes as an interview with Cooke, "Janet's World" (Sager, 1996). Although there are what are apparently direct quotations from Cooke in the article, it appears to me to be more of a profile than an interview, and I am unclear as to how much of Janet's voice, rather than Mike's, actually comes through.

The account is notable primarily for its depiction of Janet as a highly strung, neurotic, at times almost desperate, young woman, a sharp contrast to the chic impression she gave at the *Post*. The family pressures on Janet, and her driving ambition to get out from under her father's domination, and her feelings of insecurity are portrayed as the primary factors in her fabrication and subsequent undoing. One could get the impression that the events were a tragedy based almost solely on Janet's idiosyncratic personal problems. Particularity, based on presumed psychological factors, is the order of the day in this depiction of Janet Cooke.

What the Stories Missed

In the case we examine here a sequential improvement did not ensue. A whole series of people considered a phenomenon in turn, created a layer of stories about it, and missed the identical crucial points. They sequentially made the same error of omission, which we can call the error of particularity, that is, considering a phenomenon as only a thing in itself rather than also as an instance of the confluence of a set of broader social forces. Thus, they became blind to the fact that *when the same forces repeatedly interact, future instances will almost inevitably be created*. One might almost infer that the series of stories, each based on the previous ones, created a "response set" to view the original phenomenon as the previous viewers saw it: a kind of "framing" of the phenomenon. We have also noted the salient role of the various audiences in eliciting the series of stories about Jimmy.

The *New York Times'* Fabrications: Coping with A Plethora of Untrue Stories

A front page story in the 11 May 2003 *New York Times*, entitled, "Times Reporter Who Resigned Leaves Long Trail of Deception," begins:

> A staff reporter for the *New York Times* committed frequent acts of journalistic fraud while covering significant news events in recent months, an investigation by *Times* journalists has found. The widespread fabrication and plagiarism represent a profound betrayal of trust and a low point in the 152-year history of the newspaper.
>
> The reporter, Jayson Blair, 27, misled readers and *Times* colleagues with dispatches that purported to be from Maryland, Texas and other states, when he often was far away, in New York. He fabricated comments. He concocted scenes. He lifted material from other newspapers and wire services. He selected details from photographs to create

> the impression that he had been somewhere or seen someone when he had not (Barry et al., 2003).

It is clear from the account that Blair used email and cell phones ingeniously as aids in carrying out the fraud.

"And he used these techniques to write falsely about emotionally charged moments in recent history, from the deadly sniper attacks in suburban Washington to the anguish of families grieving for loved ones killed in Iraq." Jonathan Landman, the metropolitan editor of the *Times*, had expressed strong reservations about Blair based on the many errors he had found in Blair's stories, but over his protests Blair was promoted from intern to full-time employee. The paper's (understandable) commitment to "diversity" (Blair was African American) was alleged by some staff members to have been a factor in the promotion. There was a failure to check Blair's educational credentials (reminiscent of the Janet Cooke imbroglio): Blair had been a college intern, and "when he returned to the *Times* newsroom in June 1999, Ms. Rule said, everyone assumed he had graduated. He had not; college officials say he has more than a year of course work to complete."

On 6 June 2003, the *Times* ran a front page story. "Times's 2 Top Editors Resign After Furor on Writer's Fraud" (Steinberg, 2003). The article begins: "Howell Raines and Gerald M. Boyd, the top-ranking editors of the *New York Times*, resigned yesterday morning, five weeks after the resignation of a reporter set off a chain of events that exposed fissures in the management and morale of the newspaper." On 11 May the *Times* described in an extensive article how

> Jayson Blair, a staff reporter, had made errors or had committed the equivalent of journalistic fraud in at least 36 articles since October. ... Mr. Raines was the executive editor; he had been in charge of the newsroom for less than two years, during which the paper won eight Pulitzer Prizes. ... Mr. Boyd was the newspaper's first black managing editor (Steinberg, 2003).

Mr. Blair was described as having committed "deceptions, including the plagiarizing of articles from other newspapers and news agencies and the concocting of quotations" (Barry et al., 2003).

Reprise of the Janet Cooke imbroglio

The reprise of the Janet Cooke case could hardly be more complete: there was with failure to check college credentials because of a laudable and well-intentioned urgency to hire and retain members of minority groups; there was inadequate supervision of reporters; there was "general truth" and resulting verisimilitude in the fraudulent reports; and there was a lack of mentoring leading to a failure of understanding by a young reporter of the long-term significance of his behavior.

Perils of Story-telling: Particularity

It is a bit discouraging that despite the sequential story-telling in the Janet Cooke case not enough had been learned to prevent a near exact repetition on an even larger and more destructive scale in a kindred newspaper. Particularity, the intensity of the individual instance, so important in journalism, the story as a *Ding an sich*, a thing in itself, had prevented the insights that were potentially available from reaching fruition. In both cases some of the editors "knew and didn't know" that something was wrong. The journalist's need to "tell a story" militated against the more analytical stance that was also needed. It is as though the original story, and the successor stories, were so powerful as to create a "response set" or a "frame," limiting what could be understood. As a result, the editors of each newspaper "knew and didn't know" that something was wrong.

On a still more general level, no one seems to have related the Cooke and Blair episodes to the emergence of a broader societal pattern of corruption, such as became manifest in Enron, in WorldCom, and in Global Crossing, to name a few among many, an endemic of corruption more usually associated with a banana republic, a theme we shall consider in detail in Chapter 11.

The reader will have noticed that in the Blair case, unlike the Cooke deception, new technology—email and the cell phone—was crucial in creating the deceptions (Barry et al., 2003). The pattern of resorting to technology to deceive was manifest on a more high-tech level in the complex computer-enabled deceptions by Enron, WorldCom, and Global Crossing. No one seems to have discussed this parallel either.

In Sum

Story-telling, because of its particularity, makes for exciting journalism and great reader appeal but sometimes it can mask more general psychodynamic and social scientific insights. I think that a narrative analysis, by examining the components of a story, such as the protagonist, the dramatis personae, the implicit conflict the story is an effort to resolve, the crucial role of audiences, and the psychodynamic, cultural, and social structural factors implicit in the story, can help provide some of the missing insights.

8
A Systematic Study of Irreality

When small men cast long shadows, the sun is going down.
Proverb

This chapter is intended to give the reader a further idea of the reach and scope of psychodynamic inquiry into world events using social science methodologies. For example, this particular study uses *sampling, thick description, and very extensive verbatim quotation*. The material in this chapter also illustrates the *bizarreness of thought and behavior* we discussed in the protocol in Chapter 3. And this chapter will give you, the reader, a chance to see if your associations to various texts comport at all with mine, or whether instead the fabled idiosyncrasy of psychodynamic interpretations is, in fact, a reality.

I don't mean to suggest that all or most psychodynamic studies should be done using the methods in this chapter, but I do want to illustrate the possibilities.

A Word on Modern Political Versions of Irreality

I would like to be able to tell you that what I call "irreality" in the case study in this chapter was confined to the activities of the three authoritarian leaders the time period of the study, the 1990s. But this would not be true. Georgios Papadopoulos is dead but Vladimir Zhirinovsky and Jean-Marie Le Pen are very much still with us, very politically active today, as will become evident.

I would also like to be able to tell you that the deliberate induction of confusion about what is real, described in this case study, is no longer a problem. But this would not be true either.

On the current political scene, Nigel Farage, the leader of UKIP, the United Kingdom Independence Party, might be compared to Le Pen and Zhirinovsky. He is a charismatic right-wing populist and a fiery speaker, like Zhirinovsky. And like Le Pen and Zhirinovsky he is a nationalist. Like Le Pen, a key concern is to stop further immigration from European Union (EU) countries. To this end, Farage wants the UK to leave the EU entirely.

Although a much more eloquent and knowledgeable speaker than Le Pen, Zhirinovsky, or Papadopoulos, Farage is also considered by some to be a "clown" and a "buffoon." The *Telegraph* says, "Nigel Farage is a buffoon for admiring Vladimir Putin…The Ukip leader—the Kremlin's favorite British politician—is becoming increasingly ridiculous and offensive" (Rifkind, 2014). The *Mirror* says "Vote for Nigel Farage and the UKIP 'clowns' and the joke's on us" (Reade, 2013). The *London Evening Standard* (2013) says "That 'clown' Farage is covering all the bases now."

An example of the reported "clowning "is the so-called "calypso video," which uses humor, sarcasm, and calypso music to deliver a political message. But this was not nearly as extreme as the "donkey video" by Zhirinovsky, which is described later in this chapter. With Farage, as with Zhirinovsky and Le Pen, the "clowning" appears to be in the service of gaining publicity for a political agenda.

It is important to remember that being perceived by one's opponents, or even by some more other observers, as clownish, does not mean that the person is not a powerful political force or that he will not appeal to major audiences. Farage, Zhirinovsky, and Le Pen demonstrate this, and so did Papadopoulos, with his remark that Richard Nixon was a communist.

There may be some unconscious psychological connection between what may appear to some to be buffoonery and being perceived as a powerful leader by the populace at large. This is a matter that deserves a psychodynamically informed social research effort.

Here is an example of how Farage has turned the "clown" designation to his advantage. The *International Businesses Times* reports, "Nigel Farage Joins Forces with ex-Clown Beppe Grillo as Ukip and Five Star Movement Unite in EU":

> The new Europe of Freedom and Democracy Group (EFD) includes 48 MEPs [Members of the European Parliament] from countries including Sweden, France, Lithuania, the Czech Republic and Latvia. … The new group followed a meeting between the two leaders in an Indian restaurant in Brussels after which Grillo said Farage possessed a "sense of humor and sense of irony."

> Ukip stormed to victory in last month's EU election in Britain by topping the ballot and winning 24 MEP seats. ... The Five Star Movement [headed by former clown Beppe Grillo], has raged against austerity in Italy and has won 17 representatives at the European parliament in Brussels in Italian elections. Last year, it won 25% of the vote in a general election.
>
> Farage said, the Europe of Freedom and Democracy Group (EFD) will be "the people's voice" and predicted "it will operate very well." Hailing the EFD, Beppe Grillo said: "Now we will start working in committees and we will have the peoples' voice heard in the European institutions, without intermediaries" (Glover, 2014).

I would say that what has been called a buffoonish element in Farage is subsidiary to his effort to get publicity for his political agenda, which is also true of Zhirinovsky and Le Pen, as the reader will see below. Farage's primary goals are to shut off further immigration from EU countries and to get the UK to withdraw from the EU. His scornful personal attacks on EU leaders may seem bizarre to many but there is no doubt that they are seriously intended.

What do we find if we look into these speeches from a psychodynamic perspective, "listening with the third ear" for implicit themes that may be out of conscious awareness? The speeches emphasize that the people of the UK have been unfairly ignored, left out, disregarded, discarded. Could this result in a wish to get even by humiliating the opponents? Nigel Farage, at an EU council meeting, televised around the world, said to EU President Herman Van Rompuy, " You have all the charisma of a damp rag and the appearance of a low-grade bank clerk. ...Who are you? I have never heard of you. Nobody in Europe has ever heard of you" (*Guardian*, 2010).

Irreality Broadly Manifested Through the Internet and Other Modern Communications Media

But the creation of doubt as to what is real is no longer confined to political posturing. Irreality has become far more important and menacing than I perceived when Christine Gerety and I began the study described later in the chapter. We have become used to believing something is real if we read it in the newspapers or magazines. But something has changed: the Internet has arrived and has become a dominant means of communication.

Let me set forth some of the threatening and deeply disturbing manifestations of irreality, the intentional creation of doubt as to what is real, that the Internet has made possible.

What has happened is that the Internet has created what is called a "virtual reality," in which a computer simulation imitates what is real and can, unfortunately, create a situation in which the viewer loses the ability to distinguish the Internet presentation from real-life people and activities. An induced confusion about what is real, which I have called "irreality," is thereby produced.

Irreality, that is, induced confusion about what is real, is easily fostered by the Internet. It is the sequel to the irreality that can be produced, with more difficulty, by the press: you will see in the following study that a character in Ionesco's *Rhinoceros* (1960), Dudard, says, "It's in the paper, in black and white, you can't deny that..." Today, one would say, "I saw it on the Internet," a great deal more convincing than "I read it in the newspaper." An irreal persona can also be achieved in the press by a writer with sufficient talent, as we saw in Chapter 7, when we looked at Janet Cooke's fabrication of a child heroin addict. But it is so much easier with the modern Internet.

Joshua Ferris, in his novel, *To Rise Again at a Decent Hour* (2014) calls attention to the ease with which doubt as to what is real can now be created. An Internet imposter who speaks with a voice imitating the protagonist, a Manhattan dentist, competes with the him on web pages, Facebook, and Twitter as to who is the actual person. Ferris echoes Franz Kafka's questions about what is real, but this time the Internet is the source of an irreal presence. The book was short-listed for the 2014 Man Booker Prize, and has won the International Dylan Thomas Prize, indicating that the impersonation of its dentist protagonist touches a nerve in the contemporary world.

There are several manifestations of the irreal made possible by the Internet. The most dangerous is the creation of a false self by sexual predators in order to entrap children and young people for purposes of sexual exploitation.

A second manifestation is the blurring between the real and the unreal that one observes in some addicts to Internet fantasy games. Some people, mostly men, become so absorbed in the game that not only does it consume much or most of their free time, but they also take on the character they are playing so intensely that that character usurps their actual self and actual role. For example, a man as a character may flirt seriously with a woman character, and proceed as far as a fantasy Internet marriage, even though he is actually married to a real woman, whom he is neglecting.

A third kind of creation of an unreal self is achieved, for example, by a man who plays a female character in a fantasy game, and flirts with and has Internet sex with a male character. Whether either party is unconsciously aware of the deceptions involved is unknown and would be a good topic for psychodynamic inquiry.

This kind of creation of irreality, a deliberately induced confusion about whether the person is real, may possibly be involved in the sad case of the athlete Manti Te'o, a linebacker so good that he was credited with getting the Notre Dame Football team into the American national championship game. He was also a candidate for the Heisman Trophy as the outstanding American college football player of 2010, and it was predicted that he would receive millions of dollars as a signing bonus with the National Football League (NFL), and more millions from commercial endorsements of athletic products and for products for men such as shaving cream, deodorants, and even soft drinks.

American football heroes are expected to have girlfriends, and according to reports in the popular press and the media, which may be in error, although he apparently didn't date much in his years at Notre Dame, he had a long-term serious liaison with a young woman in Hawaii, with whom he reportedly talked by phone at least once a week. Ultimately, as curiosity in the press and in football fans grew as to who this girlfriend was, the media and popular press alleged that she apparently did not exist, and that the voice he was speaking to was a man pretending to be a woman, allegedly without Manti Te'o's knowledge. His sign-up value to the NFL suddenly plummeted to 10 percent of what it would have been and the potential endorsements disappeared entirely, in a sad and embarrassing dénouement.

According to the reports in the popular press and the media, which may be in error, the extent to which Te'o was deceived by a friend is not known, nor whether a deliberate deception of the press and the fans was being enacted. Sometimes one knows and doesn't know at the same time owing to the characteristics of the unconscious we have been discussing. In any case, the fans and the press apparently had come to believe in a person who perhaps didn't exist or may have been very different from the person described by Te'o.

There are other instances of irreality in the media. For example, as we shall see in Chapter 11, climate change deniers seek to create an irreal world in which there is no climate change. Most of their creations of an irreal world are fostered through Internet videos, blogs, and postings.

And so we turn to a historical study that we wish were only of historical interest rather than an early depiction of what has become a modern threat.

The Study in Brief

This chapter reanalyzes data from the doctoral dissertation of Christine Gerety (2000), done under my direction. In reanalyzing this study of world press journals, I noticed a strange parallel between the world press profiles of Vladimir Zhirinovsky, Jean-Marie Le Pen, and Georgios Papadopoulos, and the portrayal of dictators and dictatorship in the writings of Franz Kafka, Eugene Ionesco, Luigi Pirandello, and George Orwell. I called this parallel "irreality," which I defined as *induced confusion about what is real*. I found the creation of confusion about what is real to be a salient characteristic of the speeches and writings of these three leaders, as described in world press journals. I discovered that world press journalists, and these four modern writers, have independently called attention to induced confusion about what is real, but without naming it. I will use a lot of verbatim quotations from the profiles by world press journalists in presenting the study, so that readers can draw their own inferences. This will illustrate *thick description through extensive verbatim quotations*, a method I recommend.

The reader will note that this is not a direct study of the personalities of these three leaders. The research presented here concerns the *portrayals of three authoritarian leaders in the world press in English, as a result of statements by these leaders at certain times of special interest, usually during elections*. By contrast, an analysis of the actual personalities of these leaders would require a study of their entire lives, drawing on original sources in English, French, Russian, and Greek.

How the Study was Done

I formulated the concept of "irreality" after reanalyzing data from a much larger study I did with my colleague Christine Gerety, a multiyear study that culminated in her outstanding doctoral dissertation (Gerety, 2000), and so I am considerably in her debt for the present chapter. The larger study was systematic, and we tried to follow the canons of scientific procedure so the reader could have some assurance that a replication of the study was likely to yield similar results. I will set forth the methodology briefly. Much more detail is given in Meyers et al. (1997) and Meyers and Gerety (1999).

Our Search for Profiles in the World Press: Computer-aided Objective Sampling

We searched for "profile" articles in 19 leading world press sources (listed in Table 8.1). These 19 sources were chosen by an expert on the world press. We used The Lexis-Nexis Electronic and E-library databases, and an original computer algorithm to identify "profiles" objectively. An article to be considered a "profile" had to meet several objective criteria. Specifically, to qualify as a "profile" of Zhirinovsky

Table 8.1 World press data sources

International Herald Tribune	*Observer*
Herald (Glasgow)	*Time Magazine*
Los Angeles Times	*Jerusalem Post*
The Times (of London)	*Independent*
Washington Post	*National Review*
Sunday Telegraph	*Foreign Affairs*
Financial Times	*New Republic*
New York Times	*The Economist*
American Spectator	*Guardian*
European	

or Le Pen or Papadopoulos, an article had to mention his name at least five times (as counted by the computer), the article had to be about him rather than about an event such as an election (assessed when the first few paragraphs are inspected by a hypothesis-blind reader), and the article had to be at least 200 words in length (as counted by the computer).

The Profiles

We searched for the profiles within specific time periods during the 1990s. We looked at four sets of profiles in the 19 world press journals. The first set comprises all profiles of Vladimir Zhirinovsky in these journals from 1 December 1993 to 31 July 1994. This period includes the December 1993 election in which he received 24% of the vote. We found 21 profiles in this period.

The second set of data consists of all profiles of Zhirinovsky in these journals from 1 January 1996 to 31 January 1997. This period comprises the six months prior to and the six months after the second election, in June 1996, in which he received only 6% of the vote. We found 17 profiles in this period.

The third set of data comprises all profiles of the extreme right-wing French leader Jean-Marie Le Pen, from 1 January 1996 to 31 January 1997 (a time period paralleling that of the second Zhirinovsky data set; this is a period in which Le Pen also was very active politically). We found 28 profiles in this period.

A fourth set of data consists of all obituary profiles of Georgios Papadopoulos published in these 19 journals in the week immediately following Papadopoulos' death on 27 June 1999. We found 13 obituaries that met our definition of profiles given above, and, as a result, these obituaries parallel the Le Pen and Zhirinovsky profiles.

Since our study, using computer-driven selection, included all the profiles of these leaders in those journals meeting our criteria for the time period considered, our data sets have no "sampling error." That means that using these sampling methods we would get exactly the same samples if we tried again. The idea is to make sure our results don't depend on some peculiarity of particular samples that other samples wouldn't show. (However, our data could have measurement error, that is, imprecise measurement of the variables we used.)

Consulting the Profiles: A Methodological Note

The major benefit of "thick description" (presenting an abundance of raw data) is to enable the reader to look at the data themselves and decide whether they agree with the researcher's conclusions. Readers may therefore wish to consult the profiles on which the present study was based to see if they agree with the study findings. Since there were 81 separate profiles in this study, for the convenience of the readers I have listed them together at the end of the chapter in the "Further Reading" section, stratified by authoritarian leader, rather than leaving them scattered through the myriad of other references. Part of the value of this arrangement is that readers who agree with my concept of combining research methods can easily take successive stratified random samples of the profiles until they feel comfortable with their own conclusions.

What is "Irreality?"

The "irreal," as I define it, consists of the intentional abolition or serious impairment of the distinction between what is real (as defined by consensus of observers) and what is not real (as defined by consensus of observers). *Irreality is induced confusion in the audience about what is real.* The "surreal," by contrast, is a deliberate distortion of reality used for artistic effect only (for example, a watch dripping over a tree branch in a Dali painting), and understood as such by the audience.

The "irreal" constitutes a thorough and intentional blending of the real and unreal, on the part of the dictatorial leader; the distinction between the real and the unreal is explicitly rejected. This mixture of fantasy and reality is difficult for the listener to separate. As part of his creation of the irreal, the dictator implicitly or explicitly rejects the rational. A Nazi concentration camp guard is quoted as saying to the newly arrived prisoner, "Hier Ist Kein Warum" ("Here there is no why") (Levi, 1996).

Irreality must be distinguished from the use of "poetic license" by the speaker, and from the exercise of "suspension of disbelief" by the audience. Poetic license involves a distortion of reality freely granted by the reader to the writer, and understood as an artistic device by both. Suspension of disbelief is a situation where the reader willingly enters into the writer's fantasy, and for artistic purposes; the reader willingly takes as true something he or she knows to be false. In neither poetic license nor suspension of disbelief is there any confusion by writer (or speaker) and audience about what is real and what is not real. In the case of irreality, however, this confusion does exist and is knowingly induced by the writer or speaker. In the case of the irreal in literature, the protagonist, as well as the reader, may be confused about what is real.

Sources of the "Irreal" in Literature

George Orwell's book, *1984*, published in 1949, which consciously depicted Nazism and Stalinism (pointed out by Fromm, 1961), provides a detailed account of the development of the irreal. I found four key elements in the creation of the irreal by the dictator, Big Brother, in *1984*:

1. *Rewriting history*, which destroys the ability to discern what was real in the past (consider a recent example, Holocaust denial or minimization: Jean-Marie Le Pen called the Holocaust "an incident in history").

   In *1984* rewriting history is part of a larger attempt to blur the distinction between what is real and what is not real. O'Brien, an Inner Party member and a representative of the dictator, Big Brother, says to Winston, the protagonist:

   > You believe that reality is something objective, external, existing in its own right. You also believe that the nature of reality is self-evident. When you delude yourself into thinking that you see something, you assume that everyone else sees the same thing as you. But I tell you, Winston, that reality is not external. Reality exists in the human mind, and nowhere else (p. 205).

2. *"Newspeak,"* a constricted language, makes it impossible to think certain thoughts. By creating this language, the Party of Big Brother could interfere with the veridical interpretation of events by

eliminating the language necessary to analyze the events. The person was therefore left in a world in which reality has little meaning.

3. "*Doublethink*," the ability to believe firmly in two opposite propositions simultaneously. In Orwell's words, "If one is to rule, and to continue ruling, one must be able to dislocate the sense of reality" (pp. 176–7).

   This is as clear a statement as one could hope to find of the construct of irreality, a dislocation of the sense of reality so that one is in doubt as to what is real. In the world of *1984*, this is achieved through a process known as "doublethink." Party leaders, as well as followers, practiced doublethink. What started as a deliberate policy of distortion of reality took on a life of its own, and both leaders and followers became genuinely confused about what was real. Biographical records show that Orwell had Stalinism and Nazism in mind when he formulated this concept in his novel.

4. *The power of oratory to create the irreal*. Big Brother's oratory is beamed in constantly over the radio, and in mass rallies in which the audience screams agreement in unison, in a kind of mass hysteria.

Franz Kafka's Novels

Franz Kafka's *The Trial* (1925 [1988]) and *The Metamorphosis* (1915 [1986]) are powerful portrayals of irreality, situations in which the reader and the protagonist cannot be sure of what is real. *The Trial* portrays persecution by a relentless, impersonal, authoritarian bureaucracy. The protagonist, Joseph K., is accused of a crime which is never stated and which may, in fact, not have been a crime. It is never known whether he has really committed a crime, or, if he has, what that crime might be. He is run through a myriad of bizarre legal hoops and has strange relationships with people who seem to know a great deal about him, even though he believes he is meeting them for the first time. What is real and what is fantasy in this legal and social system are never disentangled. Nevertheless, Joseph K. is executed at the end of the book.

In *The Metamorphosis* a young man, Gregor, wakes up one morning to find himself suddenly transformed into a large and ugly cockroach. The story depicts the gradual abandonment and destruction of Gregor by his family. No reason or explanation is ever given for his transformation into this appalling state. He and his family accept this impossible transformation as real, and yet he retains his sense of identity and all of the psychological characteristics of a person. The protagonist and the reader are confused by the transformation but no resolution of the confusion is given. A profound blurring between the real and the unreal has occurred.

Rhinoceros, by Eugene Ionesco

Eugene Ionesco's play, *Rhinoceros* (1960), was written "with the relentless rise of Nazism in mind" (Ellison and Gooding, 1976). In this modern masterpiece, people gradually turn themselves into roaring, brutal, mindless rhinoceroses, with the grey of the rhinoceros symbolizing the Nazi uniform. The rhinoceroses represent Nazism and also express regression into primary process thinking in which reason is suspended and opposites don't contradict each other. This transformation appears to blend the voluntary and the involuntary. It is strangely parallel to the transformation in *The Metamorphosis* but this transformation into rhinos appears to be largely voluntary: people will themselves into this animalistic state. Yet there is more than a hint of the involuntary, for people do it under the influence of mass excitement and the sound of the roaring of other rhinos. In *Rhinoceros*, irreality is portrayed as being a result of mass hysteria apparently induced by oratory that stirs group emotion. Ionesco notes that in writing *Rhinoceros* he was influenced by Denis de Rougemont's account of nearly being overwhelmed emotionally while watching Hitler's Nuremberg rally. At the end of the play, the hero, Berenger, resolves never to give in to mass hysteria, and to remain the only man not transformed into a rhino.

Doublethink appears also in *Rhinoceros*: Botard, a rival of Berenger, says, "The fact that I despise religion doesn't mean that I don't esteem it highly." Here the ability to hold two contradictory ideas simultaneously is seen as a characteristic of dictatorship.

The transformation of people into rhinos has, for the protagonist, Berenger, the characteristic of irreality: he explicitly says he is confused about what is real. During an exchange of words between Berenger and Jean, another character in the play, Berenger thinks he may have only dreamed the rhino that ran through his town. Jean replies, "Asleep or awake, it's all the same thing."

The first sightings of rhinos also have this irreal quality: the characters debate whether they really saw a rhino go by.

In Act Two, Scene One:

Botard: It's all a lot of made-up nonsense.
Daisy: But I saw it, I saw the rhinoceros!

Dudard:	It's in the paper, in black and white, you can't deny that...
Botard (interrupting him):	It's obvious they were just making it up. You put too much trust in these journalists...
Daisy:	But I saw it, I saw the rhinoceros, I'd take my oath on it...
Papillon:	Well, Berenger, did you see the rhinoceros by any chance?
Berenger:	Oh, yes, I saw it alright.
Botard:	Pfff! It's possible that Mr. Berenger thought he saw a rhinoceros. ... He's got such a vivid imagination!...
Berenger:	I wasn't alone when I saw the rhinoceros! Or perhaps there were two rhinoceroses.
Botard:	He doesn't even know how many he saw...Did you see one rhinoceros, Mr. Berenger, or two rhinoceroses?
Berenger:	Well, it's hard to say!"

Pirandello's Six Characters in Search of An Author

In Luigi Pirandello's play the distinction between illusion and reality is deliberately obscured. In *Six Characters in Search of an Author* (1921 [1952]), a family comprising six members, who appear to be real people but are always called "characters," bursts in on the rehearsal of a Pirandello play (!) and demands that the Manager (who would be called a Director, in English) create a play about their lives:

In Act One:

The Father [coming forward a little, followed by the others who seem embarrassed]:	As a matter of fact...we have come here in search of an author...
The Manager [half angry, half amazed]:	An author? What author?
The Father:	Any Author, sir.
The Manager:	But there's no author here. We are not rehearsing a new piece.
The Step-Daughter [vivaciously]:	So much the better! We can be your new piece.
An Actor [coming forward from the others].	Oh, do you hear that?
The Father [to Step-Daughter]:	Yes, but if the author isn't here... [To Manager] unless you would be willing. ...

The Manager:	You are trying to be funny.
The Father:	No, for Heaven's sake, what are you saying. We bring you a drama, sir.
The Step-Daughter:	We may be your fortune.
The Manager:	Will you oblige me by going away? We haven't time to waste with mad people.
The Father [*mellifluously*]:	Oh, sir, you know well that life is full of infinite absurdities, which strangely enough, do not ever need to appear plausible, since they are true.

And again, in Act Three:

The Father:	Well, sir, if you think all those illusions that mean nothing to you now, of all those things which don't even seem to exist any more, while once they *were* for you, don't you feel that—all this present reality of yours—is fated to seem a mere illusion to you tomorrow?

This excerpt concludes our illustration of some of the roots of the irreality construct in modern literature. It seems no accident that themes of irreality appear in modern fiction: they often reflect strange menacing external events. For example, Orwell fought against General Franco's fascist armies as a volunteer soldier in the Spanish Civil War. Ionesco wrote *Rhinoceros* when he was in hiding in rural Vichy France during World War II. Kafka lived through the terrifying anti-Semitic riots in Prague in 1899, when he was 14 years old, and one wonders if being Jewish was the secret unmentionable offense of Joseph K.

W.G. Sebald (1999) in his travel novel *Vertigo*, details Kafka's 1913 trip to Venice where he saw the cell in Piombi prison (beneath the Doge's Palace), in which Casanova had been imprisoned and from which he eventually escaped. Casanova had been arrested without warning and imprisoned after a secret trial that had been unknown to him. Frederick McGavran (personal communication) has noted that the Venetian legal system echoed that in *The Trial*: accusations were brought in secret to secret courts, without knowledge of the accused, a verdict was rendered, also without knowledge of the accused, who was then suddenly arrested and imprisoned. In 1914, the year after his trip to Venice, Kafka wrote *The Trial*.

A Word on the Relationship of Literature to Social Science

We have just considered some of the implications of literature for the psychodynamically informed social scientific investigation of world events. Let us consider the matter more generally for a moment.

A vignette: A five-year-old boy says to his mother, "I want to marry you when I grow up." His mother says, "What about your father?" The little boy says, "We can throw him away." A common theme, if one listens. But this is not new. Sophocles long ago wrote about patricide and incestuous marriage with the mother. Are we really ready to say Sophocles, and Doestoyevsky for that matter, were wrong?

I think we have been overenthusiastic in making the distinction between literature, which is expressive, and science, which is objectively "true." We have made a useful distinction between the two into an unbridgeable chasm. I think there is a sense in which some of literature is "true."

A second issue is the reverse. In an interview by David Remnick, now the editor of *The New Yorker*, with the novelist Philip Roth, who was then living somewhat reclusively in upstate New York, Roth commented that he "was disappointed on reading a number of recent pieces that implied that Freud was a charlatan, or worse." Roth added, "This great tragic poet, our Sophocles" (Remnick, 2000, p. 87).

Roth's comment is profound. I think there is a sense in which some of social science, particularly some of psychology, is literature. Indeed, the Nobel Laureate Roman Rolland was so impressed with the imaginative power of Freud's writing that he nominated him in 1936 for the Nobel Prize in Literature, doubtless the first time anyone has been considered for both the Prize in Medicine (Freud was nominated 32 times for the Nobel Prize in Physiology or Medicine, but never awarded) and the Prize in Literature.

The Three Leaders

Now let us turn to the evidence of the construct of irreality in the words and actions of three dictatorial leaders, Jean-Marie Le Pen, Vladimir Zhirinovsky, and Georgios Papadopoulos.

Jean-Marie Le Pen

Le Pen is the founder and leader of France's National Front, a far right-wing political party that sees itself as "the only hope for the French people" (Front Nationale, 1998). This group depicts the French government as corrupt, and warns that the creation of an open Europe will only signal the downfall of France. Le Pen promises to represent the "true" French people who support his ideas and are in need of representation (ibid). Over a period of several years in the 1990s, Le Pen and his party received between 10 and 18 percent of the vote nationally and became powerful forces in many of France's regions, achieving the mayoralty of Lyon, for example.

Le Pen, backed by many French conservatives, declared that the use of Nazi gas chambers during the Holocaust was simply "a detail in history." He threatened to deport the three million foreign-born Arabs who live on French soil. In early April 1998, Le Pen was convicted of physically assaulting a Socialist politician, the penalty for which was the removal of his civil rights for two years; this sentence, however, could not take effect until after he had appealed the verdict, which allowed him to run for and win a position in the 1999 European Parliament.

The journalists describe Le Pen as creating "rhetorical excitement... rapidly shifting from humor to rage," leaving onlookers unsure of what was meant seriously.

Many people had written off Le Pen as a serious electoral threat, until he unexpectedly won enough votes to force a two-man runoff race for the Presidency of France in May of 2002.

Vladimir Zhirinovsky

Zhirinovsky, the leader of Russia's ultranationalist Liberal Democratic Party, was highly visible in the period covered by these world press profiles (1993–96). In 1993 he garnered 24 percent of the vote during the presidential election, while in 1996 he obtained only about six percent, suggesting a drop in his influence. But in subsequent years Zhirinovsky's party continued to be very active in the Russian parliament and consistently voiced radical right-wing ideologies. These include eradicating the Russian Jewish population, and regaining territories from former republics of the Soviet Union.

Georgios Papadopoulos

Papadopoulos, the leader of the Greek Colonels, seized power in Greece in 1967 and remained in power for seven years until being overthrown by a coup by his military chief of police in 1973, who, in less than a year, was himself overthrown. While in power he ran a regime noted for its torture of dissidents.

Study Findings from the Profiles by Journalists

Journalists' portrayal of the irreal in the words and actions of Zhirinovsky and Le Pen

In an earlier study (Meyers and Gerety, 2000), we had carefully read and reread and discussed together the 66 profiles of Zhirinovsky and Le Pen to try to identify common themes in the journalists' portrayals of these men. Considered together, these profiles, as outlined below, suggested to me that the journalists alleged *a definite sense of the presence of the irreal—the deliberate blurring of the distinction between the real and the unreal*—in the lives and programs of these two dictatorial leaders.

Aspects of the creation of irreality

One element in the deliberate creation of confusion about what is real is *the perplexing use of humor.* The journalists comment on "the sort of humorous rhetoric which [Le Pen's National] Front has made its own" (Powell, 1996, p. 12). Zhirinovsky is termed "amusing" (Beeston, 1996, p. 10). A journalist states, "His listeners seemed genuinely charmed by his sense of humor" (Fedarko, 1994, p. 38). His followers are quoted: "People enjoy Zhirinovsky's speeches. Laughter is healthy'" (Meek, 1996a, p.12). But was Zhirinovsky's threat to turn huge fans on to blow radioactive waste from Chernobyl on to the Baltic countries simply a joke, or did it presage a more serious proposal to take some sort of massive action against the Baltic countries? Should non-Russian residents of the Baltic really flee their country if Zhirinovsky wins? How real is Zhirinovsky's "clowning?" The calculating and the impulsive coexist in his person and his program. One article is titled, "Smile masks a scream of rage: Vladimir Zhirinovsky is part clown, part victim" (Lloyd and Boulton, 1993, p. 8).

Deliberate ambiguity

Deliberate ambiguity is another element in the creation of irreality in the hearer, as depicted by these journalists. Le Pen wins a suit against the press to establish that he is not a racist, yet he argues that the races are different, that black people are better at athletics but the Europeans accomplish more. Zhirinovsky says if he lets people see the good-natured intellectual he is, he will get no votes. Possible exaggeration, impossible to assess, is part of this ambiguity. "Much of Zhirinovsky's crude rhetoric appears delivered for shock value" (McElvoy, 1993, p. 5). The journalists note that Zhirinovsky "had said Baltic nationalists should get in boats and start rowing" if he won Russia's presidential race (*Herald*, 1996a). How much of this is rhetoric and how much an actual program in the manner of *Mein Kampf*? Fantasy and reality are so blended here that an irreal environment of discussion is created, and the journalists call attention to it in their own words. "Despite his astonishing display of excess, there seems to be a kind of brutal calculus behind the madness. 'If I behave like the good-natured intellectual I really am,' he [Zhirinovsky] told *Time* editors last week, 'I won't get votes. It's war out there, and I'm out to win'" (Fedarko, 1994, p. 38). A deliberate ambiguity, hard to interpret, is being created.

Deliberate parody

An element of *deliberate parody* is also part of the creation of an irreal environment of discussion, and is related to Zhirinovsky's peculiar sense of humor discussed earlier. For example, the journalists point out that Zhirinovsky has repeatedly denied having a Jewish father, despite what seems strong evidence that he did. They quote him as saying in response, "I've had several blood tests and there is no Jewish blood in me, not even 5 percent," and the journalist notes, "If the actor is skilled enough, and the audience willing to suspend its disbelief, the parody may be taken for the real thing" (McElvoy, 1993, p.5). Another says, "But it's hard to take him completely seriously. He treats the occasion as a kind of joke"; the term "farce" is used to describe his "antics," and "the journalists he treats with mixture of amusement and contempt" (DeBreadun, 1994, p.13.). One profile terms him "a kook, a clown, someone who does not fully believe what he says" (Quinn-Judge, 1994, pp. 23–5).

He is called by a journalist "a showman," and by another, "a barnstorming Bonaparte" (Fedarko, 1994, p. 38). But another journalist who interviewed him several times warns that it is all seriously meant as well: "His sincerity was frightening and disgusting" (McFaul, 1994, p. 23). Another profile has the subtitle: "Not the buffoon some might think" (Kipp, 1994, pp. 72–86).

Dramatic, outrageous, and outlandish statements for the purpose of getting media coverage

Zhirinovsky uses dramatic, outrageous, and outlandish statements in order to get media coverage, and is very successful in doing so. Journalists speak of "a calculated attempt to create a permanent sense of drama" by Zhirinovsky (McElvoy, 1993, p. 5), and often use the word "performance." The journalists accuse Zhirinovsky of using *clownishness* to manipulate the press into giving him more coverage. It is problematic that the outlandish statements reportedly attract a popular following, and may presage reality if the person is elected; no one knows where drama stops and reality begins. They term him both "bombastic" and "a fine orator-demagogue."

Provocativeness

Provocativeness by Le Pen and Zhirinovsky helps create confusion about what is real. The journalists note that Le Pen uses "a well-tried tactic: making provocative statements which prompt response from mainstream politicians and which, as a result, receive wide media coverage" (Smith, 1996a, p. 13). Consider Le Pen's comments on France's national soccer team, saying, in effect, that it isn't French because some of the players are black. "Addressing a rally in Nimes, Le Pen derided 'half of France's team' as 'foreigners' and complained that they did not know the words of the national anthem" (Shaw, 1996, p. 23). This announcement was made on the eve of an important match and gained wide media attention, especially since all the players were French citizens. Some said "Le Pen is a fascist who makes these attacks to gain publicity...Le Pen is always saying these things" (ibid). Another says, "It works every time: the National Front's leader, Jean-Marie Le Pen makes some provocative remark, and the French press delightedly pounces on it" (*The Economist,* 1996a). *But how much of such a remark is real, and would presage an attempt, for example, to ethnically purify the team if Le Pen were elected? A situation is created where it is impossible to tell. This particular kind of ambiguity is the hallmark of both of these aspiring dictators, and the world press journalists call attention to it.*

The *New York Times* weighed in, under the title, "French far right thrives on outrage" (Simons, 1996):

> It is a ploy at which Jean-Marie Le Pen is now an acknowledged master. He makes statements certain to be attacked as racist or xenophobic by French newspapers and mainstream political parties. Once assured of the spotlight, the tart-tongued leader of the far-right National Front says he was misinterpreted, then turns his guns on the entire political establishment...
>
> He did not shock the nation on Sunday by saying that "there is corruption at all levels" of the ruling conservative party. But this weekend he introduced a nasty new threat. "When we get to power," he shouted at the crowd, "all the cheats and bandits will not only have to defend their deeds but also their throats."

It is clear from a consideration of events in Europe in the twentieth century—the pogroms of Hitler against all opponents, and the Stalinist show trials—that the audience cannot rule out that this threat to the lives of establishment politicians might be real. A situation has been created where *the audience cannot be at all sure what is a real threat and what is only fantasy or rhetorical posturing.*

The creation of an irreal environment of discussion

The creation of an irreal environment of discussion does not, so far as I am aware, form a salient part of the social science literature on dictatorship, and so it constitutes a special contribution by these journalists. It is, however, depicted in modern literature, as we have seen in the writings of Orwell, Kafka, and Ionesco. Perhaps, as Orwell argues, the show trials of Stalin in the 1930s were such an enactment, where one never knew if Stalin and his prosecutors actually believed the accused were guilty.

Zhirinovsky, a spellbinder as an orator, is nevertheless given to what appear to the press to be buffoonish statements: "if I win the election, they [the citizens of the Baltic states] better get in boats and start rowing" (*Herald*, 1996a); concerning "the Baltic states, which he once suggested should be dusted with radioactive waste blown out from Russia by giant fans" (*The Economist*, 1996b); and "who has promised to father a child in each of the former Soviet republics" (Specter, 1996); and who has said "Russian soldiers will wash their boots in the warm waters of the Indian Ocean and forever change to summer uniforms" (Kipp, 1994).

Some of the confusion Zhirinovsky induces about what is real appears to the journalists to be brought about for rhetorical purposes, attention-getting bombast. However, they always raise the question of how much Zhirinovsky means it, especially in the light of his physical assaults on opponents in the Russian Duma (legislature). They suspect that he is serious when he says: "Make no mistake: I say it quite plainly—when I come to power there will be a dictatorship" (Fedarko, 1994). When he repeatedly says that Russian soldiers will wash their boots in the Indian ocean the listener is left in doubt; it may, indeed, be meant seriously as a plan for conquest.

Under the headline, "Weimar on the Volga," *The Economist* notes: "Clownish antics make it impossible to tell how much is for real" (1993, pp. 45–6).

The *American Spectator* opines: "Days before the election last December 12, he promised that under his policies every Russian woman would have a man of her own: living standards would rise, male mortality rates would plummet, and presto—a husband in every bed" (Young, 1994).

A profile in the *Washington Post* dwells at length on the induced confusion about what is real. Under the title, "Who Is Zhirinovsky? Mysteries Shroud Russian Nationalist" the *Post* argues:

> "Political impotence is finished!" Vladimir Zhirinovsky rasped at a polling station here Sunday as he cast his vote in Russia's legislative elections. "Today is the beginning of orgasm. The whole nation, I promise you, will feel orgasm next year!"...Clownish, bizarre and calculated to shock.
>
> ...his speeches and public remarks are noteworthy not only for their nostalgia for imperialism and their xenophobic rage, but also for their abundant contradictions, glaring illogic and sheer outrageousness.
>
> He wants Russia to take over enormous swaths of territory in Europe and, especially, Asia, in a "last thrust south" to warm waters that would realize the country's "great historic mission." But he says no Russian blood need be shed in the process. ...
>
> He speaks fondly of respecting human rights and building a civil society, but he has also pledged to eject non-Russian minorities from Russia. ... he has called Nazi dictator Adolf Hitler and his ideas "not that bad." "When I come to power, there will be a dictatorship. ... Those who have to be arrested will be arrested quietly at night. I may have to shoot 100,000 people, but the other 300 million will live peacefully. I have the right to shoot these 100,000. I have this right as president" (Hockstader, 1993, p. A1).

A profile in the *Los Angeles Times*, under the headline "Zhirinovsky a riddle to the world—and Russia too...Just who is he?" complains of the difficulty of knowing what is real and what is unreal with regard to Zhirinovsky's plans (Goldberg, 1993):

> Is Vladimir V. Zhirinovsky a KGB agent or isn't he? Is he or isn't he a self-denying Jew? Is he or isn't he a beneficiary of neo-Nazi funding from Germany? Is he or isn't he mentally ill? ...

[His] book ends with an apocalyptic vision, glorious to him but terrifying too for its implications: "I see Russian soldiers, gathering for this last southern crusade," he writes. "I see submarines surfacing by the shores of the Indian Ocean and paratroop ships approaching the shores, along which the soldiers of the Russian army are already marching, armored personnel carriers moving, enormous masses of tanks advancing. At last, Russia is completing its last military crusade..."

The *Guardian* describes the mystification produced by Zhirinovsky's contradictory and paradoxical pronouncements, and points out *the parallels to what it calls Hitler's* "surreal" *pronouncements*. This profile, under the headline, "Zhirinovsky, Mon Amour," states:

> We have reasons to be grateful to Vladimir Wolfovich Zhirinovsky, the son of a Russian woman and a lawyer. He is not the enemy of Poland. He merely wants to bring back the Molotov–Ribbentrop Pact because he loves the Germans, and because of this love he is prepared to share Poland with them.
>
> He is not anti-Semitic, either. He simply does not want the Jews to secretly run the Russian press and television. He would gladly see a Russian soldier washing his boots in the Indian Ocean. He wishes to see many more similar sights, which today may seem as surreal as those ideas once cobbled together by a bad painter, a private in the army, who did so in a German prison in the pages of a boring book called *Mein Kampf*... (Michnik, 1994).

A Note of Caution

Hitler and Mussolini were at first widely considered to be buffoons. But Hitler wrote in *Mein Kampf* that he promised to "hang every Jew in Munich from the lampposts." What was taken by some to be a buffoonish exaggeration, came literally to pass, 15 years later. The declared intention had an irreal quality: it was not possible to assess in 1923 whether the intention was real and whether the future state of affairs could really come to pass. Like Hitler and Mussolini, our next subject, Georgios Papadopoulos actually took power and acted out some of his menacing fantasies.

Georgios Papadopoulos

The following description of Papadopoulos' regime is quoted from the world press obituaries in our sample:

> During his time in power, Papadopoulos suspended civil liberties, and jailed thousands of people he thought to be opponents of the regime. According to an Amnesty International report, under Papadopoulos the use of torture became a standard administrative procedure to punish and intimidate suspected opponents. The European Commission on Human Rights concluded that the regime tortured prisoners as a matter of policy and denied fundamental human rights to citizens.

Irreality in the Papadopoulos obituaries

The journalists' profiles of Papadopoulos considered here consist of the 13 obituaries published in our 19 world press journals in the week immediately following his death on 27 June 1999. These obituaries meet our definition of profiles. The comments are drawn from these obituaries. They suggest to us that the journalists perceived Papadopoulos' speeches and actions as deliberately inducing a confusion about what is real:

> [Papadopoulos'] paranoid regime indulged in a baffling mixture of brutality and absurdity to enforce discipline, ranging from mass arrests, deportations and torture to a ban on long hair and mini-skirts (*The Times*, 1999).
>
> The army colonel...once said U.S. President Richard M. Nixon and two-thirds of the American Congress were communists... (*Washington Post*, 1999).
>
> During a concert in Athens by the Rolling Stones in 1967, Mick Jagger threw red flowers, and was hauled off the stage by authorities, who saw the gesture as support for communism (*Daily Telegraph*, 1999, p. 1).
>
> A list of banned books was drawn up, authors including, among many others, Shakespeare, Aristophanes, Chekhov... (Tonkin, 1999).
>
> The Colonels' practical initiatives were combined with grandiose schemes such as a plan to rebuild the Colossus of Rhodes. Their confused ideology is perhaps nowhere more evident than in the seven volumes of Papadopoulos' collected speeches, written in a farcical, pompous language, and published under the title To Pistevo Mas ('Our Credo') (Tonkin, 1999).

There is ample evidence in Papadopoulos' own speeches that he created confusion about what was real:

> I got to the point where I thought that it would move the emotions of the Greek nation, if I came in front of them as a new Gandhi and I asked them to help in the realization of the goals of our revolt, and after a successful ending I would commit suicide in front of them (Tonkin, 1999, p. 31).

In another speech he said, "Before the revolution, Greece stood at the edge of a precipice. Now, Greece has taken a big step forward."

Here we see that Papadopoulos followed the pattern we observed earlier in Zhirinovsky and Le Pen.

They are Still With Us

This study concerned the period from 1993 to 1997, a time of widespread interest in Zhirinovsky and Le Pen. Zhirinovsky was involved in election campaigns, and Le Pen was politically active as well. The study still is of current interest. The influence of these two political figures in the political scene continues even today.

In 2011, Jean Marie Le Pen's daughter, Marine Le Pen, succeeded him as the leader of the French extreme right-wing party, the National Front, and she continues his campaign against immigration and minorities. The election of 25 May in France made the National Front the leading party in France, with 25 percent of the total vote. Jean-Marie Le Pen is still making bizarre statements: that the deadly virus ebola could solve the global "population explosion" and, by extension, Europe's "immigration problem" (Willsher, 2014). And recently he recommended making an "oven load" of a Jewish singer he disliked (BBC News, 2014b). The political power of the National Front may increase as the French public reacts to the Charlie Hebdo assassinations, despite a bitter controversy emerging between Jean-Marie and Marine Le Pen (Sage, 2015; see also Gourevitch, 2015).

Zhirinovsky is also still very active, as of 2015, and is still spouting material on the border between humor and delusion, creating a sense of unreality in his listeners. He is still the leader of the Liberal Party in the Russian Duma, and still goes into long tirades with a lot of forceful hand waving and shouting. Very recently he again delved into the irreal in a statement about the 15 February 2013 meteorite strike in Chelyabinsk in central Russia, which injured about 1200 people: "Russian parliament member says meteor was actually a U.S. weapons test" (Fisher, 2013b); "'Those aren't meteors falling; it's the Americans testing new weapons,' the Russian politician said" (Koplowitz, 2013). There is no way a listener or a reader could tell if this was meant seriously or only provocatively.

Zhirinovsky's "donkey video" has also achieved notoriety.

According to Wikipedia (n.d.),

> On 6 February 2012, Vladimir Zhirinovsky, the far-right populist leader of the nationalist Liberal Democratic Party of Russia, released a 30-second election video on the Internet that featured him on a sleigh which was harnessed with a black donkey. Zhirinovsky later claimed he owned the animal and that the animal was named Proshka

> (Russian: Прошка, diminutive from Prokhor), after Mikhail Prokhorov, another candidate in the Russian presidential election, 2012. …
>
> …and that if he, Zhirinovsky, would become the President, a "daring troika" would return as a symbol of the country. … While making the proclamation, Zhirinovsky whips the animal. As the donkey does not immediately pull, Zhirinovsky shouts "It cannot move…. The whole country got stuck…" and continually shouts "Go! Go! Go!" while furiously whipping the animal into moving across the snow-covered backyard of his dacha.

The implied threat of actual violence against opponents cannot be easily dismissed because, reportedly, on more than one occasion Zhirinovsky punched another member of the Duma, the Russian legislature (*Moscow Times*, 1995; Mereu, 2005). Though disguised with heavy-handed humor, the threat of violence in the donkey video may be more than histrionics. No one knows how far Zhirinovsky will go if he attains power.

Implications for the Study of Dictatorship

The parallelism we find between themes of irreality in our world press profiles and themes of irreality in modern literature and in world press journals is impressive. These novelists and playwrights, and these journalists, are clearly trying to tell us something important: we must take account of dictatorial leaders' practices that induce confusion in the audience's mind about what is real. The device is sometimes cloaked with humor. The dictatorial leader appears aware of the confusion introduced and seems to take pleasure in it, a kind of confounding of the critics. Recent events suggest that it is safer for the audience to take irreal statements seriously, even where they are cloaked in humor, stated paradoxically, or disguised as rhetorical exaggeration.

Further investigation, discussed in Chapter 11, suggests that it is not only authoritarian political leaders who induce confusion about what it real, but it is also induced by media figures and private organizations outside of government itself.

The Study Methods Reviewed

The study presented here exemplifies two stratagems for deriving assertions about unconscious motives and fantasies. One method is *objective sampling*. This involves objective procedures to obtain textual data. One application of this sampling method would be to obtain 100 percent population samples of texts, that is, all articles or speeches by defined persons on a certain topic in a certain time period. Using this kind of sampling, Christine Gerety and I obtained all articles in specific world press journals in specific time periods dealing with specific topics and specific leaders.

In our use of this methodology, specific criteria for sampling, that is, for identifying the texts, were developed by specialists other than the researchers. The text selection was carried out by computer programs applying these criteria literally. The point of objective sampling is to give the reader some confidence that the textual data were not chosen in a biased way.

From these assembled texts, psychodynamic interpretative statements may be made.

In addition to the use of large samples of texts, objectively identified, the study used *very extensive verbatim quotations from these texts*. These were quotations from the articles in the world press showing the confusion that had been created, so that the reader can more readily judge the validity of the psychodynamic assertions. This extensive quotation is an application of the method of "thick description" (Geertz, 1973), which was described in Chapter 6.

In Chapter 9, we will consider a dramatically different approach: a remarkable collaboration among experts in assessing a major psychosocial study.

Further Reading

Zhirinovsky Profiles (1994)

Bohlen, C. (1994) Zhirinovsky and friends: quite a party. *International Herald Tribune*, Apr 6.

Clark, V. (1993) A mad pike is loose in the world's river. *Observer*, Dec 9, p. 10.

DeBreadun, D. (1994) Yearning for the bad old days of Dr. Zhivago. *Herald*, Jan 31, p. 13.

Fedarko, K. (1994) Rising Czar? *Time*, Jul 11, p. 38.

Goldberg, C. (1993) Zhirinovsky a riddle to world—and Russia too. *Los Angeles Times*, Dec 26, p. A1.

Hackett, J.T. (1994) Hitler's scheming heir in Russia. *Jerusalem Post*, Apr 15, p. 5A.

Higgins, A. (1994) Vlad the mad, and dangerous. *Independent*, May 1, p. 12

Hockstader, L. (1993) Who is Zhirinovsky? Mysteries shroud Russian nationalist. *Washington Post*, Dec 18, A1. Available at: http://www.highbeam.com/doc/1P2-980399.html (accessed 15 March 2015).

Hockstader, L. (1994) How Russia's Zhirinovsky rose. *Washington Post*, Mar 6, A1.

Judy, R.W. (1994) From anarchy to Zhirinovsky. *National Review*, 46, Mar 21, 49–52.

Kampfner, J. (1993) Vlad, bad, and dangerous to know. *Sunday Telegraph*, Dec 19, p. 25.
Kipp, J.W. (1994) A threat to Russian democracy. *Foreign Affairs*, 73, May/June, 72–86.
Lloyd, J. and Boulton, L. (1993) Smile masks a scream of rage: Vladimir Zhirinovsky is part clown, part victim, say John Lloyd and Leyla Boulton, but his contradictions cause concern. *Financial Times*, Dec 18, p. 8.
McElvoy, A. (1993) Zhirinovsky lays bare dark side of his Russian soul. *The Times (London)*, Dec 21.
McFaul, M. (1994) Nut 'n' honey. *New Republic*, 210, Feb 14, pp. 23–5.
Michnik, A. (1994) Zhirinovsky, mon amour. *Guardian*, Jan 14, p. 16.
Nove, A. (1994) Just call me Czar. *Herald*, Jan 14.
Quinn-Judge, P. (1994) Pantie-hero. *New Republic*, 210, Feb 14, p. 24.
Safire, W. (1993) Reading Yeltsin's mind. *New York Times*, Dec 20, p. A19.
Spector, M. (1994) The Great Russia will live again. *New York Times*, Jun 19, p. 28.
The Economist (1993) Weimar on the Volga. *The Economist*, Dec 18, pp. 45–6.
Young, C. (1994) Zhirinovsky up close. *American Spectator*, 27, 2.

Zhirinovsky Profiles (1996)

Beeston, R. (1996) Zhirinovsky's wild words mesmerise the workers. *The Times*, Jun 8.
Gordon, M. (1996) Zhirinovsky, with vows and gifts, woos voters. *New York Times*, Feb 12, p. A8.
Herald (1996a) Woman who tamed "Mad Vlad" says he is no monster. *Herald*, Jan 3, p. 6.
Herald (1996b) Zhirinovsky buys vote with vodka and parties. *Herald*, Feb 9, p. 11.
Heritage, T. (1996) Zhirinovsky joins race as Russia's third force. *Herald*, Apr 6, p. 10.
Hockstader, L. (1996) Russian front-runners to court Zhirinovsky's followers. *Washington Post*, Jun 6, p. A23.
Hooper, J. (1996) Odd deals in high places. *Guardian*, Jun 3, p. 7.
Khalip, A. (1996) Zhirinovsky shares Duma nostalgia for Soviet days. *Herald*, Mar 16, p. 12.
Macdonald, A. (1996) Zhirinovsky plays czar for a day. *Herald*, Feb 12, p. 8.
Macdonald, A. (1996) Zhirinovsky plays to the camera and uses silver wedding ceremony to bless his presidential campaign. *Guardian*, Feb 12, p. 11.
Meek, J. (1996a) Poor Pskov, trapped between the Soviet devil and the Baltic Sea. *Observer*, Nov 17, p. 12.
Meek, J. (1996b) Russians tune into a cocky entertainer. *Guardian*, Nov 17, p. 12.
Simon, S. (1996) Zhirinovsky renews wedding vows to woo voters. *Los Angeles Times*, Feb 12, p. A6.
Specter, M. (1996) Zhirinovsky savors Russian kingmaker role. Available at: http://www.nytimes.com/1996/06/14/world/zhirinovsky-savors-russian-kingmaker-role.html (accessed 15 March 2015).
Spector, M. (1994) The Great Russia will live again. *New York Times*, Jun 19, p. 28.
The Economist (1996) Russia: You have been warned. *The Economist*, May 18, p. 50.
Womack, H. (1996) Fascist threat or court jester? Russian poll: Zhirinovsky rides a new hobbyhorse. *Independent*, Jun 8, p. 9.

Le Pen Profiles

Anonymous (1996) Headline: talk of the streets. *Time*, Sep 30, p. 16.
Barber, T. (1996) Le Pen cries foul as front foes unite. *Independent*, Sep 24, p. 11.
Borger, J. (1997) Tremors in the Balkans: Belgrade/Le Pen finds nationalist unity lies in common hatreds. *Guardian*, Jan 22, p. 10.
Buchan, D. (1996) This week: Le Pen's case for greater popularity. *Financial Times*, Jun 24, p. 8.
Dejevsky, M. (1996) The races are unequal. It's what every Frenchman thinks privately: Openly racist remarks by Jean-Marie Le Pen, the National Front leader, have put France in a rage of indignation. *Independent*, Sep 14, p. 1.
Herbert, S. (1996) Le Pen campaigns to woo the jobless; France's hard-liners are showing a softer side. *Sunday Telegraph*, Nov 10, p. 29.
Hughes, R. (1996) Politics and sports shouldn't mix. *International Herald Tribune*, Jun 26.
International Herald Tribune (1996) French can't figure out how to nullify him. *International Herald Tribune*, Sep 30.
Jacobson, P. (1996) Le Pen's man tries to squeeze out rivals in battle for Orange. *Sunday Telegraph*, Aug 18, p. 24.
July, S. (1996) Three-prong strategy to outflank Le Pen. *Guardian*, Sep 18.
Kraft, S. (1996) Jean Marie Le Pen: The strong voice of France's far right. *Los Angeles Times*, May 26, p. M3.
Lewis, R. (1996) Bardot's book stirs cries of racism. *Independent*, Sep 25, p. 10.
Macintyre, B. (1996) Attack on French team rebounds on Le Pen. *The Times*, Jun 25.
Powell, N. (1996) Le Pen kicks own goal with care. *Herald*, Jun 29, p. 15.
Shaw, P. (1996) France let down by right-winger. *Independent*, Jun 25, p. 23.
Simons, M. (1996) French far right thrives on outrage. Available at: http://www.nytimes.com/1996/10/02/world/french-far-right-thrives-on-outrage.html (accessed 15 March 2015).
Simpson, A. (1996) Feeling the true pulse of France. *Herald*, Dec 23, p. 14.
Smith, A. (1996a) Le Pen rebuked for exploiting papal visit. *Guardian*, Sep 17, p. 13.
Smith, A. (1996b) Le Pen skillfully stokes the nationalist fire; French politicians, of both left and right, don't know what to do about the racist appeal of the "Front National"; "we are going straight towards an ethnic war." *Independent*, Jul 1, p. 15.
Smith, A. (1996c) Racist party wins over the workers. *Observer*, Nov 3, p. 21.
Swardson, A. (1996) Anti-immigrant party grows; French National Front's popularity stumps mainstream parties. *Washington Post*, Sep 29, p. A28.
The Economist (1996) France. racism, vote-catching and Le Pen. *The Economist*, Sep 21, p. 50.
Toulon, A. (1996) The friendly face of hatred. *Observer*, Jan 28.
Vandenhove, K. (1996) Politics: French court bans racism on disk. *Guardian*, Jan 18, p. 2.
Washington Post (1996) Le Pen revises racial views. *Washington Post*, Sep 30, p. A20.
Washington Post (1997) Le Pen learns lesson on Serb politics. *Washington Post*, Jan 22, p. A18.
Webster, P. (1996) Tactical voting turns tide against Le Pen. *Guardian*, Nov 19, p. 12.

Papadopoulos Profiles

Beech, H. (1999) Milestones. *Time*, Jul 12, p. 14.

Clogg, R. (1999) Obituary: Georgios Papadopoulos; key plotter of the colonels' coup in Greece, he survived with US backing but brought torture and economic ruin on his country. *Guardian*, Jun 28, p. 18.

Daily Telegraph (London) (1999) Obituary of George Papadopoulos leader of the Greek Colonels' junta who abolished the monarchy, making himself President, only to spend his last years in prison. *Daily Telegraph*, Jun 28, p. 23.

Financial Times (1999) A dictator's secret. *Financial Times*, Jul 10, p. 8

Hope, K. (1999) Papadopoulos dies at 80. *Financial Times*, Jun 28, p. 3.

International Herald Tribune (1999) Papadopoulos, ex-dictator in Greece, dies. *International Herald Tribune*, Jun 29, p. 2.

Pace, E. (1999) George Papadopoulos dies; Greek coup leader was 80. *New York Times*, Jun 28, Section B, p. 8.

Peckham, R. (1999) Obituary: George Papadopoulos. *Independent* Jun 28, Obituaries, p. 6.

The Economist (1999) George Papadopoulos. *The Economist*, Jul 3.

The Times (1999) George Papadopoulos. *The Times*, Jun 28.

Tonkin, S. (1999) Papadopoulos, ex-dictator of Greece, dies in jail at 80. *Independent*, Jun 28, Foreign News Section, p. 11.

Washington Post (1999) George Papadopoulos dies; led Greek Junta; colonel defended coup, repression as necessary to stop Communist takeover. *Washington Post*, Jun 28, p. B06.

9

The Munich Crisis Examined: An Experiment in Collaboration in Data Interpretation

This four-year experiment in collaboration in data interpretation primarily involved iterative interaction; the emergence of jointly agreed meanings through the process of symbolic interactionism; the use of informants; and elite and specialized interviewing. Very late in the collaboration it became clear that future studies of this sort might benefit from the Delphi technique; content analysis; use of non-reactive data; control for researcher bias; and Popperian disconfirmation.

David Beisel's landmark book, *The Suicidal Embrace: Hitler, the Allies, and the Origins of the Second World War* (2003), inquires into the mentalities of European leaders, the media, and the populace during the events leading up to World War II. A particular focus was the Munich crisis.

The Suicidal Embrace consists of an overall introductory chapter, a chapter for each of the European countries involved, a summary chapter, and 16 contemporary cartoons by David Low with annotations by Beisel. The scholarship is deep and broad, and the themes of the book are supported by extensive verbatim quotations from European leaders and the contemporary media. Beisel's generosity of spirit and open-mindedness made this collaboration possible.

The Suicidal Embrace has provoked an extensive discussion among psychologists and political scientists as to the proper interpretation of the data. The characterization of the Czechoslovak mentality during the Munich crisis seemed particularly controversial. At my suggestion, three social scientists undertook an extensive interactive collaboration with Beisel, involving an iterative exchange of comments and responses to comments, over four years, based on a symbolic interactionist theory of the creation of meaning.

This chapter presents their views and those of Beisel in response, culminating in a roundtable discussion at the Annual Scientific Meeting of the International Society of Political Psychology, in Istanbul in 2011. David Beisel, Ivo Feierabend, Martina Klicperova-Baker, and Jana Svehlova are the authors of their respective sections of this chapter.

The Symbolic Interactionist Viewpoint

At the outset we hoped to converge on a formulation of the psychodynamic phenomena involved in the Munich crisis or at least to clarify the different points of view if convergence proved problematical. Our method is based on the symbolic interactionist view, that *shared meanings*, and indeed our pictures of reality, *gradually evolve from a series of interactions among people*. These interactions can sometimes involve the negotiation of meanings.

Problems of Dealing With Psychodynamic Materials

Psychodynamic considerations span many strange or uncomfortable topics, such as the influence of childhood experience on the adult personality, as with Vladimir Zhirinovsky, who had a strange childhood; threats to the stability of the personality, as with cartoons of Mohammad as experienced in Islamic nations; projection of unwanted aspects of the self onto others, as in anti-Semitism; magical thinking, as in the idea that one "race" can pollute the blood of another "race," as with Nazi ideology. We have seen that unconscious guilt has been invoked to explain Marshall Pétain's failure to mount a serious defense of his actions during his trial for treason at the end of World War II (Szaluta, 1980). Explanation of world events partly in terms of unconscious processes like these presents readers with a strange set of concepts to evaluate. That can make it hard to get consensus without some sort of interactive procedure such as the one we essayed. Even this can be difficult, given issues such as the suspension of the law of contradiction in the unconscious: opposite feelings don't cancel each other out.

The Study Group

This inquiry involved, to an important extent, a group process, with group phenomena at work, including a sense of group membership that facilitated the interactions. David Beisel and the Czech political psychologists had important things in common that helped make such a group process work. A group that has some common ground for a start can argue and disagree, and gradually define and refine the nature of the disagreement and perhaps even come to agreement on some matters of importance.

The four substantive members of the study group share a commitment to understanding the Munich situation in the deepest possible way, an openness to the workings of psychodynamic factors, a commitment to scientific inquiry, and a generosity of spirit. And for the three Czechs, there were additional deep commonalities in their background. It may be helpful to detail these here.

Ivo Feierabend, Martina Klicperova-Baker, and Jana Svehlova are recognized authorities on the political psychology of modern Central Europe. They also had important personal experiences to contribute and so were informants as well as experts. Feierabend's father was in Masaryk's cabinet, and later in a postwar government cabinet, and twice had to flee for his life, once from the Nazis and once from the Communists, the second time taking young Ivo with him. Ivo Feierabend is Professor Emeritus of Political Science at San Diego State University.

Jana Svehlova's grandfather was in Benes's cabinet in wartime London. Her father went to England and fought with the Royal Air Force (RAF) in the defense of London. On his return to Czechoslovakia in 1949 he was imprisoned for ten years at hard labor by the Stalinist government as an "enemy of the state" because he had fought for the capitalist West by flying for the RAF. Svehlova founded and leads a support group, called "Daughters of Enemies of the State."

Martina Klicperova-Baker, now at the Institute of Psychology, Academy of Sciences of the Czech Republic, also lived through the Stalinist dictatorship in Czechoslovakia, in constant danger of arrest by the secret police. After the Velvet Revolution she conducted a long, recorded interview with Vaclav Havel, and presented him with an award in honor of his leadership and his contributions to the freedom of the Czech people.

The Scope of Our Collaboration

Beisel's book is a broad and deep scholarly work, extensively footnoted, and rich with verbatim quotations, covering many aspects of the events leading up to World War II. To make full use of the profound special expertise of the commentators, the collaboration focused on Czechoslovakia and the Munich crisis, as portrayed in the book itself, including its David Low cartoons. As a result of the Munich Agreement, first the Sudetenland and then the rest of Czechoslovakia was handed over to the Nazis without a shot being fired. This result is generally considered catastrophic and as a precipitator of the subsequent invasion of

Poland by the Nazis, which touched off World War II. There clearly were important psychodynamic components to this catastrophe, including emotionally driven cognitive distortions.

The Procedure for Our Collaboration

It will help the reader if we list here the phases of this complex and intense interaction.

Phase I: David Beisel gave each person a copy of the book.

Phase II: Ivo Feierabend, Martina Klicperova-Baker, and Jana Svehlova independently wrote comments on it and sent these to Beisel.

Phase III: Beisel then wrote a lengthy rejoinder to these comments.

Phase IV: This took place at a roundtable at the Annual Scientific Meeting of the International Society for Political Psychology (ISPP), in Istanbul on 9 July 2011, which was first suggested by Feierabend.

I chaired the roundtable in Istanbul, which presented the latest round of the interaction. We endeavored to find a deeper, common ground if possible. My own contribution was orchestrating the collaborative process.

The Delphi Technique and the Asch Experiments

In trying out a new method of inquiry, it is usually helpful to relate it to techniques previously used by others. This is good intellectual discipline and adds to the value of what is being done by giving it context. Moreover, reference to previous related techniques lessens the researcher's own anxiety, and by implying credibility rather than fecklessness, it may have the additional virtue of making the reader less anxious and skeptical. But, alas, I actually didn't have any previous technique in mind as we carried out the collaboration.

However, as I was writing this chapter it occurred to me to think about the Delphi technique as a way of reaching consensus among experts. Delphi involves iterative interaction among experts, each one submitting an estimate (this can be via computer if convenient), along with his or her reasoning to support it, then receiving the results and reasoning of the other experts, then submitting another estimate and further reasoning—repeated for as long as necessary to get group convergence on an estimate. I knew, however, that it is more suited to getting consensus among estimates of *quantitative* variables, such as future interest rates, or future global temperature levels, or the date when tigers will become extinct, or the appropriate limit on the national debt. I saw that Delphi is an elegant and underused procedure but at first I could not see a feasible application to the kinds of qualitative assertions characteristic of psychodynamic inquiries of all kinds.

But on further reflection I think that what that what we did can usefully be thought of as a qualitative application of the Delphi technique. I served metaphorically as the central clearing house, receiving email comments and forwarding them to David Beisel and then to the other collaborators as permission to do so was given. David Beisel then forwarded his replies to the others through me. This procedure was repeated iteratively through several rounds. In the paper I gave as Chair of the ISPP roundtable on *The Suicidal Embrace*, I, as facilitator, offered my own comments. And I believe the interaction will continue after the roundtable.

It surprises me that I did not see sooner the analogy between the Delphi technique and what we did in the collaboration. The Delphi technique is essentially a procedure for structured iterative symbolic interaction, to create shared meanings.

However, there have been complaints about Delphi in the literature, on the basis that the results are susceptible to manipulation by the person "facilitating" it. This possibility brings to mind the famous experiment carried out by the psychologist Solomon Asch at Swarthmore College (1951, 1955, 1956), described in Chapter 2. That experiment established that a false group consensus can exert pressure on individual members to change their judgments. Also relevant is the work by Irving Janis (1972, 1982) on "groupthink" in which dissenting views are overwhelmed. This may well happen in some applications of Delphi. But one thing I am sure of is that the individual experts who formed our own collaborative effort had deep and strong backgrounds in the area examined and were persuaded if at all only by rational arguments and not by emotional pressures to agree. Whatever the process we have invented may be termed, it appears to foster, rather than constrain, individual judgments.

Withal, it is apparent that what we undertook together—iterative collaboration between a social scientist and potential critics—is an experiment in the sense described by Abraham Kaplan, "poking nature with a stick to see what happens." As far as we knew, no one had yet tried this procedure with a psychodynamic oeuvre. Nobody knew if it would work or how it would turn out.

Setting Forth the Various Views

Firstly, I will set forth David Beisel's themes, and the various commentaries and responses to the commentaries.

For clarity, and to guide the reader through this intense, rich, and emotionally laden material, I will offer brief comments in italics as we go along.

Subsequently, I will look at the pattern of interactions as a whole, to see if convergence or some other phenomenon emerges from the iterative interactions.

Phase I: The Beisel Book, *The Suicidal Embrace*

The following assertions of David Beisel, among the dozens in his book, proved to be of special interest to the three Czech political psychologists (italicized headings are mine, for the purposes of summary):

1. *European leaders spoke of Europe as a human body, with a head, a torso, and various organs, and Czechoslovakia as a diseased organ, and as an appendix that might have to be cut out and removed*

   To Winston Churchill, a problem of Europe after the First World War, as he said at the time, was "a poisoned Russia, an infected Russia, a plague-bearing Russia. ..."

   Czech Ambassador Jan Masaryk said he "felt that Chamberlain spent most of his official time explaining that Czechoslovakia was a country and not a contagious disease."

   American diplomat George F. Kennan said that after the Munich crisis of 1938 the Hungarian and Polish governments helped themselves the spoils by beginning to "rend...bits...from the flesh of the stricken country."

   In the summer of 1930 the Polish press and the Polish leaders had told the world they would fight for Danzig because Danzig made up the "lungs" of the Polish economy.

   B.H. Liddell Hart said in his 1930 book *The Real War* that "Germany's arteries were subjected to an invisible pressure which never relaxed."

   In Britain, wrote one diplomatic observer at the time, Hitler's demands on Czechoslovakia were seen as a "beautiful plan of bringing about a peaceful amputation," although other people felt that

"German opinion did not favor a surgical operation for the amputation of the Sudeten."

Goring...said that "Czechoslovakia is the vermiform appendix of Europe! We shall have to operate."

When the immediate war crisis was temporarily ended by the Munich accord, Chamberlain told the House of Commons that it had been "a painful and difficult operation," but that "the operation was a success."

Nearly every book or article on the Czech Crisis sooner or later gets around to speaking of "the dismemberment of Czechoslovakia..."

Almost all scholars have concluded that Hitler's language reveals his fantasy that Germany was an organism..."the Polish Corridor...is like a strip of flesh cut from our body...a national wound that bleeds continuously, and will continue to bleed until the land is returned to us."

2. *European leaders spoke of Europe as though it were a family, with Germany as a disruptive teenager*

   The use by diplomats and the media of phrases such as "the family of nations. ... The courtship was over...the Russian game of pitting its suitors against each other...family squabbles." [Beisel advocates] "taking seriously the political cartoon of the Nazi–Soviet Non-Aggression Treaty showing Stalin as Hitler's bride, or another cartoon from the Sunday Graphic showing Hitler as Stalin's bride."

3. *The idea of "sacrifice" of Czechoslovakia*

   On 20 September 1938 *The Times* of London spoke of the "Czech government's sacrifice."

   Masaryk's son, Jan Masaryk, Czech Ambassador to London...told Chamberlain and Halifax "if you have sacrificed my nation to preserve the peace of the world, I will be the first to applaud you. But if not, gentlemen, God help your souls."

   Benes, who had succeeded Thomas Masaryk as President after Tomas Masaryk's death a year before the crisis, later declared his government had accepted the Munich solution as "a sacrifice for world peace."

4. *The perception of Czechoslovakia as "small" and "weak," and as an infant who could not survive and would have to be sacrificed*

> ...the British repeatedly spoke of Czechoslovakia (and other smaller countries) as "wretched little places...half the size of Yorkshire," "snuffling little countries," and "funny little people."
>
> ...the infant Czechoslovakia saw light on October 28, 1918.
>
> A wrong step might have killed the baby state before it was born.
>
> On the eve of Munich, Churchill gave a statement to the press in which he noted the "fatal delusion" of believing "that security could be obtained by throwing a small state to the wolves."

5. *Themes of suicide and martyrdom in the Czech leadership, media, and populace*

> But if the end of Czechoslovakia was imagined in unconscious fantasy as Europe's infant or child sacrifice, the Czechs imagined it to be their own mass suicide. "Are we to commit suicide?" asked the headlines of Czech newspapers on 2 September 1938. It was a rhetorical question since they already knew the answer.
>
> [A journalist observed that] British policy was "compelling Benes to commit suicide in order to forestall murder."
>
> That was what the powers unconsciously wanted, and such statements clued the Czechs that this was to be their fate.
>
> The Czechs seemed willing to be sacrificed...In Masaryk and Benes, Czechoslovakia and the family of Europe had found the perfect leaders to carry out the sacrifice. ... The personalities of Masaryk and Benes made them specially suitable candidates for Europe's delegated suicidal commands. ... This was clearly the case with Masaryk, whose life was obsessed with one central theme: suicide. His first published work was *Suicide and Civilization.* He regularly returned to the theme...in essays and in his book on Tolstoy and Turgenev...
>
> The historian A.J.P. Taylor speaks of Masaryk's "observation that the Czechs had a disposition to martyrdom."
>
> [Beisel then argues that Benes was "psychologically merged" with Masaryk and shared the same mentality.]

Phase II: The First Round of Comments

Having read the above materials and the relevant chapters in David Beisel's book, the Czech political psychologists commented.

II.A. Martina Klicperova-Baker Takes a Different View From Beisel's Chapter on Czechoslovakia.

Martina Klicperova-Baker says that Beisel's view is, in effect, "blaming the victim," and she "finds it absurd to speak of Masaryk as a suicide-obsessed maniac. I know him as an admirable constructive realistic pragmatic politician."

Klicperova-Baker also disagrees with the idea of a Czech martyr complex:

> although patriotic Czechs were ready to mobilize and defend the country, they never intended a martyr path...the Czechs did not go martyr-like as did, say, the Polish army when ill-equipped soldiers on horses faced German tanks...there are always more than two alternatives. ... There were plenty of other coping strategies than dying. Rational coping would be one of them...there was always gallows humor—after all, according to Oberdlik (1947) humor as a sociological phenomenon was first described in the Czechs during the Nazi occupation...only very rare suicides from desperation immediately following the Nazi occupation. ... Immense sadness from the Munich betrayal...rational coping...gallows humor and collaboration for survival, yes. But pathological suicides on any significant level? I do not think so.

II.B. Ivo Feierabend's View Also Differs From Beisel's

Ivo Feierabend feels that the interest in suicide was only a tiny part of Masaryk's personality and life:

> To try to interpret Masaryk's scholarly output, personality, statesmanship in reference to just one criterion strikes me as a reductio ad absurdum. He was a towering figure, a giant of moral integrity, what comes to mind is humanism, then life in truth (adopted later by Vaclav Havel) democracy, anti-anti-Semitism, human and minority rights, civic nationalism, pax democratica, transcendentalist religious sensibility, realism...also those who wanted to fight at Munich,

> many commanding generals wanted to, argued that Masaryk would have fought.

Feierabend adds,

> Concerning Beneš, it was said that he overplayed his role in Geneva, resented by many diplomats for his staunch defense of the Versailles order and the League of Nations. To reconcile this perspective with a suicidal or sacrificial or martyr-like inclination would be fanciful, to say the least.

Feierabend refers to the courageous military tradition of the Czechs, which he feels disproves the idea that there was "suicide or sacrifice or martyr-like inclination in the Czech mentality or in Masaryk." He says,

> The ethos of the First Republic had to do with the heroic Czechoslovak Legions of WWI [World War I] that earned the Czechoslovak independence and which fit neatly with the historical, heroic tradition of the Hussite wars. This was the proud staple of Czechoslovak socialization and my own: A rather cocky, self-assured stance (à la another small nation later on, the early Israel) with Sokol, scouting, Masaryk and patriotism with a good measure of democratic civic culture. Masaryk was the exemplar of all that.

He continues,

> How is it possible to reconcile such an ethos with the thesis of "suicide" and "sacrifice" presented in the chapter? And a corollary question: How can it be reconciled with the Czech Army, allegedly the best little army in the world, of 1.5 million soldiers, 2000 airplanes, a just finished little Maginot Line mostly in the Sudetenland and the two gung-ho mobilizations during 1938?

Finally, Feierabend argues that:

> The Czechoslovaks, their leadership and Beneš at Munich, perceived correctly that they were presented with Sophie's Choice: Alone in an impossible war with Hitler, or a truncated state at Hitler's mercy. To this day the Czechs argue the choices. How can such an extreme avoidance–avoidance conflict be mistaken for sacrifice, suicide on the part of the Czechs?

II.C. Jana Svehlova's Initial View is Rather Different From Those of Martina Klicperova-Baker and Ivo Feierabend

Jana Svehlova and Gregory Moore write:

> Beisel's chapter "Czechoslovakia" within the context of "the Origins of the Second World War," immediately invites a distinction between the fantasies of people in Slovakia and in the Czech lands. Because, as Arendt points out: "The Slovaks had come to Berlin to negotiate their 'independence' even before the Germans occupied Czechoslovakia, in March, 1939." The Czechs, according to Beisel "seemed willing to be sacrificed." He continues, using Pynsent's study of Czechs and Slovaks that "Czechs had a predisposition to martyrdom," and adds that the predisposition has become known as the "Czech martyr complex." However, it needs to be clarified whether the Czechs were *willing to be sacrificed* by someone else, by themselves, or was that a perception [or a state of denial] of their leader, President Dr. Edvard Beneš.

They continue:

> Based on Beisel's notion "fantasies are rooted in the history and linguistic formulations of a particular group at a particular moment" in his well-researched book, martyrdom is rooted in the Czech psyche as two different entities. One applies to the martyrs who are willing to sacrifice *themselves* for their causes. Czech pilots who were willing to sacrifice their lives, out of patriotism, when they joined the RAF during WWII [World War II] to fight Nazi Germany are a case in point. Even though, Czech students learn about their national martyrs differently, depending on the political climate in the country. For example, the same pilots who survived WWII and returned home became "traitors" in the postwar Czech communist lexicon. The accusation came from their willingness to sacrifice their lives by fighting with the Western Allies. Those who tortured them stayed behind. The Czech lands during the Nazi occupation were run "in 1942 by just 1,900 German bureaucrats" (Judt) because Czechs satisfied the occupiers' demands.
>
> The more appropriate opinion is Beisel's "predisposition to martyrdom," as part of the Czech identity when interpreted as self-pitying, *victimology*, and faulting others. For example, during the Stalinist era of the 1950s the Czechs executed more people than any other European communist country. Today, instead of reflecting on the past, their tendency is to say, "The Soviets did the interrogations [only a few KGB advisors were present but 250,000 people were

imprisoned]. Self-pitying is a component of the Czech discourse; it comes in many forms. I have experienced the wallowing of Czech tourists about their inadequate pensions while proudly showing their latest camera models. The self-pitying of "how much work" one has, while spending an hour on the phone talking about it, is another one.

Whereas self-pitying is a linguistic formulation of the particular group in question, Beisel's judgment elevating Czechs' admiration for Edvard Beneš to the level of admiration for their "taticek" (diminutive of father), Tomas G. Masaryk is a Western fantasy "rooted in the history and linguistic formulations of a particular group at a particular moment."

On the other hand, three dominant linguistic formulations are rooted in the Czech collective consciousness about President Edvard Beneš. One, questioning his judgment when in exile in England. He agreed to send a group of parachutists to kill Hitler's representative in Prague Reinhard Heydrich, known as "The Hangman." The assassination in 1942—in the middle of a brutal war—resulted in *Heydrichiáda,* a Czech term used for German reprisals such as murdering of thousands of Czechs, the destruction of the villages Lidice and Lezaky, and an immediate transport of a thousand Jews to a death camp. Two, the *Beneš decrees,* when in May 1945, President Edvard Beneš "declared that Czechs and Slovaks no longer wished to live in the same state as Hungarians and Germans. This sentiment, and the actions that followed, haunted Czech–German and Slovak–Hungarian relations ever since" (Judt, 2007). Three, the relationship of Beneš with Stalin, another linguistic formulation echoed by Richard Crampton: "Now Beneš was seen as the man who...had been tricked by the communists and done nothing to frustrate their machinations in 1948, and above all the man who had been mesmerized by Stalin and who had signed away half of Czechoslovakia's independence in the Moscow treaty of December 1943.

In defense of Beneš, he did not have a chance to protect his nation when Western power brokers Chamberlain and Daladier "sold" Czechoslovakia to Hitler. Beneš writes from London in November 1938, "I shall never say that I do not have a responsibility; that it is someone else's...It is true, based on our Constitution, I was not responsible; the cabinet was. But it is also true that during the crucial moments I had the greatest influence and the cabinet did not want to do anything without my decisions, but it is also true that they always agreed with my decisions..." (my translation).

However, Beisel's chapter on Czechoslovakia is not about history per se, it is about historical figures within the context of *The Suicidal Embrace.* Beisel includes that Masaryk..."was obsessed with one central theme—suicide." Is it suicide, or is it society's "illness" as the cause of suicide, that interested Masaryk? Based on Durkheim's suicide analysis, Masaryk's is the anomic one that goes along with the lack of raison d'être. Tomas G. Masaryk in *Modern Suicide* points out "suicide is a modern social disease; it is an illness of modern civilization. ... The battle or a war hits you in the eye. But those thousands and thousands that die without being noticed, nobody is noticing that...; it is perceived as something inevitable. ... Today it is already an epidemic..."

Tomas G. Masaryk died in 1937; therefore, he was spared seeing his nation "sold" by Britain and France to Hitler on that fateful day in Munich in 1938. His successor, President Beneš, according to Beisel, exclaimed that "the Czechs...[were] doomed to the sacrifice and exulting in its fate" is not rooted as a history formulation among the people he singles out. On the contrary, forty years of communist totalitarianism, and the Czech Communist Party in third place seventeen years after the *fall of the wall*, is a fantasy "rooted in the history and linguistic formulations of a particular group at a particular moment."

Phase III: David Beisel's Response to the Comments

David Beisel's response focuses on the generality of the view in Europe that Czechoslovakia was an infant within the European family: He says:

> The child-fantasy (the Czech state as a newborn) was abroad in Europe, existed in the minds of many who thought and wrote about the international situation and international affairs at the time. The fantasy of Czechoslovakia as a child existed as one of the hidden transcripts in the European diplomacy of the time: it comes from the diplomatic documents of all the greater and lesser powers, is found in personal letters, public statements, cabinet meetings and media sources all over Europe—I didn't mean for it to be understood as a view shared in collective fantasy by the Czech people as a whole... although surely how the Czechs saw themselves in terms of the organic fantasy in general (society is a body/human organism) and how they understood their specific place in the general fantasy of the international family system must have been shaped in part by the views and fantasies of the international community of which they were a part and not just from their own self-definition.

He continues,

> Was the Czech state driven to the outcome that occurred as a result of some inner flaw? Not at all: it's not a matter of changeless national character...as much as it was a matter of the historical moment and the demands of the European family of nations at that moment.
>
> It was not as a result of some deeply ingrained moral failing in the national character...it was the *British* and *French* who were, in fantasy and in their own minds the imagined parents, midwives, or nurses; *they* were the ones who, on their side, were committing what amounted to a fantasy infanticide in 1938, and repeated it again in September 1939 by betraying the "infant" Poles in the same way.

Was the Munich outcome inevitable? Beisel "Couldn't disagree more about the Czech's being presented with what amounted to a 'Sophie's Choice.'" There were plenty of alternatives if the Allies had "banded together," they would have had "clear superiority" militarily, in "number of divisions, tanks, and aircraft available in their joint forces."

And Beisel argues that the Czechs were participants in the European fantasy system, and that Masaryk played a role in guiding this participation.

> I do not think Masaryk's scholarly obsession with suicide can be so easily dismissed as irrelevant...I was intent to show his role in creating an atmosphere, an emotional tone in the 1930s, for what Czech's themselves recognized and called a collective suicide. ... There was a role he played and guided the Czech state into playing in the European fantasy-system, a role encouraged by that European fantasy system and one Masaryk was inclined to play because of certain psychological predispositions in him...
>
> This didn't happen in a vacuum, but emerged out of the interactions of the deep collective fantasies of the European family which set-up the Czechs as a suicidal victim. As every study of small group social psychology has found, the group's chosen scapegoat is chosen in some sense because she/he has something in them which makes them in some ways unconsciously "willing" to play the role.

Beisel also argues that "the acknowledged heroism of the Czechs at many points in their history does not preclude unconscious fantasies about sacrifice, suicide, and martyrdom."

Phase IV: The Istanbul Conference Roundtable

IV.A. From David Beisel's Welcoming Presentation, to Begin the ISPP Istanbul Roundtable (Abstract for ISPP Roundtable on *The Suicidal Embrace*: "Factual, Interpretive, and Methodological Issues")

> I will be commenting on the final papers produced by the panel on the various aspects on my book-length study as delineated in the Roundtable Proposal submitted by William Meyers. My commentary will focus on factual, interpretive, and methodological issues emerging from the historical study itself and those related to evidence and the specific question of how scholars can identify fantasies collective and individual, conscious and unconscious embedded in the documents. I am particularly interested in engaging in a dialogue elaborating and exploring the scholarly and psychological strengths and weaknesses and broader implications of the methodological processes which the group members collectively employed before and now continue in the roundtable.

IV.B. From My Own Roundtable Introduction ("Munich and Czechoslovakia in a Psychodynamic Context: Re-Evaluating David Beisel's *The Suicidal Embrace*")

> The historian David Beisel's study, *The Suicidal Embrace: Hitler, the Allies, and the Origins of the Second World War*, inquires into the psychological components of the tragic Munich crisis of 1938. The book provoked an extensive discussion, particularly among Czech psychologists and political scientists. Ivo Feierabend, Martina Klicperova-Baker, and Jana Svehlova are authorities on the political psychology of modern Central Europe. In addition, they have personal or family experience with the highest levels of the Czechoslovak or Czech or Slovak governments, and each has lived through Nazi or Communist dictatorships, in peril of the secret police.
>
> These social scientists undertook an extensive interactive collaboration with David Beisel, involving an iterative exchange of comments and responses to comments, over several years, based on a symbolic interactionist theory of the creation of meaning.

The roundtable presents their views and those of David Beisel in response. Among the issues examined were: Did European political leaders before WWII think of Europe almost literally as an organism, and as a body with a diseased component that might have to be amputated to save the rest? Were European nations viewed by their leaders as a family with a disruptive member, Hitler? Was Czechoslovakia viewed as a newborn that might not survive? Was there suicidal ideation in the thinking of the Czechoslovak political leaders themselves? Do the David Low cartoons illuminate the role of humor in the face of tragedy? And, can our symbolic interactionist iterative method serve to properly modify, enrich or reject psychodynamic assertions?

IV.C. From Martina Klicperova-Baker's ISPP Istanbul Roundtable Presentation ("Munich and the Czechs—A Psychological View")

A. Czechoslovakia of 1938 was placed in a negative dilemma: be dismembered "for peace for our time" (Chamberlain) or face Hitler alone and be "responsible for war" (France, England). It is unlikely that the Czechs and their elites, who had responded to the Nazi threat with mass manifestations and mobilization, were motivated by psychopathology as Beisel (2003) suggests. On the contrary, one can suppose mature patriotic, civic and democratic motivation for life, and for the defense of the republic rather than for death. When the military strategy of opposing Hitler failed, then other, mostly survivalist coping style followed. The rhetoric presenting Czechoslovakia as a child or an embryo downgraded its status and trivialized its dismemberment. The crisis of 1938 will be reviewed in points: 1. Blaming the victim. 2. Sophie's choice. 3. Revival of Hussite and legionary legacies. 4. Disappointment in democrats and democracy. 5. Nonviolent conflict resolution and a rational approach to a moral dilemma. 6. Coping and gallows humor as a sociological phenomenon, cartoons and jokes.

B. The contemporary Czech Republic and a possible Munich legacy in recent empirical findings. 1. Czech national mentalities: democrats, bonvivant social liberals, opportunists. 2. Perception of highs and lows in the Czech history. 3. Ethnic tolerance and intolerance. 4. The Czech heroes

Conclusion: Even provocative stimuli for reviewing pivotal historical points are useful for making our past alive and useful.

IV.D. From Ivo Feierabend's Roundtable Presentation ("David R. Beisel's *The Suicidal Embrace* vs. Sophie's Choice: The Czechs, Masaryk, Beneš, and the Munich Crisis.")

The apex of appeasements was reached at Munich. Telford Taylor (cited by Beisel, 204) and recently Niall Ferguson maintained that if the war had been declared that fateful September, 1938, it would have been a bagatelle compared to WWII. The Twentieth Century might have unfolded without Hitler and the Holocaust, Stalin and the Soviet superpower, the communist contagion, the atom bomb and the Cold War. Munich's irrationality makes Beisel's scholarly excursion in psychodynamic inquiry very attractive. Starting with Melanie Klein's little Richard (13) and quoting R.D. Laing, Beisel wonders "why international relations are almost always studied as economics, power, or strategic necessity, hardly ever as family relations" (32). Consequently, the "suicidal embrace" includes the "family of nations" complete with child rearing practices, the "Versailles nurses," "early traumas of humiliation," "sacrifice" and much more. The analysis is ingenious and persuasive, especially discussing Britain and Prime Minister Chamberlin with his ubiquitous umbrella. However, in Czechoslovakia, the idiom seems less than valid. There, the "suicidal embrace" was coerced. Munich presented the prosperous, democratic nation with the impossible choice to fight Nazi Germany alone, or become its vassal. The salient Czech perception of Munich was not "sacrifice" or "martyrdom," but Western zrada, i.e., both betrayal and treason, and the "family of nations" is not a part of the Czech vocabulary. Also, suicide was hardly Masaryk's obsessive "central theme" (199), but just one among many, of a prolific professor, politician and statesman. Perhaps his dedication to "truth" is noteworthy (in Hannah Arendt's sense of prohibition to lie and later the legacy of Vaclav Havel with his "life in truth," and still today the inscription "truth will prevail," on the presidential flag flying over Prague Castle). Besides, Masaryk missed the Munich crisis. As President, he abdicated in 1935 and died in 1937, while Beneš's status as his epigone is overstated.

IV.E. From Jana Svehlova's ISPP Roundtable Paper

Since she could not attend the Istanbul Conference, Jana Svehlova kindly circulated a paper several months before the Conference. I had the pleasure of reading excerpts from it on her behalf at the roundtable.

Svehlova begins by making a distinction between the Czechs and the Slovaks:

> Beisel's analysis immediately invites a distinction between fantasies of people in Slovakia and in the Czech Republic, not because Czechoslovakia split peacefully into two distinct countries in January 1993. But, as Hannah Arendt submits, "the Slovaks had come to Berlin to negotiate their 'independence' even before the Germans occupied Czechoslovakia in March, 1939."

If I understand Svehlova correctly, this quotation appears to be a way of saying that the Slovak people were less willing than the Czech people to be sacrificed, or commit suicide, or become martyrs.

Svehlova feels that "What needs to be clarified is whether the Czechs were willing to sacrifice themselves; or whether they were sacrificed by others..."

Svehlova argues that:

> Martyrdom in the Czech psyche can be interpreted as two different entities. One applies to the martyrs who are willing to sacrifice themselves for their causes. Czech (and Slovak) men, for instance, were willing to sacrifice their lives when they joined the Royal Air Force in England during World War II to fight Nazi Germany. Many left their homeland out of patriotism to help the Allies with defeating the enemy. Others, for reasons only they knew. But all of them were aware of the price luring in the sky.

Svehlova then goes on to argue that there is what I might paraphrase as a tendency to resignation, or passive or active collaboration, in the Czech mentality.

Beisel's book covers the situation up to 1939, but Svehlova believes that subsequent events cast important light on Beisel's question. While Ivo Feierabend refers to Czech heroism in World War I, before the period Beisel covers, Svehlova deals extensively with the post-1939 period during World War II (WWII), and then with the long period after 1945. So different "databases" are being referred to within the collaboration.

For example, Svehlova says:

> The same RAF pilots who survived WWII and returned home became "traitors" in the postwar Czech communist lexicon. This denunciation was hurled at them by those who stayed behind. The alleged crime was spying for the former Western friends who became an arch enemy after the Second World War during the Cold War. Some of those who tortured them in order to obtain signed admissions to

> invented charges performed their duty out of belief that the accused was a bona fide enemy of the state. Others were torturers out of fear of being found out that they were collaborators of the Gestapo. It is significant, that the Czech lands during the Nazi occupation needed to be governed only by "1,900 German bureaucrats because the natives satisfied the occupiers' demands" (Judt, 2007).

Svehlova goes on to, in effect, elaborate on Beisel's formulation and develop it further than Beisel did, relying on postwar events:

> Beisel's concept of *predisposition to martyrdom,* as part of the Czech identity invites further inquiries into notions such as resignation, *victimology,* and faulting others. For example, during the Stalinist era of the 1950s the Czechs executed more of their own people than any other European communist country. Today, instead of reflecting on the past, their tendency is to say: "The Soviets did the interrogations." Yet, archive documents show few KGB (Soviet Secret Police) advisors were present during interrogations. Since 250,000 people out of a population of ten million were imprisoned; the interrogators were mainly their Czech fellow citizens. Blaming the Nazis, the Soviets, and the Communists further silences the former immediate victims.

Evidently agreeing substantially with Beisel, Svehlova asserts:

> Sacrifice and martyrdom are components of the Czech discourse. ... Beisel illustrates the psychodynamics at play when he mentions German and Italian Foreign Ministers Ribbentrop and Ciano establishing a new Czech border in 1938, and the Czechs accepted it without a word.

As for Beneš, Svehlova quotes Richard Crampton:

> Now Beneš was seen as the man who...had been tricked by the communists and done nothing to frustrate their machinations in 1948, and above all the man who had been mesmerized by Stalin and who had signed away half of Czechoslovakia's independence in the Moscow treaty of December 1943.

Results Concerning the Three Propositions of David Beisel

It is noteworthy that there was no explicit rejection of David Beisel's central contention, that European leaders thought of Europe as an organism, a human body, with the nations representing various organs. There was one dissent from Beisel's central contention that European leaders thought of Europe as a "family of nations."

Ivo Feierabend wrote:

> The notion that specifically Bohemia is in the heart of Europe, is rather old. I have someplace, a late medieval depiction of it, a princess and her heart. The Czech language I do not think devised a "family of nations." In literal translation it sounds very strange and awkward. Perhaps, large and secure, self-congratulatory nations may do so. For the small ones, who may well fear for their existence, there are too many bullies out there, or too much disinterest.

It became evident during the collaboration that Ivo Feierabend and Martina Klicperova-Baker emphatically disagreed with David Beisel on the third proposition, the presence of strong masochistic, self-sacrificing, and suicidal themes in the thinking and writings of the Czechoslovak leadership, media, and populace, and Jana Svehlova largely and emphatically agreed with Beisel on this issue. Agreement on the third proposition could not be reached, but the issues were defined with clarity and depth, and in that sense a much greater understanding was obtained.

Results in Terms of Iterative Methodology

Early in this collaboration I had wondered if the interaction would produce a *consensus* of views, or a *vector*, in which several forces in similar directions result in one force in a particular direction, such as a developing line of analysis or inquiry. Or perhaps it would produce a *fugue*, in which a theme is repeated but with elaborations and creative variations, or a perhaps a *variorum edition* in which small textual changes are presented.

What we found was surprising: *alternative conceptualizations of events.* The dissenting and concurring formulations were psychodynamic, couched in terms of underlying psychological mechanisms. This result came about for the following reasons. Ivo Feierabend, Martina Klicperova-Baker, and Jana Svehlova were the experts in Central European political psychology. But they also served in another role. What the collaboration had created was a group of experts on the political psychology of Central Europe, who were also members of the Czech and Slovak cultures being studied. With their deep personal involvement and experiences in these cultures, they served as *co-researchers* with David Beisel. This kind of collaboration is analogous to the role of the *informant* in anthropological studies: providing insights that non-members of the culture could never provide.

As a result, what emerged was not only a series of critiques by substantive experts, but it was also much more: what emerged from the collaboration was a series of *alternative conceptualizations of events*. It was as if the psychodynamic forces within Czechoslovakia before, during, and after the Munich crisis could be viewed through different optical instruments, sensitive to different wavelengths. Our experiment in collaboration, our version of the symbolic interactionist creation of meaning, had produced *a set of portraits in different wavelengths of light*. This is different from, but perhaps deeper than, a simple consensus. Each alternative formulation offers new material and new insights. Alternative portraits of the Czechoslovak leaders Tomas Masaryk and Edvard Beneš, and alternative depictions of the Czechoslovak mentality and national culture, have been produced by our Central European specialists who are also members of the Czech or Slovak cultures.

The alternative conceptualizations from the Czech experts are presented by representatives of different generations and different academic fields, and by people with very different personal experiences in the Czechoslovak culture, and so they contrast with each other. This result is to be expected on the basis of the theory of ideology and bias. Karl Mannheim believed that no view was without bias, either in what is included and what is left out, how the issues are posed (what we today call "framing"), and in the position taken on these issues. The bias he believed would in almost all cases stem from, or at least be consistent with, the person's role and social position, and with the person's ethnic and cultural identifications.

By understanding these background factors, the reader or hearer could take the bias into account to some extent. Almost all biased formulations, according to Mannheim, also contain insights and elements of truth. By taking several into account one could obtain a more veridical overall picture. I think this is true of our alternative conceptualizations from our Czechoslovak experts responding to the work of an American social scientist.

The Role of the David Low Cartoons

The 16 cartoons by David Low, chosen from Low's classic *A Cartoon History of our Time* (1939) form a powerful part of *The Suicidal Embrace*. Primitive fantasies, family dysfunction among European nations, dismemberment of a European body, unconscious agendas, and denial of reality, are among the psychic mechanisms manifest in these cartoons. As a result, they, too, form a parallel to David's text.

It strikes me that two voices expressing these ideas are so much more powerful than just one. Two voices independently proposing these ideas rebuts the objection that these formulations are idiosyncratic, that is, characteristic of only one person.

The psychology of dissent is also involved. Solomon Asch's experiments disclosed that if one person dissents from a false group consensus, that frees others to dissent. Irving Janis' research on "groupthink" shows something similar: in order for the creation of a monolithic group viewpoint to proceed, every single dissent must be squelched. This is one reason authoritarian regimes are so vicious toward individual dissenters. If even one person dissents, others are encouraged to do so.

The inclusion of the David Low cartoons frees the writer to proceed with the challenging approach involved in psychodynamic inquiry. The cartoons also free the reader to consider this approach as a serious and credible one. It is again evident that the creation of meaning arises from the interaction among people.

The Iterative Method Assessed

The particular iterative method we used in this experiment involved substantive experts who were also members of the culture being studied. We found that this procedure generates not simple consensus but alternative psychodynamic formulations that, taken together, greatly enrich the discussion. I therefore feel safe in recommending this method as a useful procedure in cross-cultural kinds of inquiry.

My Own View of *The Suicidal Embrace*

At this point, having completed my enabling role as a Figaro figure, it is perhaps no longer inappropriate to express my own view of *The Suicidal Embrace.*

I find the book to be obviously very scholarly, carefully researched, and buttressed with myriads of footnotes, references, and, especially, verbatim quotations that I feel are very probative. This book is an important contribution.

One of David Beisel's main contentions is that the leaders of European nations explicitly thought of Europe as a family of nations. Czechoslovakia was viewed as an infant nation that might not be viable and might not survive. On the evidence presented, especially the verbatim quotations, I feel this is incontestably true of the leaders of the large nations, England, France, and Germany.

A second contention is that Europe was viewed also as an organism, a body, and that Czechoslovakia was viewed as a vermiform appendage that might have to be cut out to save the organism. Again, I think that on the evidence presented by Beisel, especially the verbatim quotations, this was incontestably true of the leaders of England, France, and Germany.

I found no evidence that the Czechoslovak leaders or media at all bought into these two metaphors or fantasies.

A third contention of the Beisel book is that the child-rearing techniques of the European nations influenced the mentality of these children when they grew up to be the nation's leaders. This general idea has been widely derided when presented by others elsewhere but, interestingly, no one has denied that the German authoritarian family structure and its influence on child rearing had a great effect on the mentality of German leaders and followers as adults. It seems to me that David Beisel overstates its importance for England and France, but given the truly weird child-rearing practices that Beisel describes for these two countries, I infer that child-rearing practices may have had a non-zero influence on the personalities, if not the policies, of the leadership in England and France.

Where there was substantial disagreement among the members of the collaboration was on the mentality of the Czechoslovak leadership and media and populace, particularly the allegation that there were important suicidal themes present. It is on this last issue that the interactive collaboration focused and from which the parallel formulations emerged.

Our Experts as Informants

It is important that our three Czech experts also served as *informants* about the Czech culture, in the social anthropological sense. Let us look at that issue a bit further.

An anthropologist often studies a culture whose language and customs the anthropologist does not know at the beginning of a long stay in the culture. This is typically handled by the use of an *informant, a member of the culture* who befriends the anthropologist and tells him or her what the rituals mean, what the customs mean, and helps to teach the anthropologist the language. What is accomplished in this way is technically called "*verstehen,*" a German word that means, in this context, an understanding by the anthropologist, attained in part through the informant, of the customs, practices, and cultural meanings in the culture being studied. Informants are also used by field sociologists within subcultures of American society: "Doc" was the informant in *Street Corner Society* (Whyte, 1943 [1993]). The informant becomes a colleague and a de facto co-researcher.

Each of our three substantive academic experts on the political psychology of Central Europe had deep personal experience with the Czechoslovak culture, having grown up there, having lived under Nazi or Communist regimes, or both, and having Czech as their native language. Even leaving aside their impressive substantive academic expertise, their membership in the Czech culture and these personal experiences qualified them as informants, and this greatly enriched the study.

Sequel: When Informants Disagree: A Startling Proposal

But the academic literature is silent on the situation where informants disagree sharply. This isn't supposed to happen. One gets multiple rich but contradictory insights. Which ones should we emphasize? As I was mulling over what to do when informants don't agree, I received a startling email from Martina Klicperova-Baker:

> Hi Bill,
>
> I browsed through internet second hand bookstores in Czech R. and I found a book which my Grandma use to have, it is a unique collection of hundred(s) of poems which were written and published in Czechoslovakia around the first mobilization and Munich. Very strong reading. I can try to make a content analysis—I think it would be also a nice illustration, in some ways a contrast to Low's caricatures.

A Sequel: Popperian Disconfirmation in the Czech Case

Martina Klicperova-Baker's decision to content-analyze the poems permits a *formal test of the validity* of David Beisel's assertion about suicidal themes in Czechoslovak culture in the Munich era. Using the *Popperian disconfirmation paradigm* discussed in Chapter 4, one could construct *formal predictions* as to material these poems *must* contain if the Beisel assertion about suicidal ideation is valid.

Why would is such a formal test helpful? Let me review the results of the consensus obtained and not obtained by the symbolic interactive collaboration. It appears to me that there is consensus about two of Beisel's main themes. First, Beisel demonstrates with extensive verbatim quotations that the leaders and media of the European nations spoke of the European nations as a family, with a disruptive adolescent, Hitler, and an infant, Czechoslovakia, who might not survive. Second, the leaders and media also spoke of Europe as an organism, a human body with a head, a heart, and lungs (Danzig was the lungs for Germany), and a vermiform appendix, an appendix, Czechoslovakia, that was infected and must be cut off. I believe Beisel's verbatim quotations are easily sufficient to convince most readers that European leaders and the media were thinking consciously and unconsciously of a family of nations, and of Europe as an organism.

However, Beisel has an additional thesis, that the thinking and speeches and writings of the leaders of Czechoslovakia, Tomas Masaryk and Edvard Benes, showed great concern with themes of suicide, and these themes also appeared in the popular media and in Czech culture generally. But the verbatim quotations were not extensive enough, or perhaps apposite enough, to convince two of the Czech political psychologists, Klicperova-Baker and Ivo Feierabend, who read the Beisel book with me. They strongly dissented. But Jana Svehlova, the third Czech political psychologist, strongly concurred with Beisel on the themes of suicide and sacrifice. The collaboration illuminated this difference and the reasons for it, but did not resolve it.

The Popperian procedure helps us here. It consists of predicting data that must exist or the hypothesis is disconfirmed. It is a great good fortune that Klicperova-Baker chanced upon a book of collected poems from the period immediately before and during the Czech crisis, a long-forgotten book her grandmother had read. Klicperova-Baker then undertook a quantitative content analysis of the poems, looking for themes of suicide or sacrifice or despair. She reports in a paper to be published that she found very few. But by Popperian prediction, there had to be many instances, or the Beisel hypothesis of suicidal ideation in the Czech media and culture stands disconfirmed. While one instance is not determinative, since there are few or no critical experiments in the social sciences, Klicperova's results strike a significant blow to the Beisel formulation of the Czech mentality.

One of the strengths of the Klicperova-Baker content analysis is that she studied not one poem but a large number of poems, a *sample* of poems. I have argued in Chapter 8 on the merits of sampling in clinically psychodynamic investigations of world events, even where 100% sampling, or true random sampling, is not possible.

Klicperova-Baker's sample was a *judgment sample,* as explained by Michael Quinn Patton in *Qualitative Research and Evaluation Methods*

(2014). Judgment samples are non-random; they are cases drawn for a specific purpose on the basis of someone's judgment. In this case, the purpose was to assemble the best poems of that era, not to serve a research purpose. This literary purpose had the effect of eliminating any researcher bias in the actual drawing of the sample, and so it strengthens Klicperova-Baker's test of Beisel's hypothesis about Czech suicidal ideation.

Prediction and Replication in the Czech Case

Martina Klicperova-Baker was an excellent informant, as well as a substantive expert. We also recognize that a Czech patriot understandably has views on the subject of the Czech mentality. A study such as hers will gain increased probative value when repeated elsewhere by other researchers with different national affiliations and different national commitments. In science generally, the results from one study or one laboratory are taken as probative only if they have been repeated with similar results by similar studies at other locations by other researchers. This repetition is called "replication."

Assessing Researcher Bias

One can see that if several people at Martina Klicperova-Baker's own laboratory independently performed a content analysis on this book of poems, it would help the probative value of her study. Consistency among raters is called "inter-rater reliability." It is reassuring if independent raters within a study turn out to agree with each other in their ratings. This is a kind of replication within a study. It makes the original study stronger. But to rule out bias by a whole research group, or other factors idiosyncratic to a particular research setting, it is still important to *replicate* the study *in other settings by other researchers*.

Implicit in all of this discussion is the Popperian prediction that the replications will produce data similar to the original data. If they do not, the study hypothesis is disconfirmed. Replication is a complex and powerful scientific procedure involving Popperian disconfirmation, and resort to replication would go far toward improving the validity and credibility of psychodynamic inquiry.

The Benefits of Unobtrusive Measures

In a classic study, Webb and Campbell (1966) explain the benefits of what they term *unobtrusive measures* and *non-reactive research.*

Unobtrusive measures are those that don't alter the situation that you want to study. Non-reactive research is research that doesn't cause change in the people studied that could affect the results.

For example, personal interviews, questionnaires, observations of teachers in the classroom all change the situation: the respondent to the questionnaire or interview starts to think anew about the issues and about the fact that he or she is being studied. The teacher in the classroom may change his or her actions because of the observer.

While admitting the contributions of reactive study procedures, Webb and Campbell suggest that we try to avoid relying on them solely. In a classic example, they suggest that instead of only asking people which museum exhibits they prefer, why not measure the wear on the floor in front of each exhibit?

How might this insight apply to our Munich study? In addition to predicting to archival data such as poems of that era, we could predict that suicide rates, and emergency hospital admissions for suicide risks, were higher in 1930 through 1938 in Czechoslovakia than in the other central European countries: Austria, Hungary, and Poland. But Austria is a special case in this comparison: as Nazi troops marched into Austria, following the Anschluss of 10 March 1938, there were waves of suicides.

Iterative Collaboration Versus Popperian Disconfirmation

In the present chapter we have illustrated the scope and persuasive power of an iterative collaborative approach rooted in the symbolic interactionist perspective. We have also seen that it may not always be sufficient in itself. Experts, and informants, can differ.

The collaborative method has the great advantage of yielding deep and rich insights. We surely found these in the correspondence and position papers in our collaboration.

However, the method of Popperian disconfirmation has the advantage of yielding a "yes or no" answer, especially if replicated, but the answer may be in the form of a rather sharply limited outcome variable.

I therefore view these two methods as complementary. A study that uses both has a greater chance of producing rich insights that are clearly valid.

Alternatives to Disconfirmation

We have found in this chapter a complex iterative collaboration that sheds a great deal of light on the problems we examined. It also presents an opportunity for a disconfirmative approach such as that taken by

Martina Klicperova-Baker in her study of the poetry in the era before and during the Munich crisis.

But is there any alternative to ultimate reliance on disconfirmation? We know from the "Law of Evidence" that corroboration by a second witness is extremely persuasive (see Best, 2014). But suppose, as in our case, the witnesses or informants do not entirely agree? Doesn't this failure to agree represent a disconfirmation of whatever assertion is being examined?

The "coherence theory of truth," expounded by one of my teachers, Professor C.I. Lewis, following in the tradition of Charles Sanders Pierce, presents a possibility. As I interpret it, coherence theory asks: "Do the various explanations or interpretations *cohere*, that is, fit together in a persuasive and stimulating way?" Not: "Do they coincide or provide one-to-one correspondence (= reliability)." Coherence theory is no longer a dominant force in modern philosophy but I find it a useful way of understanding the results of a collaborative effort. In my view, a coherence theory of truth implies a more Gestalt-like approach to confirmation and disconfirmation. If research results cohere in a way that stimulates further inquiry, the researcher may learn more than if they exactly coincided. I think this was the case in our collaboration.

As a practical application of coherence theory to weave together related explanatory propositions, one can follow the "contextualist" procedure proposed by William McGuire (1989). He suggests repeating a study with systematic planned variations to determine the boundaries within which an assertion holds. It seems to me that the boundary conditions, that is, the factors that delimit the applicability of the assertion, can be used to express the set of non-identical but cohering explanations.

A Final Boon

A final benefit from this experiment is that it has been a great pleasure working with this remarkable group of people, over a period of several years. Their extensive and generous verbatim contributions to the text of this chapter make it clear that Drs. Beisel, Feierabend, Klicperova-Baker, and Svehlova are essentially co-authors of this chapter, although they are absolved of any responsibility for my own conceptualizations and interpretations.

10
Methods for Studying Irrationality in Organizations, Institutions, and Social Movements: Overview and a Case Study: Urban Design

In this chapter I will explain some research methods that I believe will be helpful to readers who wish to do research on irrational elements in organizations, institutions, and social movements. These methods include elite and specialized interviewing; use of informants; field work; participation in the social role; participant observation; field experimentation; analysis of the logical sequence; stratified sampling; content analysis; legal research; and in-milieu studies.

I will first offer some definitions. We will discuss at some length the issue of rationality in organizations, which will lay the basis for considering a range of research methods. The chapter concludes with a detailed case study of urban design and the livability of cities.

Some Definitions

An *organization* can be defined, for our purposes, as a particular group of people linked together over a period of time, for given goals or sets of activities. An *institution* can be defined for our purposes, as a certain kind of social structure, comprising all organizations of a particular kind. A *social movement* can be defined as a sustained, organized collective effort that focuses on some aspect of social change.

For example, *The corporation* is an institution; Goldman Sachs is an organization. *The court* is an institution; The Ohio Court of Appeals is an organization. *The university* is an institution; Boston University is an organization. Climate change denial is an example of *a social movement.*

Why Studies of Organizations, Institutions, and Social Movements Involve Studying Functional Rationality

This section involves a good deal of theory, which I think you will find helpful in thinking about these research questions. I am reminded of two quotations. The social psychologist Kurt Lewin said, "There is nothing so practical as a good theory." And Albert Einstein said, "A theory should be as simple as possible. But no simpler." And so we will proceed with theory and then set forth appropriate research methods.

The sociologist of knowledge, Karl Mannheim (1940), drew a crucial distinction between *instrumental* or *functional rationality* (derived, in part, from Max Weber's concept of formal rationality), and *substantial rationality* (Weber, 1947). Mannheim defined *functional rationality* as the actions by the society that are highly organized and intended to be maximally efficient with reference to objective goals. Mannheim defined *substantial rationality* as "the capacity to act intelligently in a given situation on the basis of one's own insight into the interrelationship of events." Mannheim noted that an action may be functionally rational (such as army units assembling for war in an organized fashion) and yet be substantially irrational (the war itself makes no sense). In fact, he notes "the paralyzing effect of functional rationalization on the capacity for rational judgment" (1940, p. 58).

Many activities are, in Mannheim's terms, functionally rational in the sense of being well organized and efficient, but substantially irrational: "they make no sense," as Mannheim would put it (if he wrote in English!). We go further and consider many of them as deeply irrational in our definition, reflecting the workings of mental processes outside of conscious awareness.

The Dangers of our Society's Obsession with Functionally Rational Activities

Many others have warned us of the dangers of an excess of functional rationality. Adam Smith, in *Wealth of Nations*, worried that the division of labor would turn workers into machines: it is most efficient if each person makes only part of a pin, many times a minute, all day long.

Karl Marx also warned us that functional rationality could lead to the substantially irrational: he remarked that the capitalists would line up to sell the ropes to be used to hang them.

The great sociologist Max Weber worried about bureaucracy, a "rational–legal form of authority" whose efficiency compared with traditional or charismatic forms of authority was so great as to pose a threat to the freedom of the entire society.

The problem with bureaucracy is that it is efficient, *regardless of the purpose*. We think of Adolph Eichmann with his railway tables. And we are reminded of Rudolph Hoess, the Commandant at Auschwitz, boasting that the camp could kill 10,000 people a day.

Jacques Ellul was another major sociologist to explore the systemizing tendency. He chronicled with considerable apprehension the rapid growth of technique in modern society (Ellul, 1967). He defines a technique as "any complex of standardized means for attaining a predetermined result most efficiently" (ibid, p.vi); that is, the greatest result for a given effort, or a given result for the least effort. And "Technique itself is the totality of methods rationally arrived at and having absolute efficiency" (ibid, p. xxv). Thus, a technique is a rationalized method, and it need not be mechanical. Ellul argues that technique has become huge and ever increasing in scope, dominating our emotional and social lives, a rationality so out of control that it has become deeply irrational.

A pure example of rationality gone irrational is given by the biologist and ecologist Garrett Hardin, in *The Tragedy of the Commons* (1968), one of the most frequently cited articles in the journal *Science*. He shows that in an ecological environment like Earth, some resources are a commons, like air, water, or the green pastures at the center of an English village: there is no charge to use them but they are not unlimited. Under these circumstances it is rational for each individual to use as much as possible, grazing more and more sheep, or polluting the air or water, to maximize benefit to themselves. But this rational process will inevitably destroy the commons and all will perish. In Mannheim's terms, functional rationality pursued to the end can lead to disaster.

Functional rationality can combine with psychopathology to produce harrowing results. As we saw in Chapter 6, The Oxford historian Timothy Garton Ash (1997a, 1997b) noted that the Stasi (the East German Secret Police) had more than a quarter of a million people spying or informing on the rest of the East German population, and the Stasi files on persons under suspicion stretched 90 miles long. In Ellul's terms, rational technique unbounded made a police state possible.

It is a given that functional rationality has also made possible the enormous achievements of modern society in the realm of technology, public health, life expectancy, standard of living, literacy, and medicine. But we have also seen the huge problems posed by functional rationality when applied to substantially irrational pursuits.

Mannheim and Ellul believed that along with the many achievements of technique in our modern society come some inherent limitations to realistic understanding resulting from overcommitment to functionalism and objectification. Mannheim, in describing instrumental or functional rationality, and Ellul, in describing technique, are describing cognitive styles very similar to what later researchers called the *systemizing tendency*. In Chapter 2 we discussed Simon Baron-Cohen's research on the systemizing mind versus the empathic mind, and Nicolas Taleb's (2010) view that the oversystematizing mind may entirely miss the meaning of what is happening. The views of Baron-Cohen and Taleb are consistent with clinicians' views about the value of empathy, and are supported by the research on mentalization, empathy, introspection, and the "theory of mind" described in Chapter 2.

The Next Steps in Technique: The Algorithm and Machine Learning

An algorithm can be defined as a highly specific series of steps to attain a specified result. As such, it is a quintessential technique but one that Ellul could not foresee. With a computer to carry out the steps, many human functions that previously required judgment and empathic ability have disappeared, replaced by an algorithm, instrumented by a computer, that proved it could do it better. This is well described in David Berlinsky's brilliant book *The Advent of the Algorithm* (2001).

According to Berlinsky, the logician's definition of an algorithm is "a finite procedure, written in a fixed symbolic vocabulary, governed by precise instructions, moving in discrete steps, 1,2,3...,whose execution requires no insight, cleverness, intuition, intelligence, or perspicuity, and that sooner or later comes to an end" (ibid, p. xix). This surely characterizes a computer program, for example, or a method of solving a quadratic equation.

Berlinsky also offers a shorter and broader characterization: "An algorithm is an *effective procedure*, a way of getting things done in a finite number of steps...A machine could execute the appropriate steps. A machine *can* execute the appropriate steps. No art is involved. And none is needed" (ibid, p. xvi).

A popular exposition, *Automate This!*, by Christopher Steiner (2012), details the achievements and the job displacements owing to the ascendance of the algorithm in modern economic life.

In my view, the next step has been *machine learning*: the algorithm could be designed to look at what it had produced, note any flaws or inaccuracies in it, and modify itself to eliminate most of them in the next stage. The machine learning algorithm actually improves its accuracy as it repeatedly interacts with the data. This could be done successively so that increasing levels of accuracy of prediction or measurement could be obtained even if the resulting algorithm becomes very complex. In statistical prediction, for example, extremely complex multiway statistical interactions can be handled (see, e.g., Berk, 2012).

The Spread of Technique in Research, and a Reaction

The rationalization of our society has, of course, affected the social sciences, with their intense concern with methodology. And it has also affected some humanities studies. Statistically oriented methods have in recent times become influential in historical, literary, and classical studies. There are journals in each of these fields devoted to quantitative methods.

But it is only fair to let the reader know that the response by some humanities-oriented scholars to the growth of mathematical and quantitative methods in the social sciences has, at times, been strongly negative. One of my teachers, Professor Samuel Stouffer, and his colleagues, laid the groundwork for quantitative structured survey analysis, in their epoch-making book, *The American Soldier* (1949). Their work is immensely respected by survey analysts. But their book received the following review from another of my teachers, Professor Arthur Schlesinger, Jr., the eminent American historian: "Sociology has whored after the natural sciences from the start" (Haney, 2008, p. 57). He went on in this vein: "One comes to feel that the American soldier existed, neither in life nor in history, but in some dreary statistical vacuum." Haney says, "[Schlesinger] felt the Bill Mauldin's wartime cartoons provided a more succinct and perceptive source of insight into soldier's attitudes than did the study's array of statistics." Schlesinger was not alone. As Haney notes, the social critic Nathan Glazer, in his social science column in the magazine *Commentary*, wrote: "rarely was so little information about so large a question spread over so many pages" (ibid, pp. 56–7).

I think the researcher can conclude from the above that some intellectuals feel, not that "all paths lead to Rome," but rather that only their own path leads there. For us, however, it will be to our advantage to recognize the merits of many paths and to value a variety of methods of inquiry.

Functional Rationality Versus Empathic Understanding in Research

Despite the critics of over-rationalization, it is apparent from the growing dominance of the algorithm in many areas of our life, and from the displacement of skilled and unskilled labor by automation, that our society seems to be fleeing from empathic understanding as fast as it can.

But empathic understanding has two advantages: one is that it is related to substantial rationality, not to functional rationality. Substantial rationality refers to doing the right thing. Functional rationality refers to doing something effectively and efficiently. Functional rationality can include doing the wrong thing, such as starting a war, organizing genocide, or polluting the environment, at a very high level of effectiveness and efficiency.

A second advantage of empathy is that it is rooted in our biological nature and serves a life-fulfilling purpose: helping us understand other people. That is why it is so important in psychodynamic inquiry.

We Need Both

In order to get sufficient purchase on the problems and to establish the validity of the results, psychodynamic inquiry needs methods for empathic understanding, as in Chapters 2, 3, 7, and 9, and also a variety of modern and classic social science research methods.

Research Methods for Studying Organizations, Institutions, and Social Movements

Elite and Specialized Interviewing

Lewis Dexter (1971) is the authority on in-depth interviewing of people with special expertise, knowledge, social power, personal experiences of special interest, special points of view, or people who are in special situations, all of whom are, by definition, unsuitable subjects for standardized structured interviews.

This is a classic book but it is rarely included in the readings for methodology courses. Lewis Dexter wrote it at the suggestion of my teacher, David Riesman. It is designed for interviewing people who have special expertise or unusual experience. A tool and die maker. A scientist. A poet. An astronaut. A tree surgeon. A winner of a science talent search. A survivor of a flood or fire. A mailman.

This method is also designed for interviewing people in powerful political or economic positions. They have special knowledge or experience but are vulnerable to bad publicity and are able to protect themselves from ordinary survey interviews.

Dexter says to let the respondent tell you what is important. Don't use structured questions. What the respondent thinks is important to talk about is what you want to find out. Then ask very open-ended follow-up questions. What is it like to be a Senator from Kentucky? What is it like to be Chairman of the Senate Foreign Relations Committee? What is it like to be the CEO of a high-tech startup? What is it like to be a tool and die maker? What is it like to be a concierge in a hotel? What is it like to be a neurosurgeon?

Dexter was very successful in interviewing politicians. He explains, for example, the methods he used to get an interview with Jack Kennedy.

When my students and I studied mental health boards, interviewing the busy executives who served as board presidents, we were often told that a board president could spare only 15 minutes. But often the board president was still talking an hour and a half later: no one had listened to him or her before (Dorwart and Meyers, 1981).

In the study discussed in Chapter 8, if Christine Gerety and I had actually been in Europe with good access to political leaders in France, Greece, and Russia, at the appropriate time, elite and specialized interviewing could have provided us with excellent data.

In some situations elite and specialized interviewing can be an emotionally upsetting kind of research. The survivors of a tragic situation are elite respondents (and sometimes also informants). Notice the effect on the writer J.K. Rowling after having interviewed survivors of torture while working for Amnesty International. The final volumes of her *Harry Potter* series describe secret foreign prisons that conduct torture, and use blood tests to determine racial fitness to survive.

Use of Informants

If used properly, informants become, essentially, co-researchers. From them one can obtain verbatim accounts, as we did in Chapter 9, but we could have done more.

For example, Ivo Feierabend's father, as minister of agriculture in the Masaryk and later governments, and a very well known statesman and patriot, twice fled Czechoslovakia in the middle of the night, once from the Nazi government and once from the communist government, the second time taking young Ivo with him. They hid in the walls of a boat while escaping.

Jana Svehlova's father went from Czechoslovakia to England during World War II, and fought in the Royal Air Force in the defense of England during the blitz bombing by the Luftwaffe. On his return home to Czechoslovakia after the war, instead of being treated as a hero, her father was arrested by the communist government as a capitalist sympathizer and therefore "an enemy of the people," and put in prison far from his home for ten years. His daughter, Jana, was allowed to visit her father only for ten minutes each year of his ten-year term. After her father was released and after the communist government fell, Jana founded an organization, "The Daughters of Enemies of the State," which meets periodically to give mutual support.

In October 1944, Erno Szep, the great Hungarian poet, playwright, and novelist, was rounded up at the age of 60, along with other aging Jews, by the Fascist Arrow Cross militia, and, after a long forced march, was put to hard labor in an organized detention center. In his autobiographical account (1945 [1994]), he describes this period in a dispassionate way that has been characterized as "a meld of stupefaction and irony." An enormous amount can be learned from the clinically astute (and humanly empathic) study of the testimony of a participant as informant. The reader will note that a narrative analysis of this touching memoir, along the lines described in Chapter 7, would also be likely to be productive.

Experience in many contexts, from urban street corners (Whyte, 1943 [1993]) to distant cultures, has shown that informants are of significant value to any researcher. A close relationship lasting over time develops and they essentially become co-researchers. This was my experience in the study detailed in Chapter 9.

Informants can also be useful on a group level. In my two years as Director of Research for the Peace Corps, I conducted a number of three-day discussion sessions with groups of volunteers at their Close of Service conferences, in India, Nigeria, and Morocco. The volunteers very much served as informants for me.

Field Work

Researchers doing field work actually live in the situation they are studying, for example in an inner city depressed area, as in Herb Gans's famous study of the West End in Boston as it awaited demolition under "urban renewal" (Gans, 1962). The basic method of field work is participant observation, looking and listening and interacting with the people you are studying (and later making research notes), while being part of the ongoing scene. This is discussed in the following paragraphs.

Rosalie Wax wrote a classic guide, also at the suggestion of David Riesman, *Doing Fieldwork: Warnings and Advice* (1971 [1985]). A major part of it tells of her experience as a young graduate student in anthropology from Berkeley doing a study of an internment camp for Americans of Japanese ancestry during World War II, in 100-degree heat in our southwest desert. The study lasted a year and a half. She used a structured questionnaire as an entrée to building rapport with the inmates, and achieved a high level of trust in a situation replete with mutual distrust, violence, and even a murder. In addition to her very astute advice to field workers, Wax gives us a fine history of field work worldwide, including in modern countries, and a discussion of the scientific status of fieldwork methods.

Participant Observation

A classic study is John M. Johnson's, *Doing Field Research* (1978). Johnson's chapters are one of the most comprehensive and thoughtful presentations of the philosophical and practical arguments by field researchers, participant observers, ethnographers, anthropologists, and sociologists of the "Chicago school" of urban sociology. Like the symbolic interactionists, Johnson takes the epistemological position that it is more objective, not less, to take the meaning of the action to the subject into account, as opposed to letting the researcher totally define what is real. To illustrate his argument, Johnson describes his observation of the inner workings of a mental health clinic in California, where he was both an observer and a participant in interactions with the staff. The play of unconscious factors can be readily seen in this ethnographic memoir. A helpful recent guide is *Participant Observation: A Guide for Fieldworkers* (DeWalt and DeWalt, 2011).

Ethnography in Modern Environments

Much of participant observation and field work fits under the broader umbrella of *ethnographic methods*. It will be helpful to discuss the broad picture of modern ethnographic studies to see how the various methods we have already discussed are centrally involved in these studies. Many of these modern studies involve organizations and institutions, which are our concern in this chapter. An ethnography is a descriptive account of social life and culture in a particular social system based on detailed observations of what people actually do. It involves direct field work, that is, living in the organization or group that is being studied. It therefore is based on participant observation. This kind of research aims, above all, at thick description, discussed earlier.

Ethnographic field work methods derived from cultural anthropology have been applied to more modern cultures, such as the early studies done by the "Chicago school" of sociology, where they studied taxi drivers, fishmongers, policemen, politicians, slum dwellers, immigrants, delinquents, waitresses, street corner gangs, and the like. Ethnographic field work methods have long been used by sociologists and political scientists to study communities, and are now being applied to modern organizations,

These include large retail corporations, for example MacDonald's (Leidner, 1993), a high-tech firm (Kunda, 1992 [2006]), an information technology company (Strannegard and Friberg, 2001), and public institutions, such as city management (Czarniawska, 2000).

Narrative Ethnography

One particular method used in some ethnographic field work is *narrative ethnography*, in which the researcher recounts his experiences in the culture or organization from a personal point of view. This may sound to the reader terribly subjective; however, it can transmit large amounts of valuable information. In fact, we have already examined two examples of what can be considered narrative ethnography and the valuable information it can provide. One is Ash's famous study, *The File* (1997a), in which he recounts his investigation of his own secret police (Stasi) files in East Germany. The other is Rosalie Wax's touching account (1971 [1985]) of her travails in doing research in the wartime Japanese–American internment camps in the American Southwest.

Shadowing

Another very interesting research method used in the modern ethnographic context is *shadowing*. This involves the researcher following a person of interest throughout the day, at least in the work environment, attending all meetings and conferences, being in the office with the person as he or she works at the computer, uses the phone, talks with visitors, and the like. As a research method this is discussed by Barbara Czarniawska in her remarkably original book, *Shadowing and Other Techniques for Doing Field Work in Modern Societies* (2007). She is particularly interested in applying this method to business and governmental organizations.

My own view of shadowing is that it is greatly underused as a method of learning from a willing mentor, or learning what is involved in working in a given field. As such, it is mainly used in training physicians and nurses. From personal experience I think it would also be a great help to a person going into a position in business, government, or university administration.

But I think that as a research tool it has its limitations. The examples Czarniawska gives from her own field work chill the soul: she had terrible difficulty shadowing owing to resistance from the persons being shadowed, who had no personal ties to her and no interest in the research. An issue with the way Czarniawska enacts shadowing is that she takes the stance of an objective outside observer who appears not to rely very much on empathic communication with the person being shadowed. I think the stance of the totally outside observer would make shadowing much more difficult than it needs to be.

I think the problems involved in shadowing of any sort would be compounded if one were studying a situation that one felt had marked destructive or bizarre elements. Further, there would be the issue of protecting the person one is shadowing, a duty owed by researchers to their participants. Perhaps the reader will find a way to make this work in the realm of truly irrational social movements or organizational situations.

Participation in the Social Role

This is an unusual and drastic method not for the timorous but capable of producing outstanding research data. The first instance I know of was the upper-class social activist Beatrice Webb's stint as a factory worker in England: in 1888 she worked as a seamstress in a textile factory (Webb, 1888, 1926 [1979]). Another early example was *Black Like Me* (1961), in which the journalist John Howard Griffin, dyed his skin black (temporarily) and travelled through the South of the United States posing as an African American (called a "Negro" in those days). A classic study, very revealing of, for example, "the hate stare."

Another early example, almost as drastic, was *Pink Collar Workers*, by Louise Kapp Howe (1978), a *New York Times* journalist. Kapp Howe was a well educated, middle class person who decided to work for a year in the kinds of jobs women at the bottom of our social scale take on, jobs like working behind the counter at a diner, or taking the role of an unemployed person looking for a job, or trying to start out selling insurance. Her year-long experience reveals a great deal about this level of our society. This is reminiscent for me of my days as a dishwasher, bellhop, busboy, and waiter in the hotels in Connecticut and New York's Catskill Mountains in the summers during my college years. I wish I had written them up. Writing up that sort of experience was a forte of the "Chicago school" of sociology.

Perturbing the Environment: A Variety of Field Experiments

Because they largely solve the key problem of *external validity* and they use the experimental method with its possibilities of disconfirmation, field experiments are a powerful research tool. External validity refers to the issue of the generalizability of research findings from the laboratory to the outside world. Field experiments largely sidestep this problem by taking place in the outside world.

In the study of organizations, institutions, or social movements, the researcher is not in a position to conduct typical randomized field experiments. The latter are very useful in clinical trials in the medical field, where new drugs or clinical procedures are evaluated against known drugs or procedures. These ordinarily use random assignments, and researchers and patients are both blind as to which drug is which. All extraneous variables are controlled and made equal as much as possible.

Randomized field experiments are also extremely useful in the field of development economics, in which different crop varieties can be tested against each other, or different irrigation techniques, different uses of fertilizers, different breeds of poultry or livestock, can be evaluated against each other. In these cases random assignment to plots of land is often used to neutralize the effects of fertility differences in the land itself.

These kinds of studies are considered in great detail in an outstanding text by Alan S. Gerber and Donald P. Green, *Field Experiments: Design, Analysis, and Interpretation* (2012). Various concerns, objections, and defenses of this kind of research from a design and statistical viewpoint are discussed in excellent papers by a variety of authors in *Field Experiments and Their Critics* (Teele, 2014).

But in the study of organizations, institutions, and social movements, the researcher does not have the luxury of controlling the situation nearly well enough to meet the design criteria of a field experiment in the sense used in the above-mentioned texts. For example, the power of random assignment of cases to treatments is circumscribed and often unworkable, and extraneous variables cannot be controlled and made equal by design or by statistical adjustments.

The studies I am about to discuss here have also been called "field experiments," as we discussed in the section on replication in Chapter 4, but I would also call them "perturbing the situation," or "perturbing the environment," to distinguish them from randomized field experiments with control of external variables. Research that perturbs the environment is in accord with the "loose interpretation" of experimentation: "poking nature with a stick," as explained by the philosopher of social science Abraham Kaplan, in *The Conduct of Inquiry* (1998 [2006]). Kaplan argues, and I agree, that a great deal can be learned by perturbing a situation to see what the result will be. I think that studies that perturb the environment are greatly underused in studying organizations, institutions, and social movements.

Organizations and institutions don't exist in mathematical hyperspace, they exist in real public spaces, and their vagaries and irrationalities can be studied there. Let's look at a series of perturbations (often called "field experiments") of the urban environment. These will cast light on unconscious mental processes in the built urban environment, including repressed anger, unconscious sensitivity to social status, unspoken altruism, unconscious targeting by police officials, and unconscious racial and gender discrimination by retail clerks. Based on these examples, the reader will be able to construct "field experiments," perhaps more properly called "perturbations," in order to study an organization, institution, or social movement of interest.

What we now call *road rage,* is the irrational "access of rage" among drivers due to exaggerated response to any frustration and, perhaps, to the angst of modern life. We know that it reaches highly irrational levels as it triggers ideation and fantasies outside of conscious awareness and totally inappropriate to the situation. There have been collisions and even fatalities due to road rage.

The famous study, described in Chapter 4, of horn honking at cars that did not move promptly when a red light turned to green, found that lower-status cars were honked at sooner and more insistently. The reader will note that it was impossible to assign "subjects," these days called "participants," to various intersections having traffic lights; the participants were the drivers of any cars that happened to be there. However, the intersections having traffic lights could be selected *purposefully,* to use Michael Quinn Patton's (2014) term, based on their potential information richness. Multiple replications have established the validity and credibility of the study, and the limits of the conditions under which the study findings held. You don't get honked at if there is a gun rack in the back of your pick-up truck!

Other studies had confederates of the researcher, one man and one woman, approach a department store counter simultaneously. The man was almost always served first, an experimental demonstration of the influence of gender in commercial activities.

It has also been possible to study the targeting of certain groups by the police. Florence Heussenstamm's famous study, "Bumper stickers and the cops," (1971) was conducted in Los Angeles during a period of conflict between the Black Panthers and the police. Her students at California State College, those with perfect driving records, were given Black Panther stickers to put on their bumpers. All received such a flood of driving citations that the experiment had to be stopped before the students lost their licenses.

Field experiments are greatly underused these days, perhaps owing to university "ethics committees," whose strictures are more suitable to medical experiments than to social scientific studies like interviews or observations of people in public places. These committees, when they overstep their intended function of avoiding harm to research participants, can serve as a form of governmental control of research studies that challenge existing social arrangements.

Analysis of the Logical Sequence

This method of inquiry involves constructing a detailed account of how a particular functionally rational organization has proceeded with logical well-planned steps to achieve its substantially irrational goal. Examples can be drawn from law professor Joel Bakan's (2004) treatise on the legal history of the corporation (discussed in Chapter 11); the architectural history of the concentration camps; the construction of the terrorist bombs at the Boston Marathon from an engineering point of view; and pollution considered as a formal goal of modern life.

Legal Research

This has several meanings. The one familiar to most lawyers is a search for a series of precedents for a given legal dispute or decision. These would include previous legal decisions, by courts in the Federal system, or courts in the state where the dispute is being litigated, or, if necessary, by courts in other states. It might also include a study of common law decisions, possibly stretching far back in history, as in property law. It would also include the examination of certain legislation, such as The Uniform Commercial Code. If administrative law is involved, it would include regulations by the government agencies made pursuant to legislation. For tax law, these are so frequent that they are published weekly by Prentice Hall and by the Commerce Clearing House; the loose-leaf volumes holding them line the walls of law firms' libraries.

A second meaning of legal research is the examination of social and economic data bearing on legal decisions. For example, in *Brown* v. *the Board of Education* 347 U.S. 483 (1954) data were put in evidence that the separate schools for minorities gave an inferior education. The result was a Supreme Court decision that "separate but equal" was not equal, therefore mandating the racial integration of schools.

These two meanings are the ones prominent in Bakan's book, *The Corporation: The Pathological Pursuit of Profit and Power* (2004).

There is a third meaning, "empirical legal research." Empirical research is relevant to the functioning of a particular *organization*, such as the United States Supreme Court, or to an *institution*, such as the legal profession, the judiciary, or the legal system of a particular country. Empirical legal research focuses to a major extent on topics such as the determinants of judicial decisions, including composition of the courts; the functioning of juries; the characteristics of legal opinions; the independence of the judiciary; the relationships between the lower courts and superior courts, and between state judiciaries and the federal judiciary; the functioning of attorneys; the functioning of legislatures; the effect of client demographics on decisions and on sentencing; the specificity of legislation; the effects of judicial appointments, tenure and the election of judges; the relation between federal court decisions and the dominance of one political party or another; the relationship of the law of a particular nation to international law; and the like. Many aspects of practical empirical legal research are covered very well in a fine book by Epstein and Martin (2014).

In-the-milieu Observation of the Functioning of Organizations, Institutions, and Social Movements

Organizations, institutions, and social movements operate in physical space and physical surroundings, not in mathematical hyperspace, and they can often be studied in situ, that is, in the environment in which they function.

In what I call "in-the-milieu observation," the researcher is physically present and visible but is not part of the local social system and often does not interact much with the members of that system.

The observational methods can vary quite a bit. They can be empathic, based on introspection and listening to one's own reactions to the situation, or they can be specific, objective, and quantitative.

An example of the first recently occurred to me. While traveling, I stepped into a clothing store. The merchandise was good, the service was good but the store's walls were plastered with signs telling the customers and employees on how to live their lives in a moral and productive way. Not just one sign, but many. My initial emotional reaction required only a little introspection to access: I experienced the signs as sanctimonious and patronizing. I had never seen anything like this before, the intensity, number, and hectoring quality of the signs on the wall. I felt I sensed something deeper underneath but I didn't know what. A few weeks later I heard a rumor that the owner had been sued by some workers for wage theft.

A Case Study: In-the-milieu Urban Studies

Very different examples of *in-the-milieu research* are provided by observational studies on the functioning of open spaces in cities and suburbs.

The aim of these studies was to improve the livability of cities, the agreeableness and pleasant functions of our cities and suburbs. The reader will find it useful to understand the analytical and persuasive power of structured observation by people in the milieu or environment of interest.

Is There Irrationality in Urban Design?

Despite its appearance of complex, rule-bound organization, the urban scene is replete with manifestations of profound irrationality. Some examples will suffice to illustrate this point. One is a manifestation of the "tragedy of the commons" (Hardin, 1968), which we discussed earlier: if a commons exists, that is, a natural resource, free but limited in size, it will be to the advantage of each individual to exploit it as fully as possible. But if all do so, the commons collapses.

The open air is also a commons, and it, too, is limited in size. It pays each developer of urban office buildings to build them as high as possible. But if everyone builds tall office buildings in this way, the result is dark shadowy canyons that people try to avoid.

It also pays each user of land to pollute the surrounding air, so that the user saves the cost of disposing of the pollutants but pays only part of the price since the pollution disperses over the city. But if all users follow their individual self-interest in this way, we get Beijing, where the air is often too polluted to see clearly more than two city blocks away. People are fleeing if they can. There is something deeply destructive and self-destructive in allowing this to persist.

A second example of profound irrationality, with destructive results: in the years 1924–1968, Robert Moses, as head of The Triboro Bridge and Tunnel Authority, had control of all public highway construction over the Greater New York Area. Although Moses himself never had a driver's license, his decisions, dictatorial in style, strongly favored cars over public transit and were carried out with bizarre rigidity. Was it rational to build the 204 bridges on his Long Island freeways too low for buses to clear? This foreclosed public transit forever for millions of people by one person's idiosyncrasy, in an unappealable decision. Were there infantile grandiose fantasies of omniscience or omnipotence involved? Or unconscious hostility to ethnic groups that were too poor to afford cars in which to commute? An underlying issue is the irrationality of a system that gave so much power to one person: at one time Moses held 12 top administrative positions simultaneously. As with Kim Jong-un, a scenario for capricious decisions with destructive consequences is established.

The history of public housing in the United States presents a third instance. Built to Spartan budgetary restrictions, there was no shared space in these high rises, and, as a result, no "defensible space " (first described by Oscar Newman in 1973). Crime, vandalism, and violence of many sorts were rife in these dangerous places to live. The denizens often fled them to the comparative safety of the slums. A classic case was the Pruitt–Igoe housing project in Chicago, where, as a result of crime and consequent abandonment by the residents, 33 high-rise buildings had to be demolished. Fortunately, we have long ago stopped building high-rise housing projects. As in Scandinavia, we have found that low-rise projects that are less dense and have more semiprivate space work much better.

A thoughtful person might want to ask whether naming of the project might have embodied hostility to the impoverished urban minority residents. This thought runs through my mind after having seen a housing project in Boston, where the three dismal sections were named Bataan, Corregidor, and Wake Island—three military disasters. A far cry from Yale Street, Harvard Avenue, and Amherst Street in an upper middle class community near where I live.

When a major blunder is made it is, of course, not necessarily a manifestation of an irrational action driven by unconscious needs, drives, and fantasies. Simple miscalculations, errors in logic or in estimating probabilities, or non-optimal decisions in general, would not necessarily be irrational in my sense of the word. They could instead be the result of inherent cognitive and intellectual limitations, stress, social pressure, lack of general knowledge, or lack of specific needed data. However, *if a blunder is repeated ad infinitum, despite repeated destructive adverse consequences each time, then we may wonder if motives and forces outside of conscious awareness are involved*. In a court of law, of course, one is held to have intended *the reasonably foreseeable consequences* of one's actions, as explained in Chapter 3.

A fourth example comes to mind. Urban sprawl in some cities results in commutes of an hour or more twice a day. This imposes a heavy burden of time, energy, stress from frustration with traffic, and cost of gasoline and car maintenance, on the commuter and his or her family. Yet we continue to build suburbs further and further out from the city rather than investing in public transportation such as buses. Even existing tracks for trolleys and light rails sit unused. I would argue that our present urban development and management policies are obviously self-destructive and destructive of the environment. In that sense they seem to represent some sort of failure of reality testing, and so one wonders what deeper motivations, perhaps out of conscious awareness, may be involved. Perhaps desire for status? Gated communities would express that. Fear of physical harm? Distant gated communities could express that fear. Fantasies of having an estate, like an English lord? Ethnocentrism and fear of people considered "other"? Or some other factors entirely? We won't know until we do the research.

The abandonment of public space to vehicles and the resultant stress and pollution are a fifth example of a self-destructive and environmentally destructive series of decisions. To this problem, the research studies of Jane Jacobs, William H. Whyte, and Jan Gehl are relevant. Let us now look at those.

Jacobs used observational methods to document the use of streets in Greenwich Village in lower Manhattan. By observing her street environment she was able to explain, for example, why streets that are used more are safer. For example busy streets with places for residents to observe what is going on are much safer than empty streets with no opportunity for residents to observe events. Her book, *The Death and Life of Great American Cities* (1961 [1993]) describes her observational methods and the components of residential design that enable residents to monitor their environments.

Whyte, in his "Project for Urban Spaces," (1980) carried the observational method further, documenting with photographs, and by detailed counts, the use or avoidance of small public spaces, vest pocket parks and small plazas, and pedestrian streets, depending on how they were designed. And as an editor *of Fortune Magazine,* and the author of *The Organization Man* (1956), Whyte was knowledgeable about corporate life, so his study documented the influence of corporations on the use of public space, including plazas, small parks, atriums, and the like. He also documented corporate opposition to height restrictions on corporate buildings, and promotion of zoning variances and exceptions in pursuit of corporate profit and status. Some of Whyte's studies of corporate influences on zoning and height restrictions are a kind of legal research. Whyte explains observational methods, which included quantification of usage, and his legal analyses, in *City: Rediscovering the Center* (2009).

The Danish architect and planner Jan Gehl has applied the principles of structured observation, counts of usage, and photographic evidence to the urban environment generally. Broadly stated, his research team observes how people use public spaces: where they walk; where they sit; how long they converse with others; how they use or don't use their front yards or doorways for chatting, gardening, and reading.

Importantly, the results depend on the design of the space. Gehl's studies have found the following design factors to be important: human scale rather than skyscraper scale; shared space; semiprivate space; and "soft edges," that is, easy transitions from inside to outside. Also important are appropriate width of sidewalks; narrow retail store fronts (as on Madison Avenue in Manhattan), which encourage people to walk and look in store windows); curved streets to provide variety; benches and low walls designed so that people will actually sit on them rather than their being mere decoration in an architect's plan; well-designed bicycle paths that don't obstruct traffic and don't expose bicyclists to collisions with cars; and pedestrian streets where appropriate.

Influencing Urban Policy With Quantified Observations: Whyte and Gehl

Through his research Whyte was able to influence New York City planning and zoning decisions, and corporate decisions. The results were incentives that led to the provision and enhancement of small urban spaces, primarily small plazas, atriums, and vest pocket parks in crowded Manhattan. His use of photographs of the usage or neglect of public spaces were persuasive, but even more persuasive were the quantitative data on the usage of public spaces depending on their design and their provision of *usable* seating (including properly designed benches and ledges), fountains, trees, the availability of both shade and sunlit areas, bollards, the opportunity to observe passers-by and their surroundings, and easy access from the street without the need for stairs. *Quantified observations* presented in easy-to-read charts were highly persuasive.

Gehl and his research team were even more influential in improving the usability of the built urban environment and, consequently, the livability of cities. As I noted when we discussed sampling in Chapter 6, Gehl's research has influenced urban design and management in major cities and smaller towns around the world.

It is noteworthy that Gehl and his team relied primarily on *quantified observational data* to entice and persuade cities to modify their streets, plazas, and other public spaces. As a visually gifted architect, Gehl was able to present his quantified data in appealing visual charts and supporting photographs, which made the use of numbers more palatable and persuasive to his audiences.

Gehl, like his predecessor Whyte, was able to modify entrenched urban policies that were functionally rational but substantially irrational, and was able to use data to do it. For this reason—the ability of quantified observations to influence urban policy—it will be worthwhile to examine Gehl's methods in a bit of detail.

Life Between Buildings (2011) and *Cities for People* (2010) use these methods to reach design conclusions. In *How to Study Public Life* (2013), Gehl and Brigitte Svarre explain their observational techniques for studying life in public places in cities and suburbs, and housing complexes, public squares, cafes, streets, and plazas. A simple counter or more complex equipment is used to count the number of people, their gender, whether they are standing or sitting, what they are doing, whether they are alone or part of a group, how long they stay, their walking speed if they going down a street, and variation in all these by time of day, season, and weather, and by the availability of adequate seating, refreshments, trees to provide shade, and ease of access (Are there steps or stairs, or is it on street level?). Also measured are the surrounding commercial and cultural activity; the noise level; the amount of pedestrian traffic flowing through the space; the use of bollards; the nature and direction of pathways within and to and from the space; and the number, dimensions, design, and location of benches and low walls and other sitting places. The Gehl research team also makes extensive use of maps on which the variables above are charted. Photographic evidence is also used extensively.

There is little mention of interviews or interactions, which I think is an omission: it would be useful to know from interviews how far a person walked to reach a public place, what sort of business or residence they came from, how often they use the public space, how long they usually stay, and what they plan to do there. Brief interviews could be conducted with respondents chosen on a stratified random bases (some men, some women, some young, some old) in each of their sites, a kind of cluster sampling.

Gehl and Svarre do use "diaries," that is, extensive rather structured field notes by the members of the research team, which permit the use of qualitative approaches and interpretation by the observer.

Gehl and Svarre include a comprehensive history of the genesis and use of these methods of studying the use of public space, from 1850 up to Occupy Wall Street in 2011. Modern technical methods, including Google Street, which is free, and GPS Registration, in which people agree to participate in the study of public space by having a GPS function activated in their cell phones. A mathematical program called Space Syntax (Hiller and Hansen, 1984) produces maps showing the probability of the use of streets by drivers, bicyclists, and pedestrians, and this has become important in urban planning decisions. Their book also presents field notes, maps, and photographs drawn from studies of cities by Gehl and his research team, and examines the influence of these kinds of studies on governmental and private decisions improving the use of public space.

As an architect, Gehl is more visually gifted than most social science researchers seem to be, so his extensive use of photographs has a more powerful impact. In this way he is communicating on an empathic level, conveying the ambience and feeling tone of the places he is studying.

Gehl's work and that of his predecessors demonstrate how powerful observation can be if it is quantitative and done from within an urban milieu. Issues of sampling can be handled by the purposeful sampling methods analyzed by Patton (2014). Gehl chooses cases rich in meaning, for example by "critical case sampling," based on the researcher's judgment of which cases contain critically important information.

We have considered a variety of research methods suited to the psychodynamically oriented study of organizations, institutions, and social movements. What are the advantages of using more than one research method?

Advantages of the Multioperational, Multimethod Approach

Throughout the book I have been advocating the use of more than one research method to deal with a problem of interest. The Gehl team didn't conduct interviews to any notable extent, but they did use a wide variety of quantitative observational methods, plus extensive use of photography, which strengthened their research and added to its credibility. More broadly considered, a major advantage of the multimethod approach is that each research method may be able to reveal a different aspect of the phenomenon, one that that another approach might miss. For example, counting the number and type of persons who daily use a public space, as Gehl and Svarre do, may reveal information that an interview would not. And vice versa. Photographs are another source of information. Using a variety of methods helps compensate for the inherent limitations of any one method.

In Chapter 11 we will look at the denial of climate change, and corporate acquisitiveness, and I will suggest research methods particularly appropriate for these cases.

11

Methods for Studying Irrationality in Organizations, Institutions, and Social Movements: Overview and Two Case Studies: Climate Change Denial and Corporate Acquisitiveness

This chapter discusses two case studies, one of *a social movement, the denial of man-made climate change,* and one of *an institution, the large Anglo-American publicly traded business corporation*. Each is often destructive or self-destructive and very bizarre, suggesting the influence of irrational mental processes outside of conscious awareness. My goal in this chapter is to give the reader a more concrete understanding of what this kind of research involves and how it can be accomplished. It is my hope that the readers can apply insights gained from these examples to doing other studies of organizations, institutions, or social movements of special interest to them. The methods explained in this chapter should be helpful in those studies. They include special applications of the following methods: elite and specialized interviewing; use of informants; field work; participant observation; in-milieu observation; systematic random sampling; purposeful sampling; content analysis; and legal research of various kinds.

The First Case Study: Denial of the Reality of Man-made Climate Change, and how to Study it

Denial of the reality of climate change due, in part, to human activity is a social movement that embraces irrational activities that need to be understood in terms of ideation outside of conscious awareness.

I will outline the situation and then suggest research methods for investigating it.

The Reality of Climate Change

The impact of climate change on local weather patterns is already violent and will get worse. In 2011, Europe set records for dryness, Afghanistan for drought, China for rainfall, and the Philippines and Malaysia for massive floods from giant tropical storms. The United States had the worst year yet, even worse than 2010. The huge New England blizzard on 29 October 2011 was the earliest in over 100 years. The average annual rainfall in southwest Ohio is 40 inches, with a standard deviation (SD) of 8.4 inches; in 2011 it was 73 inches, four SDs higher. Summer heat waves broke all records, as did drought in the Southwest, tornados in the Midwest and South, and blizzards in the East and Northeast. In August 2011, Hurricane Irene, the largest ever to hit New Jersey, caused widespread damage, there and in the Caribbean.

More information on global warming and climate change keeps coming in. On 7 June 2012, the National Oceanic and Atmospheric Administration (NOAA) announced that the spring of 2012 was the warmest since records began in 1895, and was 5.2 degrees above the twentieth-century long-term average. The preceding 12 months were also the warmest on record (Zabarenko, 2012). In October 2012, Hurricane Sandy struck the United States and the Caribbean, causing at least 125 deaths in the United States, and 285 in total, flooding lower Manhattan, and leaving over 7.5 million people without power.

In a typical year in the United States there are three or four weather disasters, the costs of which exceed $1 billion each. However, in 2011, there were 12 such events, according to the NOAA, and 14 according to the Natural Resources Defense Fund. In 2012 there were another 11, and in 2013 another nine.

And in 2013, the NOAA reported an astonishing list of weather anomalies, all over the world: downpours and floods resulted in Canada's most expensive natural disaster; California had its driest year ever; the United Kingdom was at its coldest since 1962; Norway had its second wettest December ever recorded; Russia had the worst flooding ever recorded; China had the worst heat waves ever recorded.

In 2013 extending into 2014, Australia had a savage year-long heat wave, making 2013 the hottest year on record, even shutting down the Australian Open Grand Slam Tennis Tournament in Melbourne at one point in January (BBC News, 2014c); and so it went throughout most of the world (Gillis, 2015).

On 1 September 2014 the disaster tabulating service of the NOAA was shut down for political reasons.

The flooding in Pakistan and in the Kashmir area of India in 2014 was the worst in memory, killing hundreds and leaving thousands homeless. In 2014, California experienced a long and severe drought, which led to extensive fires in the agricultural Central Valley. As the temperature rises, what rain does fall evaporates faster (Rothenburg, 2014). According to NASA, and confirmed independently by the NOAA, 2014 was the warmest year since record keeping began in 1880 (NBC News, 2014; Gillis, 2015). And in 2015 as the California drought continued, the Northeast of the United States was beset by record-breaking snow storms. Boston, for example, had a "record 30-day snowfall: 94:4 inches from Jan. 24–Feb. 22, 2015, inclusive (previous record: 58.8 inches)" (Erdman, 2015).

What These Extreme Values Mean

It is important to understand what these extreme values of weather, many SDs away from the mean of a normal distribution, actually indicate. On the basis of a Gaussian normal statistical distribution they might be predicted to occur only once in thousands of years. But a distribution, normal or otherwise, is a *description or estimate* of the frequency of a phenomenon based on past experience. A normal distribution is *not a force constraining a phenomenon* to occur with only a few extreme values.

When we repeatedly get weather phenomena with values many SDs away from the mean, it implies that the phenomenon itself has changed: the climate itself has become different, and a different distribution should now be used to describe and estimate its variations. This might be a different *kind* of distribution that has more frequent extreme values. For example, Nassim Taleb (2010) argues that we should use "scalable distributions" (expressing "power laws") to describe economic and environmental events, since these distributions imply a much higher frequency of extreme values than does the Gaussian normal distribution that is traditionally used.

We Have Been Warned

Kathleen Kolbert (2011) observed:

> For decades, climate scientists have predicted that, as global temperatures rose, the side effects would include deeper droughts, more intense flooding, and more ferocious storms. The details of these forecasts are immensely complicated, but the underlying science is pretty simple. Warm air can hold more moisture. This means that

> there is greater evaporation. It also means that there is more water, and hence more energy, available to the system.
>
> What we are seeing now is these predictions being borne out. If no particular flood or drought or storm can be directly attributed to climate change—there's always the possibility that any single event was just a random occurrence—the over-all trend toward more extreme weather follows from the heating of the earth. As the cover of *Newsweek* declared last week, "weather panic" is the "new normal." The larger problem is that this "new normal" won't last. Each additional ton of carbon dioxide that's spewed into the atmosphere contributes to further warming, thus increasing the risk of violent weather.

And Thomas Friedman (2011), who has won three Pulitzers for his reporting, said,

> You really do have to wonder whether a few years from now we'll look back at the first decade of the 21st century—when food prices spiked, energy prices soared, world population surged, tornados plowed through cities, floods and droughts set records, populations were displaced and governments were threatened by the confluence of it all—and ask ourselves: What were we thinking? How did we not panic when the evidence was so obvious that we'd crossed some growth/climate/natural resource/population redlines all at once?

Friedman notes that the increasing ecological turbulence will also cause economic and political turbulence, by diminishing food supplies and access to natural resources.

Dismissing the Warnings

Our mechanisms of repression, psychological and political, have blinded us to what is happening. We know and don't know at the same time. We can't even bring ourselves to prepare for natural disasters unrelated to climate change: the areas in Japan flooded by the 2011 tsunami never should have been built upon. Previous tsunamis had left clear environmental markers, accompanied by posted warning signs, delimiting unsafe areas for settlement, but these were willfully ignored.

As long ago as the early 1970s the Club of Rome warned us of the perils of overexpansion, resource scarcity, pollution, global warming, climate change, and consequent destabilization of the world system. Its report, *The Limits to Growth* (Meadows et al., 1972) sold 12 million copies in 38 languages worldwide, but most of us tried hard to discount it anyway. Twenty-four additional studies funded by the Club of Rome have followed over the years but we continue to discount those, too, on methodological grounds, grounds of bias imputed to the authors, or any grounds we can find or imagine. We continue to reject authoritative scientific studies by the National Academy of Sciences, the Union of Concerned Scientists, The National Resources Defense Council, and other scientific groups. The overwhelming consensus among climate scientists, endorsed by the National Academy of Sciences, doesn't mean anything to many people.

Al Gore's eloquent compendium, *An Inconvenient Truth* (2006), aroused widespread rage and contempt. Whole websites, with ample funding from corporations and politically conservative groups, are devoted to denying climate change. The deniers reportedly include corporation-funded efforts, right-wing think-tanks, and billionaire-funded talk shows and media outlets.

In the late twentieth century, we had several decades of corporately funded propaganda denying that smoking cigarettes is addictive and causes cancer; it has now come to light that the cigarette companies had plenty of data that smoking causes cancer; they knew. For that denial many smokers paid a heavy price, but that denial was far less dangerous to humanity than is the current denial of climate change.

Widespread Warnings Continue to go Largely Unheeded by the Citizenry and by Legislators

It is not an issue of the scientific findings being hard to comprehend by the general public. Major thinkers from a variety of disciplines have summarized very lucidly the scientific evidence for climate change and have warned of the impending ecological catastrophe if nothing is done. They could hardly have written more clearly or emphatically. For example, the expert on urban livability, James Howard Kunstler, in *The Long Emergency* (2005), detailed in lively and pungent prose the effect on the urban fabric of pressures on energy supplies and food supplies. Thomas Friedman warned us, in detail, of the economic and political consequences of climate change in *Hot, Flat, and Crowded* (2009). The noted environmental scientist David Orr, in *Down to the Wire* (2009), again warned us. *Pandora's Seed* (2010), a brilliant book by the geographer and geneticist Spencer Wells, traced the environmental unfolding of our present emergency over thousands of years of human evolution. *The Great Disruption*, by climate change scholar Paul Gilding (2011), set forth the economic consequences that are likely to ensue, and proposed ways of adapting to lessen their impact or to adjust to them. Al Gore's huge scholarly book, *The Future* (2013), presents an encyclopedic assessment of the environmental, political, and technological forces presently at work.

But little has been done to address these issues adequately, or even directly, by politicians or the electorate in the last decades. The authors of these books express astonishment at the apathy. Massive denial by politicians and the electorate is evidently at work.

The more responsible sources among the mainstream media have repeatedly sounded the alarm. For example, the *New York Times* reports:

> The level of the most important heat-trapping gas in the atmosphere, carbon dioxide, has passed a long-feared milestone, scientists reported Friday, reaching a concentration not seen on the earth for millions of years. Scientific instruments showed that the gas had reached an average daily level above 400 parts per million...The best available evidence suggests the amount of the gas in the air has not been this high for at least three million years, before humans evolved, and scientists believe the rise portends large changes in the climate and the level of the sea. "It feels like the inevitable march toward disaster," said Maureen E. Raymo, a scientist at the Lamont-Doherty Earth Observatory, a unit of Columbia University (Gillis, 2013).

We have seen the evidence for climate change caused in large part by man. There appear to be no rational grounds for denying the overwhelming consensus of the scientific community on these matters. Why then has there been repeated denial of climate change by much of the electorate and by our elected representatives in Congress?

Outright Denial: Psychodynamic Factors

In my view, the outright denial of climate change in the face of overwhelming scientific evidence strongly suggests psychopathology at the unconscious level. As far as I can discern from the anti-climate change websites at this point, among the most extreme deniers of climate change there are paranoid theories, rage, a sense of entitlement, feelings of invulnerability and impunity, and remarkably disingenuous formulations. There may be a lot more going on: suppressed panic, dread at loss of feelings of infantile omnipotence, and perhaps Gotterdammerung fantasies about "the twilight of the Gods," a Wagnerian motif. From what I can tell, a primary factor appears to be unconsciously driven paranoid themes. But there are many possibilities, which is why scientifically valid studies are needed.

One gets the impression that one component of the denial is rooted in conspiracy theories. These are set forth in articles such as "The Goal is Power: The Global Warming Conspiracy" (Kadiec, 2011), and books like *The Greatest Hoax: How the Global Warming Conspiracy Threatens Your Future* (Inhofe, 2012). According to the popular press (e.g., http://en.wikipedia.org/wiki/Global_warming_conspiracy_theory), the roster of imagined conspirators includes climate scientists out to get funding; socialists out to destroy capitalism; agents of the Soviet Union out to weaken the United States; "Margaret Thatcher and other conservative leaders, to promote carbon-free nuclear power;" "Jacques Chirac and the secret Bilderberg Group (http://rationalwiki.org/wiki/Bilderberg_group), to use the Kyoto accords to take over the world;"; the UN in order to take over America; global eugenics groups; and the anti-globalization movement.

This list is merely drawn from the Internet, with its relative lack of quality control. It is important to put research into conspiracy theories onto a more scientific basis. As a beginning, it has been proposed that there be established a computerized worldwide database of conspiracy theories (Petit, 2012).

One wonders whether the phenomenon of *the captive mind* is also present: Do the deniers know in some corner of their mind that what they are saying is false and that climate change is a fact? Is there also an element here of *irreality*: the attempt to induce confusion in the audience about what is real? Or there may be deliberate prevarication, something practiced by the tobacco industry for decades. *There are many possibilities. We won't know until we look.* Psychodynamically sophisticated studies using social scientific methods are needed to settle such issues.

Follow the Money?

The *New York Times*, in an article titled "Deeper Ties to Corporate Cash for Doubtful Climate Researcher" (Gillis and Schwartz, 2015), reports that this scientist

> accepted more than $1.2 million...from the fossil-fuel industry over the last decade while failing to disclose that conflict of interest in most of his scientific papers. ...
>
> The documents show that in correspondence with his corporate funders [he] described many of his scientific papers as "deliverables"

> that he completed in exchange for their money. He used the same term to describe testimony he prepared for Congress. ...
>
> Historians and sociologists of science say that since the tobacco wars of the 1960s, corporations trying to block legislation that hurts their interests have employed a strategy of creating the appearance of scientific doubt, usually with the help of ostensibly independent researchers who accept industry funding.
>
> Fossil-fuel interests have followed this approach for years, but the mechanics of their activities remained largely hidden.

The Deniers Speak

Here are some illustrative statements from the deniers.

"History of the Climate Change Hoax" is the headline in a Milwaukee blog post (Hollenbeck, 2014). The author describes himself as an "Ultra-Conservative, Alpha-Male, True Authentic Leader."

An article in the *Washington Times*, "Pressing the Climate Change Hoax" (2014), speaks of it as "a fashionable hoax," and "green socialism."

An article by Rush Limbaugh (2014) speaks of "climate hypocrisy."

The *Wall Street Journal (WSJ)* speaks of "climate scientists' implausible explanations" (Ridley, 2014). The *WSJ* has been consistently skeptical about climate change, and even more skeptical that human activity has anything to do with it.

Human Events, a blog for "powerful conservative voices," wrote an article about the 20 September 2014 climate change march in New York City, one of many marches in cities around the world. It headlined its article, "Anti-Capitalist March in NYC Mentions Climate Change; Weather Remains Unchanged." The article refers to climate change as "bunkum," believers in climate change as "leftists" motivated by "hatred," using "thug tactics". It says,

> Also present for the festivities, despite having science-free agendas, were Ferguson obsessives chanting "F**k the police!", militant vegetarians, the anti-war lunatics from Code Pink, terrorist sympathizers protesting "Israeli apartheid," and the dregs of Occupy Wall Street. If you're in favor of totalitarian power, sympathetic to America's enemies, dubious about representative democracy, hostile to free markets, or you just get turned on by fantasizing about violent revolution, there was a place for you at this march (*Human Events*, 2014).

Surely all this is grist for psychodynamically informed research using social scientific methods. Let's now look at some methods that may be helpful in trying to comprehend denial of an overwhelmingly obvious and very menacing reality that is shaping history. We need to understand the unconscious fantasies and psychological mechanisms involved.

A Review of Some Basic Issues in Qualitative Research

1. *Self-disclosure*. Ordinarily, in benign situations, you will need to tell the respondents who you are and why you are there, so your being there to do the research means something to them. For suggestions, see the works by Gans (1962), Wax (1971 [1985]), and Johnson (1978).
2. *For the reader of your research* considerable self-disclosure is called for: your background, your education, and especially your biases and how you have tried to overcome them in the study.
3. *A natural history of the study*. Tell the reader the vicissitudes, changes, adjustments, compromises, and research insights that occurred during the study.
4. I hope you will find *the protocol* suggested in Chapter 3 to be of some help in listening for unconscious themes.
5. In any case, you want *thick description*: lay it on with a trowel so the reader can get an idea of whether he or she might conclude the same things from the data.
6. Go for *verbatim quotes, lengthy ones,* not summaries or paraphrases. Aim for redundancy, not parsimony, in recording your data and writing up your research. This will help the reader decide whether to believe you.
7. Devote some attention to telling the reader how you are *sampling* to get the data. That will make the result clearer to you and to the reader. For an example of outstanding judgment and precision in sampling to get data sources, see Susan Sorenson's analysis of public health data sources (Sorenson et al., 2014)
8. Give some thought to *integrating your findings with well-researched social science concepts, and to comparing the verbal responses you get with items from relevant well-validated attitude scales,* as illustrated in Chapters 5 and 6. Scales for social dominance, dogmatism, and ethnocentrism seem particularly relevant here but you can think of others. In Chapter 2 we saw items from one of the scales for empathy. A low score on empathy is expected from the deniers based on their lack of concern for the environment their children will share, but this is an empirical question; we may be surprised. Do you find echoes in your own data? Or not? The reader needs to know.

Some Methods Particularly Appropriate for Studying a Social Movement From a Psychodynamically Informed Perspective

1. *Elite and specialized interviews* with key figures in the denial movement. If access were granted, using Lewis Dexter's (1971) recommendations for getting access, this could be illuminating. One would have to be sure to protect the confidentiality of the interviewees, however.
2. *Use of informants* within the movement. This might be feasible if you were open about your own views but wanted to know more. Again, you would need to protect the confidentiality of your informants. Potential informants could be chosen by snowball sampling, maximum variation sampling, criterion sampling, or other forms of *purposeful sampling* (see Patton, 2014).
3. *Participant observation*. It is a preferred method if your presence as a researcher can be safely disclosed to the subjects of the research. But I don't recommend *undisclosed* participant observation in conflictful or hostile environments, such as some social movements or some political rallies, where it would be very awkward indeed if your deception was discovered. Even in a benign environment acting as an "undisclosed participant observer" involves a high degree of dissimulation and deception, which would likely make you feel uncomfortable and unethical. Long ago, I considered doing a field study of a small splinter group of socialists in Boston, mostly bookish elderly lower-middle class people, quite sincere and opposed to violence. I couldn't have been accepted if I had acknowledged that my purpose was to do a doctoral thesis. That would have been perceived as much too "bourgeois." Although I liked the people, I gave up after two meetings because I felt too uncomfortable with the impending deception.
4. *Systematic study of published statements*. This is a promising approach. The study should use thick description and very extensive verbatim quotations, similar to the methods used in Chapter 8. The materials examined could include speeches, blogs, opinion columns, video presentations, and pamphlets, possibly using machine-aided content analysis. These published statements could then be examined using the protocol suggested in Chapter 3, or by one you deem more suitable to this situation. The results might then be compared to items from relevant attitude scales. As in elite and specialized interviewing, consulting scales such as dogmatism, ethnocentrism, and social dominance would likely be helpful in interpreting your data, as would looking at an empathy scale, on which a low score would be expected.

The Second Case Study: Legal Research as Part of a Psychodynamically Sophisticated Inquiry Into the Corporate World

Legal research is a method particularly revealing in this area. But many of the research methods we have looked at in this chapter, and in earlier chapters, also apply to inquiry into corporate irrationality and will be helpful to the researcher in this area.

The Problem We Face

The modern corporation represents one of the most advanced embodiments of the functional rationality we have been discussing. As we saw in Chapter 10, Max Weber pointed out the connection between bureaucracy and functional rationality, Karl Mannheim showed the connection of functional rationality to industrialization, and Jacques Ellul explained the connection of technique to functional rationality. Let us consider here what light legal research can shed on this relationship. This inquiry will also serve to illuminate the connection between psychodynamic inquiry and legal scholarship.

The most famous study in this genre is by the eminent legal scholar Joel Bakan. His book, *The Corporation: The Pathological Pursuit of Profit and Power* (2004) has been translated into 20 languages. I am very much indebted to his exposition in what follows. Bakan offers insights into unconscious processes in the corporate world. He argues that we have, step by step, created a Frankenstein monster of immense power, an amoral entity, a psychopathic institution that can feel no empathy or remorse. (For the specific impact on children, see Bakan, 2011). Bakan demonstrates that the corporate psychopathic personality stems from the legal nature of *the large Anglo-American publicly traded business corporation*. Corporate officers have a legal duty and responsibility *only* to the stockholders. They have *no* legal duty to the customers nor to employees. Legally, no concern *should* be shown for the welfare of customers or employees, unless it directly or indirectly promotes profits, or is compelled by specific legislative regulations. Such regulations, such as occupational safety laws, laws requiring labeling, and laws forbidding certain additives, have universally been opposed by these corporations. Bakan shows that this opposition makes logical sense given that the corporation is designed to be totally selfish and amoral, and is *legally required to be so* unless compelled by outside forces. In this summary of Bakan's work I have used "profits" as a generic category that also includes market share, competitive position, return on investment, and stock price, as was long ago pointed out by George Katona (1951).

How did we create this monster, now too strong and efficient for us to control? "Corporations now dominate society and government" (Bakan, 2004, p. 3). *The Corporation* gives the history of the legislation and court rulings, over the centuries, that have permitted the large Anglo-American publicly traded business corporation to obtain overwhelming political and social power.

(The following discussion follows very closely Joel Bakan's masterful exposition, in abbreviated form). Firstly, in England starting in about 1690, corporations were given *the power to sell stock to the general public in unlimited amounts*. Next was given *the right of limited liability*, which was not possessed by individuals or partnerships: the owners of the corporation couldn't be held liable for debts or civil damages greater than the value of the stock they owned. This occurred in England in 1856 and in the United States over the latter half of the nineteenth century. These court and legislative decisions gave corporations the power to amass huge amounts of capital and therefore to dictate the terms of economic transactions. The huge influx of capital also gave the large Anglo-American publicly traded business corporation great political power.

Then *were lifted the restrictions on mergers, acquisitions, owning stock in another company, and on doing business for only a single purpose*. In the United States these changes became law in the two decades starting with 1890. Corporate charters, starting with Delaware, lifted "unpopular restrictions on corporations, so a corporation, instead of being restricted to doing business for a specific purpose, could *do business for any and all purposes." A wave of consolidation* of large numbers of medium-sized corporations into far fewer giant corporations followed. "Between 1898 and 1904, more than 1800 corporations were consolidated into 157" (ibid, p. 14). With thousands of stockholders for each corporation, *the actual control passed to the corporation itself*, with its board of directors and top executives. An autonomous institution was being created.

Then, by the end of the nineteenth century, *the corporation became a person under the law*, with all the rights of a real person under the Fourteenth Amendment, originally enacted "to protect freed slaves." The key Supreme Court decision was *Santa Clara County vs. Southern Pacific Railroad,* 118 U.S. 394 (1886). No longer did the corporation exist under the theory that it was a grant from the state; now it had all the rights of a real person.

Corporations soon saw the effectiveness of *large-scale public relations campaigns* in the media, in which they sought to persuade the consumers and citizenry that the corporation was their friend and had their best interest at heart. Billions were spent and are being spent in this effort. The legal justification is that these campaigns protect the market share and profitability of the corporation. *Corporate donations to political figures* ensured easy access and influence by their *well-financed lobbyists.*

Then, "In the mid-1970s the Supreme Court extended First Amendment protection *to corporate financing of elections involving ballot initiatives,* a decision that opened the door to corporations' near-complete takeover of the electoral process" (*Bellotti First National Bank of Boston v. Bellotti,* 435 U.S. 765 (1978); Bakan, 2004, p. 103).

And so through lavish corporate contributions to politicians, well-financed tax-deductible lobbying, and direct funding of the electoral process, the corporations got control of the legislatures. (As I would put it, we now have the best legislatures money can buy.)

The unions, once a countervailing force, have been greatly weakened by *corporate policies of automation and outsourcing,* made possible by the corporation's ability to raise enormous amounts of capital.

Bakan is not alone is his view of the large publicly traded Anglo-American business corporation. He quotes Supreme Court Justice Louis Brandeis in a 1933 Supreme Court judgment, writing that "corporations were Frankenstein monsters capable of doing evil" (Louis K. Liggitt Co. et al. v. Lee, Comptroller et al., 288 US 517, 1933, pp. 548, 567).

After the publication of Joel Bakan's 2004 book, a landmark Supreme Court decision, *Citizens United v. Federal Election Commission,* 558 U.S. 310 (2010) ruled that corporations, as legal persons, have the *First Amendment free speech right to spend unlimited funds to influence elections by advertisements, films and media efforts of all sorts, and to advocate the election or defeat of candidates.* Many see this decision as tantamount to handing the electoral process over to huge corporations, with their almost unlimited financial resources.

In 2014 came *Burwell v. Hobby Lobby Stores Inc.,* in which the Supreme Court ruled *that a corporation can be exempt from a law—in that case, the Affordable Care Act's requirement that employers pay for contraception—that its owners sincerely object to on religious grounds if there is any less restrictive means of achieving the law's ends.* The Supreme Court ruled that requiring family-owned corporations to pay for insurance coverage for contraception under the Affordable Care Act violated a federal law protecting religious freedom. It was, a dissent said, "a decision of startling breadth."

The 5-to-4 ruling, which applied to two companies owned by Christian families, opened the door to many challenges from corporations over laws that they claim violate their religious liberty.

According to the *New York Times* (Liptak, 2014), the decision, issued on the last day of the term, "reflected what appears to be a key characteristic of the court under Chief Justice John G. Roberts Jr.—an inclination toward nominally incremental rulings with vast potential for great change..."

The *Times* noted that Justice Ruth Bader Ginsburg's dissent attacked the majority opinion as "a radical overhaul of corporate rights...which could apply to all corporations and to countless laws...Although the court attempts to cabin its language to closely held corporations, its logic extends to corporations of any size, public or private...Corporations could now object to health coverage of vaccines, or paying the minimum wage, or according women equal pay for substantially similar work."

And so, by a long series of judicial decisions and legislation expanding the powers of corporations and removing controls on them, a monster too powerful to control, and dangerous because psychopathic, was created.

Again, all of this applies to *large, Anglo-American publicly traded business corporations*. And Bakan is very clear that it is not primarily the problem that corporate executives are psychopathic personalities. Although some of them are psychopaths in business suits, most are responsible people outside the corporate environment. According to Bakan's analysis, *the real psychopathy is in the corporation itself, an institution that is legally compelled to be selfish*, and which, as a result, has all the characteristics of the psychopathic personality. According to Bakan, it is "amoral, power-oriented, manipulative, superficial in its dealings with the public, unconcerned with their effect on the environment or about externalities of any kind, deceptive in describing their activities, refusing to take responsibility for their actions, unable to feel empathy or remorse, unable to control their rapacity, and endlessly dissimulating, sanctimonious and hypocritical."

What comes to my mind as particularly egregious examples are Enron, Morgan Stanley, Goldman Sachs, the oil company polluters, the American corporations that did business with Hitler in the 1930s, IBM's provision and administration of identity cards to the South African dictatorship before its fall; and the sale by American corporations of torture equipment to Latin American dictators.

Others have also chronicled the corporate pursuit of profit to the exclusion of ethical considerations. During the Spanish Civil War, Texaco sold oil only to the Franco forces. DuPont sold Franco 40,000 bombs and evaded the American Embargo by shipping via Germany. All letters from American subsidiaries in Germany to their offices in the United States after 1933 had to have "Heil Hitler" at the bottom of the letter. (See the description in Alan Furst's historical novel, *Midnight in Europe*, 2014., p. 34.)

Bakan notes that IBM "jumped when Hitler sought its technical assistance in running the Nazi extermination and slave labor programs. IBM provided the Nazis with Hollerith tabulation machines that used punched cards to do their calculations" (2004, p. 88). He cites Edwin Black (2001): "The head office in New York had a complete understanding...that their machines were in the concentration camps generally and they knew that the Jews were being exterminated...IBM technicians serviced the machines, IBM engineers trained their users, and IBM supplied punch cards for the machines, according to Black, at least until 1941 when the U.S. declared war on Germany."

Bakan notes that corporate ruthlessness has resisted a large number of legislative attempts to control it. There has been resistance to child labor laws, workplace safety laws, pollution controls, and cigarette sales. In the 1911 Triangle Shirtwaist Factory fire in Manhattan, the locked-in workers, mostly immigrant women, were burnt alive (Bakan, 2004, p. 71). This disaster stirred a movement for legislation for workplace safety precautions. This legislation was vigorously resisted by large corporations lobbying the Congress.

For years the cigarette manufacturers gave testimony to Congress that smoking was not carcinogenic and not addictive, until the research studies overwhelmed them. Finally, it was discovered from internal memos that the tobacco companies had known all along that the cigarettes were carcinogenic and they had been trying to develop tobacco plants whose tobacco would be more addictive.

It appears to me that, at present, the denial from the cigarette era is being repeated with regard to global warming due to human activity. As in the cigarette era, the overwhelming scientific consensus is being debunked by heavily funded corporate lobbyists.

In recent years, sweatshops in California have been found to be using undocumented immigrant workers in underpaid and dangerous work environments. A number of large prestigious American corporations, especially in the clothing and garment field, have been criticized for relying on child and captive labor in developing world suppliers; however, as a result of public pressure and adverse publicity they have made some attempts to rectify this situation.

In response to these corporate excesses, there is also a long tradition in the United States of the attempt to control corporate power. There have been some popular movements that have at least limited corporate power to some extent I am indebted to the legal scholar, Professor Bradford Mank, for the following examples:

> In the 1890s there was the Populist Movement, William Jennings Bryan orated on the use of silver vs. gold as the standard, with the famous "Cross of Gold" speech.
>
> In the early 1900s, there was the Progressive Movement. Antitrust Laws broke up Standard Oil. There were Food & Drug Safety Laws, and the Federal Trade Commission Act of 1914. Theodore Roosevelt and Woodrow Wilson were influences in this direction,
>
> In the 1930s there was FDR's [Franklin D. Roosevelt's] New Deal. The Securities and Exchange Commission was set up. The Glass–Steagall Act limited commercial banks from investment banking. (But this was rescinded in the late 1990s, permitting excesses that eventually led to the 2008 financial crisis.) In 1935 the passage of the Wagner Act created the National Labor Relations Board, although the Taft–Hartley Act in 1947 put some limits on the Wagner Act.
>
> In the 1970s there were passed environmental laws: Clean Air, Clean Water, and the Superfund. There were also campaign finance reforms, although many of these were limited by the courts.
>
> In 2010: Dodd–Frank Wall Street Reform and the Consumer Protection Act was passed, and in 2011 the Consumer Financial Protection Bureau was established (all Mank, personal communication).

So there are countervailing psychological currents that also need to be researched.

In considering Joel Bakan's work it is important to emphasize that his legal history concerns large, publicly traded Anglo-American business corporations.

For example, it does not apply to small corporations, such as those that sell the recumbent trikes I use, or to the small plumbers and electricians I use, or my local tire store that does not charge people when they stop by to have more air put in their tires.

It does not apply to corporations that are not publicly traded, nor to non-profits, which, nonetheless, have a corporate bureaucratic structure. Nor does it apply well to some modern continental European corporations subject to considerable government control, as in France, Germany, and Scandinavia. It does not apply well to corporations that, by law, have labor representation on their boards of directors, as in Germany. And it doesn't apply well to those American corporations with a strong sense of community responsibility, like Starbucks, and some of the socially conscious, or "green," investment funds.

But it does apply within the realm of corporations of the type that Joel Bakan, a professor of corporate law, has specified: "large, Anglo-American publicly traded business corporations." And it certainly applies also to the Chinese corporations that have sold toxic toothpaste, toxic baby milk, and toxic toys, but Bakan does not provide data on this realm.

And, as we have seen, some corporate executives carry personally this strange mentality of ruthless exploitation combined with dissimulation and hypocrisy. Bernie Madoff defrauded non-profits, even Jewish non-profits focused especially on helping members of his own religious group. Some were forced by his depredations to shut down entirely. It is not just Madoff. For example, a number of executives from Tyco International, Enron, WorldCom, and Goldman Sachs, and from some of the hedge funds, have been indicted and convicted. The executives of Global Crossing got away free.

In looking at these data one must also remember Bakan is outlining a legal structural imperative for exploitation, not a universal law of human nature for corporate employees.

From an organizational point of view, the situation is very complex and researchers need to take this into account. In very large corporations, with many thousands or millions of stockholders, management is essentially separated from the individual shareholders and, to a major extent, can pursue its own agenda, disregarding its fiduciary duty to the shareholders. For example, in the cases of Enron, WorldCom, and Global Crossing, the victims of the fraud were the individual shareholders. Also victimized were many lower- and middle-echelon individual employees, who held as their main assets shares of company stock. They lost everything when the firms went under, including their stock, their jobs, and their pensions.

Exploring the strange mental processes that drove these disasters is the role of the kind of research I am proposing. Is there a failure of the ability to test reality, to see what is real, outside of themselves? Or is it grandiosity, or narcissism, or a psychopathic inability to empathize with others? Are there Gotterdammerung self-destructive fantasies? Or revenge motives of some kind? Or some strange sense of entitlement? Or contempt for others? Or a sense of impunity? Or are they driven by an exalted sense of individual destiny based on some narcissistic anti-empathic ideology, such as that of Ayn Rand? We won't know until we do the research.

But psychodynamic understanding is inevitably complex. For example, people have deep ambivalences, hating and loving at the same time. The movie *Joyeux Noel* depicts the first Christmas in 1914 during World War I

(Carion, 2005). The two warring sides declared a cease fire and celebrated Christmas together. They then resumed fighting and terrible bloodshed followed. Deep ambivalences and psychodynamic complexity bespeak the need for psychodynamically sophisticated social science research.

There are also some major exceptions to the picture that Joel Bakan presents, corporations that have resisted a blind adherence to the maximum exploitation model called for by the legal status of the modern corporation. There are firms that sell mostly organically grown food, or Starbucks, which emphasizes fair trade in coffee.

CVS, the second largest U.S. drugstore chain, on 1 October 2014 stopped selling cigarettes, a policy decreed by their CEO, Larry J. Merlo. But their competitor, the giant Walgreen's, remains adamant, with their wall of cigarette packs displayed directly behind their checkout counters, making it convenient for people to risk getting cancer. Perhaps in response to the CVS initiative, Walgreens has recently adopted a policy whereby every employee tells the customer to "Be Well!" as they check out. The employees appear sincere but the corporation continues to sell cigarettes at the checkout counters. In my experience at least, Walgreen's pharmacy department is well organized, highly efficient, and they offer and aggressively promote flu shots during the fall flu season, a valuable service to our society. The flu shots are free if you have insurance, since the Affordable Care Act requires that all complying insurance policies cover them. They also have a nurse on duty for consultation in some of their stores. Cigarettes, and flu shots and nurses. Is there ambivalence here? Are there two mentalities competing within some corporations?

Manipulativeness, dissimulation, and hypocrisy, exemplified by the charming, convivial, and avuncular Bernie Madoff, are part of the corporate syndrome described by Joel Bakan. But not for *all* corporations. Perhaps for the institution *corporation* but surely not for some of its organizational exemplars. As we noted above, there are major exceptions to the corporate amorality Bakan describes.

To choose another example, Bill Gates has established a foundation that has donated $28 billion to address education and world health problems. Warren Buffett, who plays bridge with his friend Bill Gates, has contributed $2.8 billion to the Bill and Melinda Gates Foundation. As far as I can tell, these gifts reflect sincere altruistic motives.

But what about the charitable donations of ruthless tycoons like Andrew Carnegie, who became generous only after he had crushed his rivals? These donations appear different, but we simply don't know, and we need to know in order to understand the modern corporation.

I think we have never really understood this combination of altruism and avarice. For example, Henry Ford was proud that his manufacturing system, with its use of interchangeable parts, made it possible for millions of people, "the average person," to own a car, transforming American society. Yet he was a life-long anti-Semite (Meyers, 1955). There are and always have been deep psychological waters in the area of the corporate mentality.

Large charitable donations by the super rich typically use money derived from their corporate enterprises. This appears to be something of a paradox in view of the avarice and ruthlessness of many of the corporations Bakan describes. What are the motivations and fantasies, some of them no doubt outside of conscious awareness, involved here?

A classmate of mine established a foundation with the assets from the engineering firm he founded, propelled by motives that were clearly altruistic, as could be seen from his past history of community involvement. The politically active ultra-conservative David Koch, of Koch Industries, has donated millions to establish the Koch Cancer Research Building at Johns Hopkins. He has also donated millions to establish the David H. Koch Institute for Integrative Cancer Research at M.I.T., his alma mater, where he had been a star basketball player. This is clearly not a "let them eat cake!" ethos, but what is it? We simply don't know how the psychopathy of some of the "large Anglo-American publicly traded business corporations" Bakan describes, some with their assets registered in the Cayman Islands to avoid United States taxes, relates to the generosity of some of their major stockholders.

Many corporate employees volunteer in their local communities with real concern, not for a public relations purpose. An executive in a large podiatry practice in the Midwest ventures into the central city ghetto one evening a week to work on the feet of the homeless (which are usually in terrible condition). He does this out of a sense of religious duty, which, in his case, trumps other considerations. Other executives I know volunteer at hospice facilities, something one would not expect if "community service" were merely being rendered by corporate policies to maintain good public relations in support of profits.

As we can tell from Bakan's study, the legal history of the "large Anglo-American publicly traded business corporation" tends to drive that institution toward amorality in the pursuit of power and profits. But, as we have seen, there appears to be a vast range of motivations among the corporate employees and owners themselves. As Timothy Garton Ash (1997a) put it, we don't know "what makes one person a Stauffenberg and another a Speer."

And we need to know. In organizational, institutional, and social movement areas like these, we need psychodynamically informed research using social science research methods.

The Big Picture: The Range of Destructive, Self-destructive, and Bizarre Activities on the World Scene

Corporate ruthlessness and denial of climate change are only two examples of the deeply irrational actives on the world scene. In earlier chapters we considered social violence, as at Tuam, Bethany, the Magdalene nurseries, and the Rotherham human trafficking; authoritarian leadership as with Kim Jung-un, Zhirinovsky, Le Pen, Papadopoulos, and Pétain; genocide, as in the extermination of the "unfit" in Germany, followed by Auschwitz and the other concentration camps; national conflict as in the Munich crisis; and terror, as in the Dresden firebombing, and the torture and murder of captives, as with ISIS. We need to be careful that we don't wipe ourselves out before climate change has a chance to do us in.

My goal in this book has been to explain methods by which these problems might be investigated, methods that combine psychodynamic inquiry with social scientific procedures. I feel that given the world situation, there is a great need for investigators who are proficient both in psychodynamic psychology and in social science research methods. We really do need to look deeply into the irrationalities on the world scene, and we need to do it in a scientifically valid and credible way.

Appendix

An Experimental Test of Accurate Empathy

I will outline here six experiments on creativity that I did long ago, which I now see have an additional significance: *they provide experimental evidence that empathic understanding can be accurate*. Firstly, I will present experimental evidence indicates that *differences in empathic tendency do exist between certain professional groups*. These results support the assertions of Baron-Cohen et al. (1985) to that effect.

Secondly, I will present detailed experimental evidence using a variety of validated outcome measures and a variety of experimental participants, which places the Baron-Cohen research in a new perspective: I find that when instructed to replicate the thought patterns of another professional or social group, some people can do so to an impressive extent. This replication of the thought patterns of another professional or social group, through the empathic method, represents mentalization of a high order, and appears to be what is involved in empathic understanding.

This work is drawn from my doctoral dissertation at Harvard (Meyers, 1963), and is available from the Harvard University Library; it was also published as an educational audio tape by the University of California at Berkeley.

In reading this appendix it is important to remember that the changes in scores reported here are not measures of increased creativity of the participants; they are measures of their ability to empathize with the attitudes and visual preferences of another social group.

Experiment I: Differences in Intraception/Extraception Among Professional Groups

Here, I present evidence from my own research (Experiment I) that artists and scientists differ on the Intraception/Extraception Scale (I/E Scale), which appears to be a measure of systemization versus empathic thinking akin to mentalization.

Experiment I used this measure, which was devised at Harvard by Henry Murray (1938). Intraception he defined as the tendency to think subjectively, in holistic terms, to care very much about the emotions of people, to be swayed by emotions in making decisions, to be interested in the spiritual, to indulge in grand plans and fantasies, to rely on intuition, and to adopt a romantic view of life. Extraception he defined as the opposite of intraception, that is, the objective, rationalistic approach, the emphasis on facts, details, practicality, objectivity of judgments, interest in things scientific, economic, material, or mechanical, reliance on reason, and tendency to be conventional rather than unconventional.

Experiment I found that a sample of ten graduate students in physics scored much higher in the direction of extraception than did a sample of eight art students. The art students scored much higher in the direction of intraception than did the physics students. These results suggest differences between professions in the proclivity to mentalize. And these results are consistent with Simon Baron-Cohen's research showing that the professions differ along a systemizing versus empathizing dimension.

This study provides evidence that certain professional or social groups do differ in the tendency to take an introspective stance toward their world. Since the participants were in the normal realm psychologically (as opposed, for example, to people with autism or Asperger's syndrome), I take these differences to indicate *preferences* in how they see the world, and preferences in willingness to introspect and to exhibit empathic responses freely, not primarily differences in *ability* to do these things.

Experiment IIA

Having found impressive evidence in Experiment I the fact that artists and scientists differ in intraceptive versus extraceptive tendency, I proceeded to find out if this difference in artistic and scientific thinking was known in our culture and, if known, could be reproduced by ordinary people, that is, non-artists and non-scientists. A group of participants, 29 in number, was chosen from the Harvard–Radcliffe undergraduate populations. Participants were divided into two groups, I ($N = 14$) and II ($N = 15$), in such a way that there were no fine arts concentrators in group I and no physical science concentrators in group II.

Each participant was asked to take the I/E Scale answering it "as an artist would" (if he or she was in group I), or "as a scientist would" (if he or she was in group II.) No participant knew what instructions other participants had.

The I/E Scale is scored in such a way that intraception gives a high score and extraception gives a low score. The result was that group I, with the "artist" instructions, scored far in the intraception direction (68.8) and the group with the "scientist" instructions scored far in the extraception direction (18.9), a difference statistically significant beyond the .001 level.

This is an important result since it provides evidence that when asked to do so, *ordinary people, that is, non-artists, can empathize sufficiently with artists to answer emotionally laden questions strongly in the direction that actual artists do.* It also indicates that *when asked to do so, ordinary people, that is, non-scientists, can answer emotionally laden questions strongly in the direction that actual scientists do.*

These results imply that a motivated person can, in certain circumstances, empathize accurately with the distinctive thought processes of a member of another professional or social group.

Experiment IIB

It is wise to demonstrate a research finding across a variety of outcome measures so that the findings are *robust* (not likely to vary much across modest changes in circumstances) and have *external validity* (are likely to apply to the world outside the research laboratory). Therefore, they *should not be restricted to one dependent variable,* even one so relevant as intraception–extraception. And they should *apply to some other research populations* beyond artists and scientists at universities.

Therefore, in Experiment IIB we consider a somewhat different social and professional group, namely people defined by our society as highly creative and original, from the 1950s and 1960s. Such people in Frank Barron's studies, described in detail in Chapter 2, included Pulitzer Prize winners, National Book Award winners, Nobel Laureates, famous architects, and the like (Barron, 1963). We can ask whether ordinary people can accurately empathize with some of their *attitudinal preferences.* The test used on Experiment IIB was Barron's Originality Test, made up of responses to attitudinal items that are answered differently by people defined by our society as highly creative and original.

In the present experiment we wish to see if ordinary subjects, when asked to do so by role-playing instructions, can produce responses yielding high scores on the Barron Originality Test (Barron, 1955), which is an *attitudinal measure. If they can produce high scores, it implies that they can empathize sufficiently and accurately with the attitudes of participants in Barron's studies to give similar responses.* But a finding that at least some ordinary people have the ability to emphasize accurately would suggest that inquiry that includes attention to unconscious processes, which depends on accurate empathy, might be done successfully. Let us find out.

The participants were 39 undergraduate students at Harvard and Radcliffe.

Participants in group A1 were given the Barron Originality Test and asked to answer it (standard instructions).

Participants in group A2 were given the Barron Originality Test and asked to answer it "as a very creative and original person would."

Each participant in group A3 was given the Barron Originality Test with standard instructions. When he or she had finished, each participant was given the Barron Originality Test a second time, with instructions to answer it "as a very creative and original person would."

The results were that the participants in group A2, with the empathy-based instructions, scored much higher on the Barron Originality Test than did the participants in group A1, which had the standard instructions.

Moreover, the participants in group A3, which had first the standard instructions and then the empathy-based instructions, scored much higher on the Barron Originality Test with the empathy-based instructions than they had earlier with the standard instructions.

These results imply that, when motivated to do so, people at the undergraduate level can under certain circumstances empathize accurately with a socially defined group, namely persons designated as highly creative and original by our society.

Experiment III: Empathizing With the Visual Preferences of People Socially Defined as Creative and Original

Experiment III used tests of *visual preferences* that characterize people socially defined as creative and original.

The Welsh Figure Preference Test consists of 400 black and white abstract line drawings (Barron and Welsh, 1952). The participant in the experiment is asked to indicate whether he "likes" or "dislikes" each of the drawings. A minority of items, about 60 in number, form subscales dubbed the Barron Welsh Art Scale (BW) and the Revised Art Scale (RA) (Barron and Welsh, 1952; Welsh, 1959).

Judged by their content, these two subscales measure a preference for complex asymmetrical "dynamic" drawings that seem to ask for further organization, and a dislike for simple, symmetrical, balanced, static, and completely organized drawings. The scales were therefore considered measures of "preference for complexity" by their originators (Barron, 1952a, 1953).

Further research gave evidence of impressive validity (Welsh, 1959). These tests can distinguish students in creative writing classes from other students; artists from non-artists; art students rated as high in ability from art students rated as having lower ability; "independents" from "yielders" in the Asch situation (a measure of a person's tendency to conform to a group consensus that is patently false); Ph.D. candidates rated "original" by faculty from Ph.D. candidates rated "unoriginal," both in the sciences and in other graduate fields; and medical school seniors rated "original" from medical school seniors rated "unoriginal" by the medical school faculty. What is important for us is that these individuals typically scored high on the BW and RA scales. These findings supported the idea that creative people prefer to deal with complexity, and that the BW and RA scales are measures of preference for complexity.

I used the BW and the RA scales in the present experiment as measures of a visual preference presumably associated with creativity, and characterizing creative people. I hoped to show that participants, either psychologically naïve or sophisticated, when asked to answer these scales as a creative person would, can actually do so. If the participants can actually do this, it will show that people actually can "mentalize," that is, they are able to empathize accurately and validly with a socially defined group sufficiently well to produce, on request, the kind of thought processes characteristic of people in that social group.

A strength of the study is that instead of using the BW and RA scales alone, the first 200 items of the Welsh Figure Preference Test were used instead. Of these, only 30 were items from the BW or RA scales; hence, the 30 relevant items were only 15 percent of the 200 items the participants were asked to judge. This means that the relevant items were hidden among a much larger group of items, making the task of the participants much more challenging since they had no idea that only a minority of items were relevant.

Group A, of five people aged between 20 and 30, was composed of psychology graduate students at Harvard and Boston University. It was intended to include people fairly sophisticated in psychology.

Group B, of five people, was intended as a group of "lay" people of good intelligence. All were college graduates. Three were working as secretaries, one as a city planner, and one as a graduate student in chemistry. They were selected so that none had any appreciable undergraduate training in psychology nor any special interest in it. None had ever been in psychotherapy or psychoanalysis.

No participant in either group knew that this research pertained to creativity.

The study hypothesis was that the overall group of ten participants would improve their scores after being given role-playing instructions, and that this would also be true for the both subgroups of five, group A and group B. There were two administrations of the tests, the first time with standard instructions, and the second time with instructions to "answer it as a very creative and original person would." On the first administration, the participants had no clue that the testing related to creativity; on the second administration they were led to believe that all items pertained to creativity. Under such challenging conditions, could either group improve its scores from the first administration to the second?

The improvement was very large and hence statistically significant despite the small numbers of participants.

Examination of the test results produced by the participants in each administration revealed that the participants seemed to have an almost uncanny sense of which items pertained to creativity. Very few of the irrelevant items were answered differently in the second (role-playing instruction) administration compared with the first administration.

This study provides strong evidence that people can actually "mentalize," that is, they are able to empathize accurately and validly with a socially defined group sufficiently well to produce on request the visual preferences characteristic of people in that social group.

Experiment IV

This is an experiment using a Combined Attitude Test, which uses data relating to deeply held personal and social attitudes.

The Combined Attitude Test is comprised of items from three attitude scales. One was the Originality Test, described in Experiment II.

A second component of the Combined Test is the Complexity Questionnaire, made up of questions answered differently by high versus low scorers on the BW and the RA scales (Barron, 1953).

A third component, the Independence of Judgment Scale, consists of items answered differently by people who resist a false group consensus in a group situation (Barron, 1952b).

Barron and Asch concluded that originality and independence of judgment are part of the same personality orientation.

Design of Experiment IV

Participants were recruited as volunteers from two classes in educational psychology at the Harvard Graduate School of Education. After the experiment, inquiry revealed that none of the participants was familiar with the psychological study of creativity.

There were two administrations in this experiment, spaced a week apart. In the first administration, all were given the Barron Combined Attitude Test with standard instructions to answer in terms of their own preferences After the first administration, the 13 participants were divided into two groups, group C ($N = 7$) and group N ($N = 6$). In the second administration, group N was given the Barron Combined Attitude Test, again with the same instructions as before. Group C was asked to "take these tests as you feel an exceptionally creative and original person would."

The result I found was that group C, with the creative instructions, increased significantly in score on the Barron Combined Attitude Test. No increase was found in group N, which had neutral instructions on both administrations.

The results of Experiment IV again indicate that people can empathize with the mentality of a defined social group, in this case exceptionally creative and original people, sufficiently well to reproduce accurately the scores of such people on relevant attitude tests. This demonstrated capacity to empathize accurately, which is an indication of mentalization, bodes well for clinically informed inquiry.

Experiment V

This experiment is a replication of Experiment IV with the same design and the same tests but with a somewhat different population of subjects: 12 undergraduate science concentrators at the Massachusetts Institute of Technology. This experiment extends our study of mentalization to another branch of the academic subculture, with the hope of increasing the generality of our findings.

The administration of each session, the order of testing, and the instructions were identical to Experiment IV. As in Experiment IV, it was found, from the first administration to the second, that group C increased in scores on the Barron Combined Questionnaire; no increase was found in group N.

Taken together with the results of the three previous experiments, this result strengthens our conclusion that *people can empathize with the mentality of a defined social group, in this case exceptionally creative and original people,* sufficiently well to reproduce accurately the scores of such people on relevant attitude tests. This demonstrated capacity to empathize accurately, which is an indication of mentalization, again bodes well for clinically sophisticated inquiry.

Experiment VI

This experiment was conducted by Frank Barron and Timothy Leary, using as participants 20 students at the Rhode Island School of Design, a highly regarded art school on the college level. The group was given the Barron Combined Attitude Test in March, with standard instructions, and again in May with instructions to answer it "as you feel an exceptionally creative and original person would." Their Barron Combined Attitude Test scores increased from an average of 46.8 on the first administration with standard instructions to an average score of 50.6 on the second administration with the creative instructions. With this large a sample, the difference was highly statistically significant. This result is consistent with the results of the first five experiments, all of which showed results in the predicted direction and all but one at a statistically significant level.

Experiment VI, with its large sample, drawn from a population of art students, demonstrates *that people can empathize with the mentality of a defined social group, in this case exceptionally creative and original people,* sufficiently well to reproduce accurately the scores of such people on relevant attitude tests. This result again provides evidence that accurate empathy with the mental life of a defined social group is, *under certain circumstances*, psychologically feasible.

Strength and Robustness of the Experiments

The experimental method is the most powerful research strategy for deciding contentious scientific disputes. All these studies were *experiments or quasi-experiments*, with hypotheses, manipulation of an independent variable, measurement of outcomes, and statistical tests of the significance of the results. In some experiments there was random assignment of cases to treatments; in others, groups of known composition were compared, for example, artists and scientists; and in others the test–retest design was used in which a group was compared with itself under different instructions.

It is a major strength of this series of experiments that the results are *consistent* across all the experiments.

Contributing to the robustness of the studies is the fact that they demonstrate the phenomenon of accurate empathy with *several* defined social groups: "artists," "scientists," and "exceptionally creative and original people."

Also giving robustness to the findings is that they are not confined to one outcome test: a variety of instruments were used. The first of these was the I/E Scale. Coming from an entirely different tradition were the BW and the RA, nested within the much larger Welch Figure Preference test, and using visual preferences rather than verbal attitude items. The Originality Scale, a verbal attitude measure was first used separately, and later combined with the Preference for Complexity Attitude Scale and the Independence of Judgment Scale, in the Combined Attitude Scale.

And all the above measures have been shown by Barron and McKinnon to discriminate well among real social groups, using item analysis and cross-validation.

Another strength of the studies is the diversity of the more than 100 participants included. Study populations included art students at Boston University, graduate students in physics at Harvard, psychology graduate students at Harvard, secretaries, a city planner, undergraduate students at M.I.T., and art students at the Rhode Island School of Design. One of the experiments demonstrated that both psychologically sophisticated and lay subjects are able to empathize accurately. (But all of the participants had at least some college education. We really have no evidence at all that high school drop-outs, for example, can empathize accurately in the test situation. They may be able to, but we don't know.)

The studies were done at different times and in different settings; the findings are not specific to a particular time and place, as would be the case in a single mass experiment in a single location. Replicated results are essential to science. For this reason, as the methodologist Lee Cronbach has pointed out, in the social research arena a "fleet of small studies" with some variation in participants, outcome measures, and settings is preferable to a single large social study in one setting with only one kind of participant and only one outcome measure. In methodologist Donald Campbell's terms, these experiments form a "patched-up design," a relatively strong design in which a particular strength of one study compensates for a particular vulnerability of another, and vice versa.

For example, we used both *test–retest,* and *after-only* designs. The test–retest design dispels the threat of bias from *selection,* the possibility the results were different because the groups were different to begin with. With a test–retest design, the groups are being compared to themselves, their own previous scores. The after-only design dispels the threat from the *practice effect,* the possibility that the change in scores is simply owing to the participant taking the test a second time with experience from the first time. There is no second time in an after-only design. This also dispels the threat from *instrument decay,* the possibility that if a test instrument is used more than once on the same participants it doesn't work so well, they tire of it. In the after-only design, it is used only once.

I think it is fair to infer from the studies shown in this appendix that accurate empathy with the mental life of a defined social group is, under certain circumstances, psychologically feasible.

References

Ackerman, D. (1989) O Muse! You do make things difficult! Available at: http://www.nytimes.com/books/97/03/02/reviews/ackerman-poets.html (accessed 12 March 2015).

Adorno, T.W., Frenkel-Brunswick, E., Levinson, D. and Nevitt Sanford, N. (1950) *The Authoritarian Personality* (New York: Harper).

Allport, G. (1954) *The Nature of Prejudice* (New York: Basic Books).

American Law Institute (1981) *Restatement (Second) of Contracts*, Paragraph 351.

Andrews, J. (2014) Foreclosure from Freud to Fannie Mae. In: Chancer, L. and Andrews, J. (eds) *The Unhappy Divorce of Sociology and Psychoanalysis*, pp. 269–83 (Basingstoke: Palgrave MacMillan).

Appleyard, D. and Lintell, M. (1972) The environmental quality of city streets: The resident's viewpoint. *Journal of the American Institute of Planners*, 38, 84–101.

Asch, S.E. (1951) Effects of group pressure on the modification and distortion of judgments. In: H. Guetzkow (ed.) *Groups, Leadership and Men*, pp. 177–90 (Pittsburgh, PA: Carnegie Press).

Asch, S.E. (1955). Opinions and social pressure. *Scientific American*, 193, 35.

Asch, S.E. (1956) Studies of independence and conformity. A minority of one against a unanimous majority. *Psychological Monographs*, 70, 1–70.

Ash, T.G. (1997a) *The File: A Personal History* (New York: Random House).

Ash, T.G. (1997b) The Romeo file. *The New Yorker*, April/May, 162–71.

Bakan, D. (1967a) The mystery–mastery complex in contemporary psychology. In: Bakan, D. (ed.) *On Method: Toward a Reconstruction of Psychological Investigation*, pp. 94–112 (San Francisco, CA: Jossey-Bass).

Bakan, D. (1967b) A Reconsideration of the problem of introspection. In: Bakan, D. (ed.) *On Method: Toward a Reconstruction of Psychological Investigation*, pp. 94–112 (San Francisco, CA: Jossey-Bass).

Bakan, J. (2004) *The Corporation: The Pathological Pursuit of Profit and Power* (New York: The Free Press).

Bakan, J. (2011) *Childhood Under Siege: How Big Business Targets Children* (New York: Free Press).

Balconi, M. and Lucchiari, C. (2007) Consciousness and emotional face recognition. *Journal of Psychophysiology*, 21, 100–8.

Baron-Cohen, S., Wheelwright, S., Skinner, R., Martin, J. and Clubley, E. (2001) The autism-spectrum quotient (AQ): Evidence from Asperger syndrome/high functioning autism males and females, scientists and mathematicians. *Journal of Autism and Developmental Disorders*, 31, 5–17.

Baron-Cohen, S., Leslie, A.M. and Frith, U. (1985) Does the autistic child have a theory of mind? *Cognition*, 21, 37–46.

Baron-Cohen, S., Tager-Flusberg, S. and Cohen, D. (eds) (2000) *Understanding Other Minds: Perspectives from Developmental Cognitive Neuroscience* (New York: Oxford University Press).

Barron, F. (1952a) Personality style and perceptual choice. *Journal of Personality*, 20, 358–401.

Barron, F. (1952b) Some personality correlates of independence of judgment. *Journal of Personality*, 21, 288–9.

Barron, F. (1953) Complexity-simplicity as a personality dimension. *Journal of Abnormal and Social Psychology*, 48, 163–72.

Barron, F. (1955) The disposition toward originality. *Journal of Abnormal Psychology*, 51, 478–85.

Barron, F. (1958) The psychology of imagination. *Scientific American*, 199, 150–6.

Barron, F. (1963) *Creativity and Psychological Health* (Princeton, NJ: Van Nostrand).

Barron, F. and Welsh, G. (1952) Artistic perception as a possible factor in personality style: Its measurement by a figure preference test. *Journal of Psychology*, 33, 199–233.

Barry, D., Barstow, D., Glater, J.D., Liptak, A. and Steinberg, J. (2003) Correcting the record; Times reporter who resigned leaves long trail of deception. Available at: http://www.nytimes.com/2003/05/11/us/correcting-the-record-times-reporter-who-resigned-leaves-long-trail-of-deception.html (accessed 13 March 2015).

BBC News (2014a) Rotherham child abuse scandal: 1,400 children exploited, report finds. Available at: http://www.bbc.com/news/uk-england-south-yorkshire-28939089 (accessed 18 February 2015).

BBC News (2014b) French national front widens in anti-semitism row. Available at: http://www.bbc.co.uk/news/world-europe-27786901 (accessed 12 March 2015).

BBC News (2014c) Heatwave halts Australian Open tennis matches. Available at: http://www.bbc.com/news/world-asia-25743438 (accessed 15 March 2015).

Beisel, D. (2003) *The Suicidal Embrace: Hitler, the Allies, and the Origins of the Second World War* (New York: Circumstantial Productions).

Berger, P. and Luckmann, T. (1966) *The Social Construction of Reality: A Treatise in the Sociology of Knowledge* (Garden City, NY: Doubleday).

Berk, R. (2012) *Criminal Justice Forecasts of Risk: A Machine Learning Approach* (New York: Springer).

Berlinsky, D. (2001) *The Advent of the Algorithm: The 300-Year Journey From and Idea to the Computer* (New York: Harcourt).

Best, A. (2014) *Wigmore on Evidence*, 4th ed. (New York: Aspen).

Best, A. and James, D. (2007) *Basic Tort Law: Cases, Statutes and Problems* (New York: Aspen Publishers).

Binion, R. (1976) *Hitler Among the Germans* (New York: Elsevier).

Black, E. (2001) *IBM and the Holocaust: The Strategic Alliance Between Nazi Germany and America's Most Powerful Corporation* (Lake Arbor, MD: Crown Books).

Blumer, H. (1956) Sociological analysis and the variable. *American Sociological Review*, 21, 683–90.

Blumer, H. (1969) *Symbolic Interactionism* (Englewood Cliffs, NJ: Prentice Hall).

Bradlee, B. (1995) Janet Cooke. In: Bradlee, B. (ed.) *A Good Life: Newspapering and Other Adventures*, pp. 435–53 (New York: Simon and Schuster).

Bromwich, D. (2011) Niall Ferguson's choice. A review of Ferguson's *Civilization: The West and the Rest. New York Review of Books*, Dec. 8.

Brooks, C. and Warren, R. (1938 [1976]) *Understanding Poetry* (New York: Holt, Rinehart and Winston).

Burgess, E. (1926) *The Urban Community* (Chicago, IL: University of Chicago Press).

Busch, F. (ed.) (2008) *Mentalization: Theoretical Considerations, Research Findings, and Clinical Implications* (New York: The Analytic Press).
Carhart-Harris. R. and Friston, K.J. (2010) The default-mode, ego-functions and free-energy: a neurobiological account of Freudian ideas. *Brain*, 133, 1265–83.
Carion, C. (dir.) (2005) *Joyeux Noel*. Nord-Ouest Productions.
Carnegie Science (2009) Zeroing in on Hubble's Constant. Available at: http://carnegiescience.edu/news/zeroing_hubble_s_constant (accessed 12 February 2015).
Carson, S. (2011) The unleashed mind: Why creative people are eccentric. *Scientific American*, 22, 4–5.
Chancer, L. and Andrews, J. (eds) (2014) Introduction. In: *The Unhappy Divorce: From Marginalization to Revitalization*, pp. 1–14 (Basingstoke: Palgrave).
Choe, S.-H. (2013) North Korea says leader's uncle was executed as a traitor. *New York Times*, Dec 12.
Cooke, J. (1980) Jimmy's world. *Washington Post*, Sep 28.
Cronbach, L. (1981) *Toward Reform of Program Evaluation* (San Francisco, CA: Jossey-Bass).
Czarniawska, B. (2000) *A City Reframed: Managing Warsaw in the 1990s* (London: Routledge).
Czarniawska, B. (2007) *Shadowing and Other Techniques for Doing Field Work in Modern Societies* (Copenhagen: Copenhagen Business School Press).
Davies, N. (1998) *Europe: A History* (London: Oxford University Press).
DeBreadun, D. (1994) Yearning for the bad old days of Dr. Zhivago. *Herald* (Glasgow), Jan 31.
DeWalt, K.M. and DeWalt, B.R. (2011) *Participant Observation: A Guide for Fieldworkers* (Lanham, MD: AltaMira Press).
Dexter, L. (1971) *Elite and Specialized Interviewing* (Chicago, IL: Northwestern University Press).
Dilthey, W. (1978) *Descriptive Psychology and Historical Understanding* (R.M. Zaner and K.L. Heiges, transl.) (The Hague: Martinus Nijoff).
Doob, A.N. and Gross, A.E. (1968) Status of frustrator as an inhibitor of horn-honking responses. *Journal of Social Psychology*, 76, 211–18.
Doolan, P. (2009) The argument with end. Available at: www.pauldoolan.com/2009/11/history-argument-with-end.html (accessed 13 March 2015).
Dorwart, R. and Meyers, W. (1981) *Citizen Participation in Mental Health: Research and Social Policy* (Springfield, IL: Charles Thomas).
Dowd, M. (2003) Pros at the con. *New York Times*, Nov 2.
Durkheim, E. (1897 [1997]) *Suicide* (New York: The Free Press).
Egan, T. (2004) Paul Ryan's Irish amnesia. Available at: http://www.nytimes.com/2014/03/16/opinion/sunday/paul-ryans-irish-amnesia.html (accessed 18 February 2015).
Ellison, R. and Gooding, S. (eds) (1976) *Eugene Ionesco: Rhinoceros*, Deuxieme Edition. (New York: Holt, Rinehart, and Winston).
Ellul, J. (1967). *The Technological Society* (New York: Random House).
Epstein, L. and Smith, A. (2014) *An Introduction to Empirical Legal Research* (Oxford: Oxford University Press).
Erdman, J. (2015) New England record snow tracker: One of the snowiest seasons in Boston, Providence, Bangor. Available at: http://www.weather.com/news/news/new-england-boston-record-snow-tracker (accessed 15 March 2015).

Falk, A. (2005) *Fratricide in the Holy Land: A Psychoanalytic View of the Arab–Israeli Conflict* (Madison, WI: University of Wisconsin Press).

Faust, D. (1996) *Mothers of Invention: Women of the Slaveholding South in the American Civil War* (Chapel Hill, NC, and London: University of North Carolina Press).

Fay, S. (1928) *The Origins of the World War* (London and New York: MacMillan).

Fenichel, O. (1945) *The Psychoanalytic Theory of Neurosis* (New York: W.W. Norton).

Ferris, J. (2014) *To Rise Again at a Decent Hour* (Boston, MA: Little Brown).

Feynman, R. (1984) *Surely You Are Joking, Mr. Feynman* (New York: W.W. Norton).

Fisher, M. (2013a) Kim Jong Un just had his own uncle killed. Why? *Washington Post*, Dec 12.

Fisher, M. (2013b) Russian parliament member says meteor was actually a U.S. weapons test. *Washington Post*, Feb 15.

Fleischmann, M. and Pons, S. (1989) Electrochemically induced nuclear fusion of deuterium. *Journal of Electroanalytical Chemistry*, 261, 301–8.

Framingham, J. (2011) Minnesota Multiphasic Personality Inventory (MMPI). Available at: http://psychcentral.com/lib/minnesota-multiphasic-personality-inventory-mmpi/0005959 (accessed 12 March 2015).

Friedman, T. (2009) *Hot, Flat, and Crowded* (New York: Picador Books).

Friedman, T. (2011) The Earth is full. *New York Times*, Jun 7.

Frith, U. (2008) *Autism: A Very Short Introduction* (Oxford: Oxford University Press).

Fromm, E. (1941) *Escape from Freedom* (New York: Holt, Rinehart, and Winston).

Fromm, E. (1961) Afterword. In: Orwell, G. *1984* (New York: Signet New American Library Edition).

Frosh, S. (2002) *Key Concepts in Psychoanalysis* (New York: New York University Press).

Frosh, S. (2010) *Psychoanalysis Outside the Clinic: Interventions in Psychosocial Studies* (London: Palgrave MacMillan).

Furst, A. (2014) *Midnight in Europe* (New York: Random House).

Gans, H. (1962) *The Urban Villagers* (New York: The Free Press).

Gardner, M. (1999) *Weird Water & Fuzzy Logic: More Notes of a Fringe Watcher* (Amherst, NY: Prometheus Books).

Garner, B.A. (2009) *Black's Law Dictionary*, 9th ed. (Eagan, MN: Thompson West Publishers).

Gay, P. (1985) *Freud for Historians* (New York and Oxford: Oxford University Press).

Gay, P. (2010) *Modernism: The Lure of Heresy* (New York: W.W. Norton).

Geertz, C. (1973) Thick description: Toward an interpretive theory of culture. In: Geertz, C. (ed.) *The Interpretation of Cultures: Selected Essays*, pp. 3–30 (New York: Basic Books).

Gehl, J. (2010) *Cities for People* (New York: Island Press).

Gehl, J. (2011) *Life Between Buildings: Using Public Space*, 6th ed. (New York: The Island Press).

Gehl, J. and Svarre, B. (2013) *How to Study Public Life* (New York: Island Press).

Gerber, A. and Green, D. (2012) *Field Experiments: Design, Analysis, and Interpretation* (New York: W.W. Norton).

Gerety, C. (2000) Psychological constructs, dictators, and the world press. Ph.D. Thesis, University of Cincinnati Library.

Geyl, P. (1948) *Napoleon, For and Against* (New Haven: Yale University Press).
Gilbert, M. (1986) *The Holocaust: A History of the Jews of Europe During the Second World War* (New York: Holt, Rinehart and Winston).
Gilbert, M. (1989) *The Second World War: A Complete History* (New York: Henry Holt).
Gilbert, M. (1999) *A History of the Twentieth Century* (New York: William Morrow).
Gilbert, W. and Sullivan, A. (1994) *The Pirates of Penzance* (Hertfordshire: Wordsworth Editions).
Gilding, P. (2011) *The Great Disruption* (New York: Bloomsbury Press).
Gillis, J. (2013) Heat-trapping gas passes milestone, raising fears. *New York Times*, May 10.
Gillis, J. (2015) 2014 Breaks heat record, challenging global warming skeptics. Available at: http://www.nytimes.com/2015/01/17/science/earth/2014-was-hottest-year-on-record-surpassing-2010.html?_r=0 (accessed 3 March 2015).
Gillis, J. and Schwartz, J. (2015) Deeper ties to corporate cash for doubtful climate researcher. Available at: http://www.nytimes.com/2015/02/22/us/ties-to-corporate-cash-for-climate-change-researcher-Wei-Hock-Soon.html (accessed 3 March 2015).
Glover, D. (2014) Nigel Farage joins forces with ex-clown Beppe Grillo as Ukip and Five Star Movement unite in EU. Available at: http://www.ibtimes.co.uk/nigel-farage-joins-forces-ex-clown-beppe-grillo-ukip-five-star-movement-unite-eu-1453383 (accessed 13 March 2015).
Goffman, E. (1963) *Stigma: Notes on the Management of Spoiled Identity* (New York: Prentice-Hall).
Gore, A. (2006) *An Inconvenient Truth: The Planetary Emergency of Global Warming and What We Can Do About It* (Emmaus, PA: Rodale).
Gore, A. (2013) *The Future: Six Drivers of Global Change* (New York: Random House).
Gough, H. (1976a) A measure of individual modernity. *Journal of Personality Assessment*, 40, 3–9.
Gough, H. (1976b) Further validation of a measure of individual modernity. *Journal of Personality Assessment*, 41, 49–57.
Gourevitch, P. (2015) Le Pen's moment. Available at: http://www.newyorker.com/news/news-desk/le-pens-moment (accessed 2 March 2015).
Green, P. (1991) *Alexander of Macedon, 356–323 B.C. A Historical Biography* (Berkeley, CA: University of California Press).
Griffin, J. (1961) *Black Like Me* (Boston, MA: Houghton Mifflin).
Guardian (2010) Ukip's Nigel Farage tells Van Rompuy: You have the charisma of a damp rag. Available at: http://www.theguardian.com/world/2010/feb/25/nigel-farage-herman-van-rompuy-damp-rag (accessed 21 April 2015).
Guardian (2014) Rotherham abuse: Report finds 1,400 children were victims. Available at: http://www.theguardian.com/society/live/2014/aug/26/rotherham-abuse-report-finds-1400-children-were-victims-live-coverage (accessed 18 February 2015).
Hadamard, J. (1944) *The Psychology of Invention in the Mathematical Field* (Princeton, NJ: Princeton University Press).
Haley, J. (1973) *The Power Tactics of Jesus Christ and Other Essays* (New York: Avon).
Hall, A. (2004) Perspective taking in language learning and teaching. Available at: http://www.forumonpublicpolicy.com/archive06/hall.pdf (accessed 12 March 2015).
Hall, P. (1998) *Cities in Civilization* (New York: Pantheon Books).

Haney, D.P. (2008) *The Americanization of Social Science* (Philadelphia, PA: Temple University Press).

Hardin, G. (1968) The tragedy of the commons. *Science* 162, 1243–8.

Harper, F.V. (1945) Book review: Res Ipsa Loquitur: Presumptions and burdens of proof. *Virginia Law Review*, 210, 32.

Hartmann, H., Kris, E. and Loewenstein, R. (1951) Some psychoanalytic comments on culture and personality. In: Wilbur, G. and Muensterberger, W. (eds) *Psychoanalysis and Culture* (New York: International Universities Press).

Hassin, R. (2014) Mining the unconscious. Available at: http://www.psychologicalscience.org/index.php/publications/observer/2014/april-14/mining-the-unconscious.html (accessed 12 March 2015).

Havel, V. (1991) *Open Letters: Selected Writings 1965–1990* (New York: Knopf).

Havel, V. (1992) *Summer Meditations on Politics, Morality and Civility in a Time of Transition* (New York: Knopf).

Hermant, N. (2013) Edward Snowden: Putin confirms NSA whistleblower in transit area of Moscow airport; rules out handing him over to US. Available at: http://www.abc.net.au/news/2013-06-26/putin-confirms-nsa-whistleblower-snowden-still-at-moscow-airport/4780468 (accessed 12 March 2015).

Hesse, H. (1927 [2002]) *Steppenwolf* (New York: Picador).

Hesse, H. (1943 [1975])*The Glass Bead Game* (Harmondsworth: Penguin).

Heussenstamm, F. (1971) Bumper stickers and the cops. *Transaction*, 8, 32–3.

Hiller, B. and Hansen, J. (1984) *The Social Logic of Space* (Cambridge: Cambridge University Press).

Hitler, A. (1923) *Mein Kampf* (transl. R. Mannheim) (Boston, MA: Houghton Mifflin).

Hodgson, J. and Lewthwaite, J. (2007) *Tort Law* (Oxford: Oxford University Press).

Hogan, D. and Aretha, D. (eds) (2003) *The Holocaust Chronicle: A History in Words and Pictures* (Lincolnwood, IL: Publications International).

Hollenbeck, R. (2014) History of the global warming hoax? Available at: http://www.southmilwaukeenow.com/blogs/communityblogs/275688881.html (accessed 12 March 2015).

Howell, J. (1992) *Hard Living on Clay Street* (Prospect Heights, IL: Waveland Press).

Hughes, E. (1971) The natural history of a research project. In: Hughes, E. (ed.) *The Sociological Eye*, pp. 530–41 (New Brunswick, NJ: Transaction Books).

Huizenga, J. (1993) *Cold Fusion: The Scientific Fiasco of the Century* (New York: University of Rochester Press).

Human Events (2014) Anti-Capitalist march in NYC mentions climate change; weather remains unchanged. Available at: http://humanevents.com/2014/09/22/anti-capitalist-march-in-nyc-mentions-climate-change-weather-remains-unchanged/ (accessed 3 March 2015).

Inhofe, J. (2012) *The Greatest Hoax: How the Global Warming Conspiracy Threatens Your Future* (Washington, DC: WorldNetDaily).

Inkeles, A. and Smith, D.H. (1974) *Becoming Modern; Individual Change in Six Developing Countries* (Cambridge, MA: Harvard University Press).

Ionesco, E. (1960) *Rhinoceros & Other Plays* (New York: Grove Press).

Jacobs, J. (1961 [1993]) *The Life and Death of Great American Cities* (New York: Random House).

Janis, I. (1972) *Victims of Groupthink: A Psychological Study of Foreign Policy Decisions and Fiascoes* (Boston, MA: Houghton Mifflin).

Janis, I. (1982) *Groupthink: A Psychological Study of Policy Decisions and Fiascoes* (Boston, MA: Houghton Mifflin).

Johnson, J. (1978) *Doing Field Research* (New York: The Free Press).
Judt, T. (2005) *PostWar: Europe Since 1945* (Harmondsworth: Penguin).
Judt, T. (2010) Captive minds, *New York Review of Books*, Sep. 30.
Kadiec, C. (2011) The goal is power: The global warming conspiracy. Available at: http://www.forbes.com/sites/charleskadlec/2011/07/25/the-goal-is-power-the-global-warming-conspiracy (accessed 13 March 2015).
Kafka, F. (1915 [1986]) *The Metamorphosis* (New York: Bantam Books).
Kafka, F. (1925 [1998])*The Trial* (New York: Schoken Books).
Kahl, J. (1968) *The Measurement of Modernism: A Study of Values in Brazil and Mexico* (Austin, TX: University of Texas Press).
Kandel, E.R. (2007) *In Search of Memory: The Emergence of a New Science of Mind* (New York: W.W. Norton).
Kaplan, A. (1998 [2006]) *The Conduct of Inquiry: Methodology for Behavioral Science* (New Brunswick, NJ: Transaction Books).
Kapp Howe, L. (1978). *Pink Collar Workers* (New York: Harper Collins, Avon).
Katona, G. (1951) *Psychological Analysis of Economic Behavior* (New York: McGraw-Hill).
Keegan, J. (ed.) (1999) *World War II: A Visual Encyclopedia* (London: PRC Publishing).
Kelman, H. (1958) Compliance, identification, and internalization: Three processes of attitude change. *Journal of Conflict Resolution*, 1, 51–60.
Kolbert, K. (2011) Talk of the town. *New Yorker*, Jun 13.
Koplowitz, H. (2013) No death penalty for Dzhokhar Tsarnaev? Prosecutors may seek life in exchange for more information on Boston bombings. Available at: http://www.ibtimes.com/no-death-penalty-dzhokhar-tsarnaev-prosecutors-may-seek-life-exchange-more-information-boston.
Kouvelas, E.D. and Akinosoglou, K.S. (2014) Unconscious: neuroscience meets psychoanalysis. Conference paper, University of Patras, Greece.
Kris, E. (1952a) *Creativity and Madness: New Findings and Old Stereotypes* (Baltimore, MD: Johns Hopkins University Press).
Kris, E. (1952b) *Psychoanalytic Explorations in Art* (New York: International Universities Press).
Kuhn, T. (1962 [1996]) *The Structure of Scientific Revolutions* (Chicago, IL: University of Chicago Press).
Kunda, G. (1992 [2006]) *Engineering Culture: Control and Commitment in a High-Tech Corporation* (Philadelphia, PA: Temple University Press).
Kunstler, J.H. (1993) *The Geography of Nowhere* (New York: Simon & Schuster).
Kunstler, J.H. (2005) *The Long Emergency: Surviving the End of Oil, Climate Change, and Other Converging Catastrophes of the Twenty-First Century* (New York: Simon & Schuster).
Lagerkvist, P. (1944) *The Dwarf* (New York: Hill and Wang).
Langer, W. (1931) *European Alliances and Alignments: 1871–1890* (New York: Alfred A. Knopf).
Larsen, J.K., Brand, N., Bermond, B. and Hijman, R. (2003) Cognitive and emotional characteristics of alexthymia: A review of neurobiological studies. *Journal of Psychosomatic Research*, 54, 533–41.
Latane, B. and Darley, J. (1969) Bystander 'apathy.' *American Scientist*, 57, 244–68.
Le Bon, G. (1896) *The Crowd: A Study of the Popular Mind* (New York: Macmillan).
LeDoux, J. (2002) *How Our Brains Become Who We Are* (New York: Viking).

Lefkowitz, M., Blake, R.R. and Mouton, J.S. (1955) Status of actor in pedestrian violation of traffic signals. *Journal of Abnormal and Social Psychology*, 51, 704–6.

Leidner, R. (1993) *Fast Food, Fast Talk: Service Work and the Routinization of Everyday Life* (Berkeley, CA: University of California Press).

Lerner, D. (1958) *The Passing of Traditional Society: Modernizing the Middle East* (Glencoe, IL.: The Free Press).

Levi, P. (1996) *Survival in Auschwitz: The Nazi Assault on Humanity* (transl. S. Woolf (New York: Simon and Schuster).

Lewis, C.I. (1946) *An Analysis of Knowledge and Valuation* (La Salle, IL.: Open Court).

Liddell Hart, B.H. (1948) *The Other Side of the Hill: Germany's Generals, Their Rise and Fall, With Their Own Account of Military Events, 1939–45 (Grand Strategy)* (London: Cassell and Co.).

Liddell Hart, B. (1948 [1971]) *The German Generals Speak* (New York: Harper Collins/William Morrow).

Liddell Hart, B. (1970) *History of the Second World War* (Old Saybrook, CT: Konecky & Konecky).

Lieblich, A., Tuval-Mashiach, R. and Zilber, T. (1998) *Narrative Research, Reading Analysis and Interpretation* (Thousand Oaks, CA: SAGE).

Limbaugh, R. (2014) RFK Jr.'s climate hypocrisy exposed. Available at: http://www.rushlimbaugh.com/daily/2014/09/22/rfk_jr_s_climate_hypocrisy_exposed (accessed 3 March 2015).

Linn, R. (2004) *Escaping Auschwitz: A Culture of Forgetting* (Ithaca, NY: Cornell University Press).

Liptak, A. (2014) Supreme Court rejects contraceptives mandate for some corporations. Justices rule in favor of Hobby Lobby. *New York Times*, Jun 30.

Loewenberg, P. (2002) *Decoding the Past: The Psychohistorical Approach* (New Brunswick, NJ: Transaction).

Loewenberg, P. (2009) Face in Chinese culture and in Sino-American diplomacy. Paper presented at the Annual Scientific Conference of the International Society of Political Psychology, Dublin, 2009.

London Evening Standard (2013) That "clown" Farage is covering all the bases now. Available at: http://www.standard.co.uk/news/londoners-diary/that-clown-farage-is-covering-all-bases-now-8603052.html (accessed 22 February 2015).

Low, D. (1939) *A Cartoon History of our Time* (New York: Simon and Schuster).

McGuire, W. (1983) A contextualist theory of knowledge: Its implications for innovation and reform in psychological research. *Advances in Experimental Social Psychology*, 16, 1–41.

McGuire, W. (1989) A perspectivist approach to the strategic planning of programmatic scientific research. In: Gholson, B., Shadish, W.R., Jr., Neimeyer, R.A. and Houts, A.C. (eds) *The Psychology of Science: Contributions to Metascience*, pp. 214–45 (New York: Cambridge University Press).

McLaughlin, N. (2014) Escapes from freedom: Political extremism, conspiracy theories, and the sociology of emotions. In: Chancer, L. and Andrews, J. (eds) *The Unhappy Divorce of Sociology and Psychoanalysis*, pp. 161–89 (Basingstoke: Palgrave Macmillan).

Macleod, S. (2005) Mrs. Hitler and her doctor. *Australasian Psychiatry*, 13, 412–14.

Mannheim, K. (1936) *Ideology and Utopia: An Introduction to the Sociology of Knowledge* (transl. L. Wirth and E. Shils) (London: Routledge and Kegan Paul).

Mannheim, K. (1940) *Man and Society in an Age of Reconstruction* (transl. E. Shils) (New York: Harcourt, Brace & World).

Manning, P. (2014) The ethnographic spiral: Reflections on the intersection of life history and ideal-typical analysis. In: Chancer, L. and Andrews, J. (eds) *The Unhappy Divorce of Sociology and Psychoanalysis*, pp. 220–34 (Basingstoke: Palgrave Macmillan).

Mead, G.H. (1934) *Mind, Self, and Society* (Chicago, IL: University of Chicago Press).

Meadows, D.H., Meadows, D.L., Randers, J. and Behrens, W.W., III. (1972) *The Limits to Growth* (New York: New American Library).

Mearsheimer, J. (1988) *Liddell Hart and the Weight of History* (Ithaca, NY: Cornell University Press).

Meyer, M.A. (1994) Air traffic: The environmental quality of city streets: The residents' viewpoint. M.A. thesis, Department of Psychology, University of Cincinnati.

Meyers, W. (1955) Similarities in the thought of Henry Ford and Thorstein Veblen. B.A. thesis, Harvard University Libraries.

Meyers, W. (1963) The concept of creativity: An experimental critique. Ph.D. dissertation, Harvard University Libraries (HU 90 8411.5B).

Meyers, W. and Gerety, C. (1999) Acquiescence and threat in world press perceptions of dictators. In: 22nd Annual Scientific Meeting of the International Society for Political Psychology, Amsterdam, the Netherlands.

Meyers, W. and Gerety, C. (2000) Why don't you just read them? A narrative analysis of world press profiles of aspiring dictators. In: 23rd Annual Scientific Meeting of the International Society for Political Psychology, Seattle, WA.

Meyers, W.R., Dorwart, R.A. and Kline, D. (1977) Social ecology and citizen participation: A problem for planners. *Journal of the American Institute of Planners*, 43, 2.

Meyers, W., Gerety, C., Elmore, A. and Dember, W. (1997) Zhirinovsky, social science constructs, and the world press. In: Annual Scientific Meeting of the International Society for Political Psychology, Krakow, Poland.

Milgram, S. (1974) *Obedience to Authority* (New York: Harper & Row).

Milosz, C. (1953 [1990]) *The Captive Mind* (New York: Vintage).

Mlot, C. (1998) Probing the biology of emotion. *Science*, 1998, 28, 1006–7.

Montagu, A. and Matson, F. (1983) *The Dehumanization of Man* (New York: Mcgraw-Hill).

MSNBC (2007) Filipino devotees crucify, whip themselves. Available at: http://www.msnbc.msn.com/id/17978154/ns/world_news-asia-pacific/#.TtLLlWC4KoA (accessed 12 March 2015).

Mukherjee, S. (2011) *Emperor of All Maladies: A Biography of Cancer* (New York: Scribner).

Murray, H.A. (1938) *Explorations in Personality* (New York: Oxford University Press).

Nagel, E. (1967)What is true and false in science. *Encounter*, 29, 70.

NBC News (2014) Planet sees warmest September ever recorded: NASA. Available at: http://www.nbcnews.com/science/environment/planet-sees-warmest-september-ever-recorded-nasa-n225836 (accessed 13 March 2015).

Neuliep, J. and McCroskey, J. (1965) The development of a U.S. and generalized ethnocentrism scale. *Communication Research Reports*, 14, 385–439.

Newman, O. (1973) *Defensible Space: Crime Prevention Through Urban Design* (New York: MacMillan).

Orac (2006) Mrs. Hitler and her doctor. Available at: http://scienceblogs.com/insolence/2006/04/mrs_hitler_and_her_doctor.php (accessed 13 March 2015).

Orr, D. (2009) *Down to the Wire: Confronting Climate Collapse* (Oxford: Oxford University Press).

Orwell, G. (1949) *1984* (New York: Harcourt).

Palgi, Y. (2002) *Into the Inferno: The Memoir of a Jewish Paratrooper Behind Nazi Lines* (New Brunswick, NJ: Rutgers University Press).

Park, R.E., Burgess, E., Roderick D. and McKenzie, R. (1925) *The City* (Chicago, IL: University of Chicago Press).

Patton, M.Q. (2014) *Qualitative Research and Evaluation Methods*, 4th ed (Thousand Oaks, CA: SAGE).

Petit, G. (2012) A modest proposal for an international database on conspiracy theories. In: International Society for Political Psychology Annual Scientific Meeting, Chicago, 7 July 2012.

Pettigrew, T. (ed.) (1980) *The Sociology of Race Relations: Reflection and Reform* (New York: Free Press).

Pick, D. (2012) *The Pursuit of the Nazi Mind: Hitler, Hess, and the Analysts* (Oxford: Oxford University Press).

Pine, F. (1990) *Drive, Ego, Object, Self: A Synthesis for Clinical Work* (New York: Basic Books).

Pirandello, L. (1921 [1952]) Six characters in search of an author. In: Pirandello, L. (ed.) *Naked Masks: Five Plays by Luigi Pirandello*, Act I, Act III (New York: Penguin Books).

Poincaré, H. (1913 [2001]) Mathematical discovery. In: Gould, S.J. (ed.) *The Value of Science*, pp. 387–400 (New York: The Modern Library).

Polonsky, M. (2001) *The Poetry Reader's Toolkit* (Lincolnwood, IL: NTC).

Popper, K. (1935 [1968, 2002]), *The Logic of Scientific Discovery* (London and New York: Routledge).

Pratto, F., Sidanius, J., Stallworth, L.M. and Malle, B.F. (1994) Social dominance orientation: A personality variable predicting social and political attitudes. *Journal of Personality and Social Psychology*, 67, 741–63.

Quinn-Judge, P. (1994) Pantie-hero. *New Republic*, 210, 24.

Ray, J. (1982) Toward a definitive alienation scale. *The Journal of Psychology*, 111, 67–70.

Reade, B. (2013) Vote for Nigel Farage and UKIP "clowns" and the joke's on us. Available at: http://www.mirror.co.uk/news/uk-news/brian-reade-ukip-vote-nigel-1864678 (accessed 22 February 2015).

Reik, T. (1948) *Listening with the Third Ear: The Inner Experience of a Psychoanalyst* (New York: Farrar, Straus).

Remnick, D. (1996) *The Devil Problem* (New York: Random House).

Remnick, D. (2000) Into the clear. *New Yorker*, May, 86–7.

Reuters (2011) Filipinos re-enact Jesus's crucifixion in Easter ritual. Available at: http://www.reuters.com/article/2011/04/22/us-philippines-crucifxions-idUSTRE73L0XU20110422 (accessed 18 February 2015).

Ridley, M. (2014) Whatever happened to global warming? Available at: http://www.wsj.com/articles/matt-ridley-whatever-happened-to-global-warming-1409872855 (accessed 3 March 2015).

Rifkind, M. (2014) Nigel Farage is a buffoon for admiring Vladimir Putin. Available at: http://www.telegraph.co.uk/news/politics/ukip/10737184/Nigel-Farage-is-a-buffoon-for-admiring-Vladimir-Putin.html (accessed 22 February 2015).

Rokeach, M. (1954) The nature and meaning of dogmatism. *Psychological Review*, 61, 194–204.

Rosenberg, M. (1969) *The Logic of Survey Analysis* (New York: Basic Books).

Rothenburg, B. (2014) Del Potro falls, hours after 100-degree heat causes halt in play. Available at: http://www.nytimes.com/2014/01/17/sports/tennis/heat-becomes-a-decisive-factor-at-australian-open.html (accessed 16 March 2015).

Sage, A. (2015) French Jews turn to Le Pen after Muslim attacks. Available at: http://www.thetimes.co.uk/tto/news/world/europe/article4363294.ece (accessed 2 March 2015).

Sager, M. (1996) Janet Cooke. *GQ Magazine*, June, 200–11.

Sammet, K. (2001) Book review: *Psychohistory: Theory and Practice. Journal of the History of the Behavioral Sciences*, 39, 316–17.

Sanger, D.E. and Sang-Hun, C. (2013) North Korea issues blunt new threat to United States. Available at: http://www.nytimes.com/2013/01/25/world/asia/north-korea-vows-nuclear-test-as-threats-intensify.html?pagewanted=all&_r=0 (accessed 18 February 2015).

Schell, O. (2002) A new leader for the *New Yorker*: David Remnick in conversation with Dean Orville Schell. Available from: Graduate School of Journalism, University of California at Berkeley.

Schore, A. (2009) The paradigm shift: The right brain and the relational unconscious. Plenary Address to the American Psychological Association, Toronto, Canada, 8 August 2009.

Sebald, W. (1999) *Vertigo* (New York: New Directions).

Service, R. (2000) *Lenin: A Biography* (Cambridge, MA: Harvard University Press).

Simmel, G. (1950) The metropolis and mental life. In: Wolff, K. (transl.) *The Sociology of Georg Simmel*, pp. 409–24 (New York: Free Press).

Sorenson, S.B., Joshi, M. and Sivitz, E. (2014) A systematic review of the epidemiology of nonfatal strangulation, a human rights and health concern. *American Journal of Public Health*, 104, e54–61.

Sowell, T. (2013) Of Stuyvesant, tests, and Tiger Moms. Available at: http://nypost.com/2013/04/10/of-stuyvesant-tests-and-tiger-moms/ (accessed 13 March 2014).

Spencer, K. (2012) For Asians, school tests are vital steppingstones. Available at: http://www.nytimes.com/2012/10/27/education/a-grueling-admissions-test-highlights-a-racial-divide.html?pagewanted=all&_r=1&* (accessed 18 February 2015).

Spreng, N., McKinnon, M., Mar, R. and Levine, B. (2009) The Toronto Empathy Questionnaire: Scale development and initial validation of a factor-analytic solution to multiple empathy measures. *Journal of Personality Assessment*, 91, 62–71.

Srole. L. (1956) Social integration and certain corollaries: An exploratory study. *American Sociological Review*, 21, 709–16.

Staub, E. (1989) *The Roots of Evil: The Origins of Genocide and Other Group Violence* (Cambridge: Cambridge University Press).

Steinberg, J. (2003) Times's 2 Top Editors Resign After Furor on Writer's Fraud. Available at: http://www.nytimes.com/2003/06/06/business/media/06PAPE.html (accessed 13 March 2015).

Steiner, C. (2012) *Automate This! How Algorithms Came to Rule Our World* (New York: Penguin Group).

Stewart, J. (2011) *Tangled Webs: How False Statements Are Undermining America: From Martha Stewart to Bernie Madoff* (London and New York: Penguin Books).

Stouffer, S. (1949) *The American Soldier*, 2 vols (Princeton, NJ: Princeton University Press).

Strannegard, L. and Friberg, M. (2001) *Already Elsewhere—Play, Identity and Speed in the Business World* (Stockholm: Raster Forlag).

Strous, R. (2006) Hitler's psychiatrists: Healers and researchers turned executioners and its relevance today. *Harvard Review of Psychiatry*, 14, 30–7.

Suedfeld, P. (2010) The cognitive processing of politics and politicians: Archival studies of conceptual and integrative complexity. *Journal* of Personality, 78, 1669–702.

Suedfeld, P. and Jhangiani, R. (2009) Cognitive management in an enduring international rivalry: The case of India and Pakistan. *Political Psychology*, 30, 937–51.

Sutherland, J. and Sutherland, B. (2010) *World War II* (London: Flame Tree Publishing).

Sweetser, F. (1965) Factor structure in Helsinki and Boston. *Acta Sociologica*, 8, 205–25.

Szaluta, J. (1978) Marshal Pétain and the French Army mutiny of 1917: A study in leadership and political personality. *Third Republic*, 6, 181–210.

Szaluta, J. (1980) Apotheosis to ignominy: The martyrdom of Marshall Pétain. *Journal of Psychohistory*, 7, 415–63.

Szaluta, J. (1990) The correspondence between Maréchal and Madame Pétain 1913–1949. A psychoanalytic interpretation. *American Imago*, 47, 169–96.

Szep, E. (1945 [1994]) *The Smell of Humans: A Memoir of the Holocaust in Hungary* (transl. J. Batki) (Budapest, London, New York: Central European University Press).

Taleb, N. (2005) *Fooled by Randomness: The Hidden Role of Chance in Life and in the Markets* (New York: Random House).

Taleb, N. (2010) *The Black Swan: The Impact of the Highly Improbable*. 2nd ed. (New York: Random House).

Tarde, G. (1903) *The Laws of Imitation* (New York: Henry Holt).

Tassel, J. (2007) The global empire of Niall Ferguson. *Harvard Magazine*, 109, 36.

Taubes, G. (1993) *Bad Science: The Short Life and Weird Times of Cold Fusion* (New York: Random House).

Taylor, F. (2004) *Dresden: Tuesday, Feb. 13, 1945* (New York: Harper Collins).

Taylor, F. (2009) "Post-war myths:" The logic behind the destruction of Dresden. Available at: http://www.spiegel.de/international/germany/0,1518,607524,00.html (accessed 13 March 2015).

Teele, D. (ed.) (2014) *Field Experiments and their Critics* (New Haven, CT: Yale University Press).

Tetlock, P. (2006) *Expert Political Judgment: How Good is it? How can We Know?* (Princeton, NJ: Princeton University Press).

Thomas. W.I. and Thomas, D.S. (1928) *The Child in America* (New York: Knopf).

Thomas, W.I. and Znaniecki, F. (1918–1920) *The Polish Peasant in Europe and America* (Chicago, IL: The University of Chicago Press).

Thornton, L. (2014) Paedophile gang's abuse lasted 16 years as authorities feared being labelled racist if they tackled it. Available at: http://www.mirror.co.uk/news/uk-news/rotherham-child-abuse-scandal-paedophile-4113152 (accessed 18 February 2015).

Thrasher, F. (1927) *The Gang: A Study of 1,313 Gangs in Chicago* (Chicago, IL: University of Chicago Press).

Travis, R. (1993) The MOS Alienation Scale: An alternative to Srole's Anomia Scale. *Social Indicators Research*, 28, 71–91.

Troldahl, V. and Powell, F. (1965) A short form dogmatism scale for use in field studies. *Social Forces*, 44, 211–14.

Tukey, J. (1977) *Exploratory Data Analysis* (Reading, MA: Addison-Wesley).

Velasquez-Manoff, M. (2014) What happens when the poor receive a stipend? Available at: http://opinionator.blogs.nytimes.com/2014/01/18/what-happens-when-the-poor-receive-a-stipend/?_r=0 (accessed 18 February 2015).

Washington Times (2014) Editorial: Pressing the climate hoax. Available at: http://www.washingtontimes.com/news/2014/sep/1/editorial-pressing-the-climate-hoax/ (accessed 3 March 2015).

Wax, M. (1967) On misunderstanding Verstehen: A reply to Abel. *Sociology and Social Research*, 51, 323–33.

Wax, R. (1971 [1985]) *Doing Fieldwork: Warnings and Advice* (Chicago, IL: University of Chicago Press).

Webb, B. (1888) The pages of a workgirl's diary. *Nineteenth Century*, 24, 301–14.

Webb, B. (1926 [1979]) *My Apprenticeship* (Cambridge and New York: Cambridge University Press).

Webb, E. and Campbell D.T. (1966) *Unobtrusive Measures* (New York: Rand McNally).

Weber, M. (1921) Politik als Beruf. In: Weber, M. (ed.) *Gesammelte Politische Schriften*, pp. 396–450 (Munich: Drei Masken).

Weber, M. (1947) The types of authority and imperative coordination. In: Weber, M. (ed.) *The Theory of Social and Economic Organization* (transl. A.M. Henderson and T. Parsons), pp. 324–92 (Oxford: Oxford University Press).

Wells, S. (2010) *Pandora's Seed: The Unforeseen Cost of Civilization* (New York: Random House).

Welsh, G. (1959) *Welsh Figure Preference Test. Preliminary Manual*, research ed. (Palo Alto, CA: Consulting Psychologists Press).

Whyte, W.F. (1943 [1993]) *Street Corner Society: The Social Structure of an Italian Slum*, 4th ed. (Chicago, IL: University of Chicago Press).

Whyte, W. (1956) *The Organization Man* (New York: Simon & Schuster).

Whyte, W.H. (1980) *The Social Life of Small Urban Spaces* (New York: Project for Public Spaces, 2001).

Whyte, W.H. (2009) *City: Rediscovering the Center* (Philadelphia, PA: University of Pennsylvania Press).

Wikipedia (n.d.) Vladimier Zhirinovsky's donkey video. Available at: http://en.wikipedia.org/wiki/Vladimir_Zhirinovsky's_donkey_video (accessed 22 February 2015).

William Alanson White Institute (2007) *The Future of the Stock Market* (New York: William Alanson White Institute).

Wirth, L. (1928) *The Ghetto* (Chicago, IL: University of Chicago Press).

Wirth, L. (1929 [1989]) Preface. In: Mannheim, K. (ed.) *Ideology and Utopia* (transl. L. Wirth and E. Shils), pp. x–xxx (New York: Harcourt Brace).
Wirth, L. (1964) *On Cities and Social Life: Selected Papers* (Chicago, IL: University of Chicago Press).
World Post (2015) Sudan flogging video sparks outrage. Available at: http://www.huffingtonpost.com/2010/12/13/sudan-video-of-woman-bein_n_795859.html (accessed 18 February 2015).
Worth, R.F. (2006) Blast at Shiite shrine sets off sectarian fury in Iraq. Available at: http://www.nytimes.com/2006/02/23/world/23iraq.html?pagewanted=all&_r=0 (accessed 13 March 2015).
Zabarenko, D. (2012) Warmest U.S. spring on record: NOAA. Available at: http://www.reuters.com/article/2012/06/07/us-climate-warmth-usa-idUSBRE8561BK20120607 (accessed 15 March 2015).
Zimbardo, P. (2007) *The Lucifer Effect: Understanding how Good People Turn Evil* (New York: Random House).
Zizek, S. (2010) Part II...Slavoj Zizek: Far right and anti-immigrant politicians on the rise in Europe. Available at: www.democracynow.org/blog/2010/10/18/part 2 (accessed 13 March 2015).

Index

CPSIA information can be obtained
at www.ICGtesting.com
Printed in the USA
LVOW13*2154090117
520319LV00007B/128/P

9 781137 524898